THINK . . .
READ . . .
REACT . . .
PLAN . . .
WRITE . . .
REWRITE . . .

FIFTH
EDITION

THINK ...
READ ...
REACT ...
PLAN ...
WRITE ...
REWRITE ...

A READER-WRITER WORKTEXT

W. Royce Adams

Santa Barbara City College

Holt, Rinehart and Winston, Inc.
Fort Worth   Chicago   San Francisco
Philadelphia   Montreal   Toronto
London   Sydney   Tokyo

Publisher: Charlyce Jones Owen
Developmental Editor: Tod Gross
Project Editor: Mark Hobbs
Production Manager: Kathleen Ferguson
Art & Design Supervisor: John Ritland
Text Designer: Caliber Design Planning, Inc.
Cover Designer: Rhonda Campbell

Cover photograph by Jim Salvati. Reprinted by permission of The IMAGE Bank.

Library of Congress Cataloging-in-Publication Data

Adams, W. Royce.
    Think, read, react, plan, write, rewrite: a reader-writer worktext / W. Royce Adams.—5th ed.
      p.   cm.
    Includes bibliographical references and index.
    1. English language—Rhetoric. 2. College readers. I. Title.
PE1408.A318   1989
808′.042—dc20   89-34335
                                     CIP

ISBN: 0-03-030817-8

Requests for permission to make copies of any part of the work should be mailed to: Copyrights and Permissions Department, Holt, Rinehart and Winston, Inc., 6277 Sea Harbor Drive, Orlando, FL 32887.

Address for Editorial Correspondence: Holt, Rinehart and Winston, Inc., 301 Commerce Street, Suite 3700, Forth Worth, TX 76102

Address for Orders: Holt, Rinehart and Winston, Inc., 6277 Sea Harbor Drive, Orlando, FL 32887. 1-800-782-4479, or 1-800-433-0001 (in Florida)

Printed in the United States of America

0 1 2 3 039 9 8 7 6 5 4 3 2 1

Holt, Rinehart and Winston, Inc.
The Dryden Press
Saunders College Publishing

PREFACE TO THE FIFTH EDITION

Written primarily for college students who need to cross from the developmental level into the mainstream, this fifth edition of TRRPWR can serve as either a review or an introduction to the three basic stages of writing: prewriting, drafting, and revision. Each of the nine units covers at least one of the tasks required and generally taught as necessary skills in these three stages of writing.

The **Think, Read, React,** and **Plan** sections deal with various aspects of the prewriting stage. Students are asked in each unit to think about a broad topic, such as learning experiences, language, self-awareness, creative thinking, work, honesty, technology, the media, or relationships, and narrow it down to a thesis they can handle. All the unit topics are wide enough in range to allow for student identification with some aspect of the subject. A reading selection dealing with the unit's topic is followed by questions on comprehension, writing style, and structure as a way to provide information, stimulate thinking, and serve as a teaching tool for reading and writing skills. Then students are presented with prewriting methods such as brainstorming, freewriting, and clustering as a means for exploring, planning, and organizing ideas for an essay of their own.

Each **Write** section presents students with a different skill in writing first drafts, such as how to write introductory paragraphs, the various rhetorical modes used in development, and how to write concluding paragraphs. Strong emphasis is placed on development.

The **Rewrite** sections, much more developed than previous editions, are divided into three parts: revise, edit, and proofread. As with the **Write** sections, each unit presents new information in the areas of coherence, mechanics, and punctuation. At the end of each unit, a new revision checklist provides reminders of what has been learned in previous units. The end result is an understanding of the totality of the cyclical writing process and its often erratic nature.

The maintenance of a writing journal is heavily stressed. Of course, instructors may choose to ignore or omit the writing journal entries. However, those who tend to feel this way may want to look at Boynton/Cook's *The Journal Book* (Upper Montclair, N.J., 1987), edited by Toby Fulwiler, which reveals the many contributions proper journal keeping offers.

Recognizing that many students may need more drills than those provided within each unit, additional practices on each skill taught are given in a special section. Nine supplemental readings, each one related to one of the unit's themes, also are provided to show another slant and provoke more thinking.

The answers to the Practices appear in an Answer Key that may be obtained from your local Holt representative or from the English Editor, College Department, Holt, Rinehart and Winston, Inc., Suite 3700, 301 Commerce Street, Fort Worth, Texas, 76102.

I would like to thank Charlyce Jones Owen, Tod Gross, and Mark Hobbs for their excellent editorial help and support with this edition. My thanks also are extended to the following reviewers for their helpful comments and suggestions: Joan Brand, Cincinnati Technical College; Henry Burgess, Carroll College; Beth Camp, Linn-Benton Community College; Natalie Daly, The Writer's Shop; Carolyn Kellog, The University of Wisconsin at Oshkosh; Shelby Kipplen, The Michael J. Owens Technical College; Vincent Lopresti, The University of Wisconsin at Oshkosh; Elizabeth Nelson, Saint Peter's College; Marti Singer, Georgia State University; Frank Torres, California State Polytechnic University at Pomona; W.C. Truckey, Lewis and Clark Community College.

TO THE STUDENT

I remember my nervousness and tension the first day of my college freshman English class. My writing skills had never been outstanding, and English was never a subject dear to my heart. It was just another requirement I had to take. My regard for the subject took an even deeper dip when the instructor gave us the first assignment: an essay on hickory-nut hunting. I wasn't sure what the difference was between a hickory nut and a walnut, let alone how one goes about hunting for hickory nuts. How was I going to write an essay on something I knew nothing about?

A trip to the library was no help. I learned a little about hickory nuts but not about how to hunt them. I asked a couple of students in the class if they knew how to hunt hickory nuts, but if they did they weren't about to tell me. I was stuck. I felt stupid. I was starting to panic. I just knew I was going to fail the class.

Staring at a blank sheet of paper, I waited for the Great God of Writing to zap my pen into action. Nothing happened, of course. Think, I told myself in panic. Had I ever seen hickory nuts growing? Where would it have been? I found myself thinking about where I was the summer before the semester had started, wishing I were still there. As in many previous summers, I had walked and climbed the bluffs along the Mississippi River near Alton, Illinois. But I didn't remember seeing hickory nuts. I began writing down some of the things I did remember seeing on my last hike: the muddy river itself, with its frequent, slow-drifting barges; the train tracks on which I practiced balancing acts; the exploring of damp, cool caves; the simmering stillness; the copperheads sunning on boulders; the big, colorful Piasaw bird said to have been painted on a cliff by Indians a hundred years ago. I wrote several pages, but none of it had to do with hickory-nut hunting. Desperate for something to turn in to the English instructor, I ended my paper by saying something similar to "I gathered few hickory nuts that day."

Perhaps you can imagine my fear and embarrassment at the following class session. I just knew my paper would be given back with a note saying, "See me!" and I would be asked to leave the class. Instead, the instructor began the class by reading my paper aloud. My face flushed as I slid lower in my seat. And it was even worse when afterward one of the students said, "The essay's not even about the subject." To which the instructor replied, "And that's what makes it so good."

Had I heard correctly? How could this be? I hadn't even written about hickory-nut hunting! All of us were confused.

He explained to the class that the assignment had been intentionally narrow and uninspiring. He wanted to see what we could do with such an unexciting topic. Unknown to me, I had stumbled on what the professor called a main key to good writing: Make the topic your own. Unable to do anything else, I had written about something I knew. I had not tried to write what I thought the teacher wanted to hear. Little did he know that it was an accident.

When the paper was handed back, my pleasure faded again because of all the markings. He liked what I had done with the subject, but I still had much to learn about writing. With his help, I learned, slowly gaining confidence as well as experience in the writing process. Today, I'm still learning how to write better.

I tell this personal narrative because many of you probably feel now as I did then about writing. For me, English was just another one of those degree requirements. I wasn't born an English teacher or a writer. In fact, even in graduate school I never planned to be either. Still, that assignment, that one essay, changed my life.

Although there are numerous approaches and theories about teaching composition, those found in this book have been helpful to many students. Some methods and assignments will appeal to you more than others, but this text has been written in the hope that it might help change your life for the better in some way.

By the way, there are no assignments in this book on hickory-nut hunting.

CONTENTS

GETTING THE MOST FROM THIS BOOK

UNIT 1

UNIT 2

UNIT 3

UNIT 4

UNIT 5

UNIT 6

UNIT 7

UNIT 8

UNIT 9

REWRITE . . .
    the first drafts.   261

PRACTICES IN . . .

SUPPLEMENTAL READINGS

INDEX

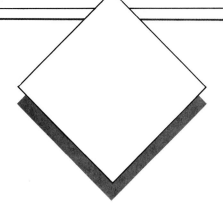

GETTING THE MOST FROM THIS BOOK

GETTING THE MOST FROM THIS BOOK

Before using this book, you should understand what the writing process entails and how the organization of this textbook relates to it.

◆ THE WRITING PROCESS

The writing process is usually broken into three major parts: *prewriting, writing,* and *rewriting*. **Prewriting** involves such activities as thinking about a subject, deciding what you want to say and to whom, making certain you have enough information on the topic, considering how you might best say what you know, and writing rough drafts. **Writing** involves organizing and developing your ideas into paragraphs that are logically presented, fully developing your thesis, and making sure what you say is clearly stated. **Rewriting** requires looking closely at what you have written; revising by adding, moving, or removing information; rewriting sentences and paragraphs if need be; editing your sentence structure; and proofreading for punctuation, grammar, and spelling mistakes.

Writing is a process that is not always exact. It would be easy to explain if writing went from step A to B to C and so on. But it doesn't. In *Write to Learn*, Donald Murray says that if we could draw a picture of the writing process, it would look something like the this:

Murray's point is well taken. Writing can seem to flow easily one minute and grind to a halt the next. You think you are on the right track at one point, only to discover that you are not. Sometimes you write a paragraph that you fall in love with, but then you come to realize that it doesn't fit the point you are trying

2

to make and have to toss it out. Other times you sit in frustration, unable to write a word, when suddenly all you wanted to say comes gushing forth. Such is the nature of writing.

Don't be discouraged when your writing seems to take a negative turn. Time away from the composing process is just as important as the time you put in. Start working on writing assignments long before they are due. Realize that you will need time away from what you write so that you can come back to it with a fresh look. As you work your way through this book, apply what you learn to your own writing.

Most of the essays you will be asked to write require answers to two basic questions: What point do I want to make about my topic? What support of that point or idea is needed to make myself clear? If you can answer these two questions, you will be on safe ground.

Writing is not only a process; it is also a skill that requires practice. Even the best writers struggle their way through these three stages. There is no getting around the fact that good writing is hard work.

◆ THE ORGANIZATION OF THIS BOOK

All the information necessary for writing an essay is in this book. However, there is no way a book can present an exact sequence of the writing process. When you write, you are dealing with your mind, and only you are in control of that. But to make learning to write as easy as possible, the various parts of the process are presented in stages. Each unit is divided into six basic sections, **Think, Read, React, Plan, Write,** and **Rewrite,** and each section relates in some way to the writing process.

The Prewriting Stages

The **Think** sections, part of the prewriting phase, represent the point where good writing begins. Before you can write about a subject, you have to think about it. Each unit asks you to think about a selected topic that is intentionally too broad to write about. Questions related to the unit's broad topic are asked to help you focus on narrower viewpoints. Sometimes suggestions for finding additional information are provided for you.

Frequently the questions in the **Think** section are seed questions, meaning that you will continue to think about them long after you have answered them. In fact, you may express your opinion in an essay only to discover later that you've changed your mind. That's good and healthy. Changing our minds based on reliable information keeps us from becoming narrow-minded. There may be times when you don't have a ready answer to a question and need to learn more about the topic. That, too, is part of the prewriting process.

Most students will never write essays once they leave college. Although it is important to learn to write well to succeed in college, the real value in learning to write is that it forces you to think through an issue. Analyzing your thoughts and feelings, thinking about more than one side of an issue, organizing information, and expressing yourself clearly are all skills you will use long after you leave college. Composition classes are frequently the only classes that actually teach you to think rather than to memorize information for tests.

Even though the **Think** stage is presented as the first stage in the writing process, thinking occurs continually as you write. At one point you may be thinking about ideas, at another point about organization, and at still another about what punctuation to use.

The **Read** sections, also part of the prewriting stage, provide reading selections that relate to the unit's broad writing topic and expose you to the ideas of others. You are not expected to agree with what these authors say but to *think* about what they say. At times you may want to disagree with an author in an essay of your own. At other times, you may agree with the writer but still have more to say on the subject. The reading selections can serve as a stimulus for ideas, as background information on some aspect of the unit topic, and as examples of various writing techniques and styles that authors use.

Research has shown a direct relationship between reading and writing. Those who read widely and frequently tend to write well. In many ways the skills involved in reading and writing essays are the same. When you write, you provide a thesis or main idea about your topic and then support it with your reasons or facts. When you read, you look for the author's thesis and the supporting ideas. When you write, you must critically evaluate your facts, opinions, and sources. When you read, you must do the same with the author's. You will become more aware of these relationships as you work your way through this book.

At times, reading selections or passages in them may seem to pose a comprehension problem. Expect difficulty in reading as part of the reading process. Don't be too quick to dismiss some readings as too difficult for you. You're not expected to know everything, but it is expected that you make every effort to read a selection more than once. Rereading is part of good reading. Just as good writing requires many rewrites before arriving at a final draft, good reading often *requires* several readings before arriving at good comprehension. Read a selection through once just to get a general idea of it. Then read it again, looking up unfamiliar words. Read all or parts of the selection aloud. Doing so usually makes what seemed difficult much easier.

Read with a pen in your hand and take notes as you read. Underline major ideas. Use numbers to identify each major idea's supporting points. Write your reactions and questions in the margins so you don't forget them. Ask yourself at least three questions: What does the reading selection say? What does it mean? What does it matter? Use answers to those questions to summarize the main points in your own words. How much attention and care you give to reading is up to you, but the more attention you give to it, the better your own writing will get.

It is also profitable to get together with two or more classmates and, using your reading notes, seriously discuss your interpretations and comprehension problems. Bring your questions about a reading selection to class. If you don't allow yourself to be challenged by what you might think as "too difficult," you will never expand your thinking, reading, and writing skills. Learning doesn't occur by merely sitting in a classroom. You have to become actively involved in the learning process.

The two parts of the **React** sections will develop your critical thinking and reading skills. One part asks you to react to the reading selection by writing a summary or your personal evaluation in your journal. In the second part, two sets of questions are presented. One set deals with your literal and critical comprehension, asking you to separate facts from opinions; to recognize propaganda; to examine the style, tone, and attitude of the authors you read. The other set of questions deals with your personal reactions and evaluations of the authors' ideas and writing styles. Reread for answers to the questions; you will find that your reading comprehension will improve. The skills you gain from such activities can be used in your own writing.

In addition, some of your beliefs about things may be challenged. A good education should shake you up a bit. It should force you to examine what you have taken for granted, to see things from a new perspective, to make certain that what you think is really based on your own thoughts and not those of others who may have influenced you in the past.

The last section of the prewriting phase of writing is **Plan.** Here you will learn various ways to think through a possible topic, to come up with ideas, and to organize those ideas even before you begin to write the first words of your essay. You will learn to brainstorm, freewrite, cluster, do PMIs, and ask questions that ensure that what you have to say has substance. Once you learn some of these techniques, you'll begin to blend them and develop your own way of doing things.

The Writing Stage

Once you have finished the prewriting stage, you are ready to write. The **Write** sections of each unit introduce you to one or two particular aspects of writing that you should consider: how to write introductory paragraphs, supporting paragraphs, concluding paragraphs, stronger sentences, transitional elements, and the like. Each unit teaches something new to consider about your writing skills. Unit by unit, you'll begin to understand more completely what an essay is and how to use language.

During the writing stage, don't worry too much about errors in punctuation and spelling. Concentrate more on developing your ideas, organizing your paragraphs, and expressing yourself clearly. Think about the audience to whom you are writing. Try different methods of expressing your ideas to see which one works best. Your first essay drafts shouldn't be thought of as the final version. That will come next.

Writing a first draft does not always start with writing the opening paragraph and working through to the end. At times you might have ideas for your concluding paragraph and will write that before your opening. At other times you may write supporting paragraphs before your introduction. Sometimes it's best not to begin with the introductory paragraph. Often the last paragraph you write may end up being your introduction. The main thing at this stage is to get your ideas into words on paper.

Sometimes "writer's block" occurs and nothing seems to get written. When you feel stuck, just start writing anything that comes to mind, whether or not it makes sense. The very act of writing words, any words, frequently gets you in the mood for writing and starts your mind working. Even when what you write has nothing to do with your subject, the act of physically writing often breaks the spell.

The Rewriting Stage

Once you are satisfied that you have developed your essay thesis, organized your support, and stated things with clarity, you are ready to revise, edit, and proofread for a final draft. At this point you need to consider your readers. The **Rewrite** sections provide you with information on development, coherence, grammar, mechanics, and punctuation. As you look for such things as subject-verb agreement, proper pronoun usage, and punctuation placement, you may find yourself back at the writing stage or even the prewriting stage. That's all part of the total writing process.

Each unit's **Rewrite** section provides a checklist to follow based on what you learn as you work through this book. The checklist reminds you to apply what you learn about thesis and paragraph development, transitional words, pronoun usage, punctuation, and the like. Frequently, actual student essays are provided for you to study and evaluate.

Many beginning writers break down at this stage. They don't want to make the extra effort that will help readers understand and enjoy their finished product. But attention to this stage can be, at a practical level, the difference between an A and a D.

◇ THE WRITING JOURNAL

We suggest that you get a spiral notebook 8½ by 11 inches that you use only for this class. Throughout the text you will be asked to make writing journal entries along with textbook entries. The journal entries are usually writing assignments, such as reactions or summaries of the readings, practices in paragraph writing, and first drafts of essays. Frequently, you will be asked to do freewriting, brainstorming, clustering, and other practices to plan and explore possible topics. Keeping these practices in one place—your journal—will be convenient for you and your instructor, who may want to check your work periodically.

◆ THE PRACTICES

For every writing skill taught in each unit, there are more practices in the back of the book. They are placed there so that they don't interrupt the development of each unit. You may not even need to do some of them. Doing them will depend on your needs and the instructor's desires.

◆ WHY WRITE ESSAYS?

Good writing requires good thinking and organizational skills, and although learning the essay form and correct punctuation is something every literate person should do, it is the development of your thinking processes that is ultimately more important. Most of your writing may end when school is over, but your ability to think clearly, to make critical judgments, to open your mind to new ideas, to be aware of the world around you and your place in it will continue the rest of your life. We hope this book will help you along that path.

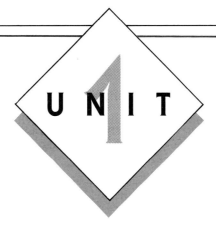

UNIT 1

PEANUTS by Charles M. Schulz

Learning is finding out what you already know. Doing is demonstrating you know it.

Richard Bach, *Illusions*

THINK . . .

about learning experiences.

◆ WRITING JOURNAL ENTRY

Later in this unit you will be asked to write an essay that expresses your feelings or concerns on some aspect of learning. In your writing journal, (1) write your definition of learning and (2) discuss your best educational or learning experience. Write thoughtful statements; they may be useful later as an idea for an essay of your own.

◆ TEXTBOOK ENTRY

In the blanks provided, answer the following questions. Take time to think before writing.

1. What are some things you would like to learn more about? _____

    _____

    _____

    _____

2. Pick one of the items mentioned in the preceding question and explain why you want to learn more about it. _____

    _____

    _____

    _____

3. What do you hope to learn from attending college? _____

    _____

    _____

    _____

4. What do you hope to learn from this class? _____

    _____

    _____

    _____

By the year 2000, 2 out of 3 Americans could be illiterate.

Read that again, just to be sure you read it correctly.

Because, believe it or not, it's true.

Even today, about one American adult in three can't read adequately. And, each year that goes by, reading skills continue to decline while the standards for literacy keep rising. By the year 2000, Americans will need greater reading skills than ever before, but fewer Americans will have them. If these trends continue unchecked for two decades, *U.S. News & World Report* envisions an America with a literacy rate of only 30%. Which means that the average person with three grandchildren could find that two of them are considered illiterate.

Before that America comes to be, you can stop it by joining the fight against illiteracy today. It takes no special qualifications. If you can read, you can tutor or help us in countless other ways. You'll be trained to work in programs right in your own community, sharing the satisfaction of seeing people learning and growing. And you'll know that you're not just helping them but their children and grandchildren, too. Because you're stopping illiteracy before it reaches them.

So join the effort. Call the Coalition for Literacy toll-free **800-228-8813.** You'll be fighting illiteracy for generations to come.

Volunteer Against Illiteracy.
The only degree you need
is a degree of caring.

 Ad Council   Coalition for Literacy

VOLUNTEER AGAINST ILLITERACY CAMPAIGN
MAGAZINE AD NO. VAI-1830-84—7" x 10" [110 Screen]
Volunteer Agency: Benton & Bowles, Inc., Volunteer Coordinator: Robert F. Lauterborn, International Paper Co.

CM-SPEC
12/84

5.   Which of the following do you need to learn more about?
_____ a. finding an appropriate topic and thesis for an essay
_____ b. organizing your ideas
_____ c. writing good sentences
_____ d. writing good paragraphs
_____ e. using correct punctuation
_____ f. developing a better vocabulary
_____ g. finding a pen and paper
_____ h. developing self-confidence in English

READ . . .

about learning to write essays.

Every well-written essay or article contains a *thesis*, or a main idea about the subject the author wants the reader to accept or think about. A thesis is not the same thing as a subject or topic but rather what the author feels or says about the subject. For instance, the *subject* of the selection you are about to read has to do with writing essays in college. As you read, look for the author's thesis, the main point he is trying to make about writing essays. Prepare to read by doing the following:

1.   Read the title of the reading selection. In your own words, explain what you think it means.

_____

_____

_____

2.   Skim read over the essay, noting the headings. Write the title of each heading in the spaces below.

_____

_____

_____

_____

_____

3. Read only the first paragraph and then answer these questions:
    a. To what audience do you think the author is writing? Why do you think

    so? _____

    _____

    _____

    _____

    b. What do you think you will learn from reading this essay?

    _____

    _____

4. The meaning an author intends may be lost if the reader does not understand
    the author's use of certain words and phrases. Make sure you understand the
    following words. The number after the word is the number of the paragraph
    where the word appears:
    a. *tedious* (6 and 12) = dull; boring; tiresomely long
    b. *trivial* (8) = of little importance; commonplace
    c. *trite* (9) = overused; lacking originality
    d. *vacuity* (10) = emptiness of mind; stupidity
    e. *indispensable* (10) = essential; important
    f. *inconstancy* (1) = changing
    g. *elation* (15) = happiness; joy
    h. *abolition* (16) = the end of or removal of some thing
    i. *abstract* (17) = not concrete; a general statement or idea that needs support
    j. *anecdotal* (18) = illustrated or explained through an interesting or humorous
        story
    k. *adept* (20) = highly skilled or expert
    l. *warily* (22) = cautiously; carefully
5. Now read the essay. Underline what you think are key points to remember,
    and make notes in the margins as an aid to better reading.

HOW TO SAY NOTHING IN 500 WORDS

Paul Roberts

Nothing About Something

1   It's Friday afternoon, and you have almost survived another week of classes. You
are just looking forward dreamily to the weekend when the English instructor says:
"For Monday you will turn in a five-hundred word composition on college football."

2   Well, that puts a good big hole in the weekend. You don't have any strong views
on college football one way or the other. You get rather excited during the season and
go to all the home games and find it rather more fun than not. On the other hand, the

class has been reading Robert Hutchins in the anthology and perhaps Shaw's "Eighty-Yard Run," and from the class discussion you have got the idea that the instructor thinks college football is for the birds. You are no fool, you. You can figure out what side to take.

3   After dinner you get out the portable typewriter that you got for high school graduation. You might as well get it over with and enjoy Saturday and Sunday. Five hundred words is about two double-spaced pages with normal margins. You put in a sheet of paper, think up a title, and you're off:

WHY COLLEGE FOOTBALL SHOULD BE ABOLISHED

College football should be abolished because it's bad for the school and also bad for the players. The players are so busy practicing that they don't have any time for their studies.

This, you feel, is a mighty good start. The only trouble is that it's only thirty-two words. You still have four hundred and sixty-eight to go, and you've pretty well exhausted the subject. It comes to you that you do your best thinking in the morning, so you put away the typewriter and go to the movies. But the next morning you have to do your washing and some math problems, and in the afternoon you go to the game. The English instructor turns up too, and you wonder if you've taken the right side after all. Saturday night you have a date, and Sunday morning you have to go to church. (You shouldn't let English assignments interfere with your religion.) What with one thing and another, it's ten o'clock Sunday night before you get out the typewriter again. You make a pot of coffee and start to fill out your views on college football. Put a little meat on the bones.

WHY COLLEGE FOOTBALL SHOULD BE ABOLISHED

In my opinion, it seems to me that college football should be abolished. The reason why I think this to be true is because I feel that football is bad for the colleges in nearly every respect. As Robert Hutchins says in his article in our anthology in which he discusses college football, it would be better if the colleges had race horses and had races with one another, because then the horses would not have to attend classes. I firmly agree with Mr. Hutchins on this point, and I am sure that many other students would agree too.

One reason why it seems to me that college football is bad is that it has become too commercial. In the olden times when people played football just for the fun of it, maybe college football was all right, but they do not play football just for the fun of it now as they used to in the old days. Nowadays college football is what you might call a big business. Maybe this is not true at all schools, and I don't think it is especially true here at State, but certainly this is the case at most colleges and universities in America nowadays, as Mr. Hutchins points out in his very interesting article. Actually the coaches and alumni go around to the high schools and offer the high school stars large salaries to come to their colleges and play football for them. There was one case where a high school star was offered a convertible if he would play football for a certain college.

Another reason for abolishing college football is that it is bad for the players. They do not have time to get a college education, because they are so busy playing football. A football player has to practice every afternoon from three to six, and then he is so tired that he can't concentrate on his studies. He just feels like dropping off to sleep after dinner, and then the next day he goes to his classes without having studied and maybe he fails the test.

(Good ripe stuff so far, but you're still a hundred and fifty-one words from home. One more push.)

Also I think college football is bad for the colleges and the universities because not very many students get to participate in it. Out of a college of ten thousand students only seventy-five or a hundred play football, if that many. Football is what you might call a spectator sport. That means that most people go to watch it but do not play it themselves.

(Four hundred and fifteen. Well, you still have the conclusion, and when you retype it, you can make the margins a little wider.)

These are the reasons why I agree with Mr. Hutchins that college football should be abolished in American colleges and universities.

4   On Monday you turn it in, moderately hopeful, and on Friday it comes back marked "weak in content" and sporting a big "D."

5   This essay is exaggerated a little, not much. The English instructor will recognize it as reasonably typical of what an assignment on college football will bring in. He knows that nearly half of the class will contrive in five hundred words to say that college football is too commercial and bad for the players. Most of the other half will inform him that college football builds character and prepares one for life and brings prestige to the school. As he reads paper after paper all saying the same thing in almost the same words, all bloodless, five hundred words dripping out of nothing, he wonders how he allowed himself to get trapped into teaching English when he might have had a happy and interesting life as an electrician or a confidence man.

6   Well, you may ask, what can you do about it? The subject is one on which you have few convictions and little information. Can you be expected to make a dull subject interesting? As a matter of fact, this is precisely what you are expected to do. This is the writer's essential task. All subjects, except sex, are dull until somebody makes them interesting. The writer's job is to find the argument, the approach, the angle, the wording that will take the reader with him. This is seldom easy, and it is particularly hard in subjects that have been much discussed: College Football, Fraternities, Popular Music, Is Chivalry Dead?, and the like. You will feel that there is nothing you can do with such subjects except repeat the old bromides. But there are some things you can do which will make your papers, if not throbbingly alive, at least less insufferably tedious than they might otherwise be.

Avoid the Obvious Content

7   Say the assignment is college football. Say that you've decided to be against it. Begin by putting down the arguments that come to your mind: it is too commercial, it

takes the students' minds off their studies, it is hard on the players, it makes the university a kind of circus instead of an intellectual center, for most schools it is financially ruinous. Can you think of any more arguments just off hand? All right. Now when you write your paper, *make sure that you don't use any of the material on this list.* If these are the points that leap to your mind, they will leap to everyone else's too, and whether you get a "C" or a "D" may depend on whether the instructor reads your paper early when he is fresh and tolerant or late, when the sentence "In my opinion, college football has become too commercial," inexorably repeated, has brought him to the brink of lunacy.

8   Be against college football for some reason or reasons of your own. If they are keen and perceptive ones, that's splendid. But even if they are trivial or foolish or indefensible, you are still ahead so long as they are not everybody else's reasons too. Be against it because the colleges don't spend enough money on it to make it worth while, because it is bad for the characters of the spectators, because the players are forced to attend classes, because the football stars hog all the beautiful women, because it competes with baseball and is therefore un-American and possibly Communist inspired. There are lots of more or less unused reasons for being against college football.

9   Sometimes it is a good idea to sum up and dispose of the trite and conventional points before going on to your own. This has the advantage of indicating to the reader that you are going to be neither trite nor conventional. Something like this:

> We are often told that college football should be abolished because it has become too commercial or because it is bad for the players. These arguments are no doubt very cogent, but they don't really go to the heart of the matter.

Then you go to the heart of the matter.

Take the Less Usual Side

10   One rather simple way of getting interest into your papers is to take the side of the argument that most citizens will want to avoid. If the assignment is an essay on dogs, you can, if you choose, explain that dogs are faithful and lovable companions, intelligent, useful as guardians of the house and protectors of children, indispensable in police work—in short, when all is said and done, man's best friends. Or you can suggest that those big brown eyes conceal, more often than not, a vacuity of mind and an inconstancy of purpose; that the dogs you have known most intimately have been mangy, ill-tempered brutes, incapable of instruction; and that only your nobility of mind and fear of arrest prevent you from kicking the flea-ridden animals when you pass them on the street.

11   Naturally, personal convictions will sometimes dictate your approach. If the assignment subject is "Is Methodism Rewarding to the Individual?" and you are a pious Methodist, you have really no choice. But few assigned subjects, if any, will fall in this category. Most of them will lie in broad areas of discussion with much to be said on both sides. They are intellectual exercises, and it is legitimate to argue now one way and now another, as debaters do in similar circumstances. Always take the side that looks to you hardest, least defensible. It will always turn out to be easier to write interestingly on that side.

12   This general advice applies where you have a choice of subjects. If you are to choose among "The Values of Fraternities" and "My Favorite High School Teacher" and "What I Think About Beetles," by all means plump for the beetles. By the time the instructor gets to your paper, he will be up to his ears in tedious tales about the French teacher at Bloombury High and assertions about how fraternities build character and prepare one for life. Your views on beetles, whatever they are, are bound to be a refreshing change.

13   Don't worry too much about figuring out what the instructor thinks about the subject so that you can cuddle up with him. Chances are his views are no stronger than yours. If he does have convictions and you oppose them, his problem is to keep from grading you higher than you deserve in order to show he is not biased. This doesn't mean that you should always cantankerously dissent from what the instructor says; that gets tiresome too. And if the subject assigned is "My Pet Peeve," do not begin, "My pet peeve is the English instructor who assigns papers on 'my pet peeve.'" This was still funny during the War of 1812, but it has sort of lost its edge since then. It is in general good manners to avoid personalities.

Slip Out of Abstraction

14   If you will study the essay on college football [in paragraph 3], you will perceive that one reason for its appalling dullness is that it never gets down to particulars. It is just a series of not very glittering generalities: "football is bad for the colleges," "it has become too commercial," "football is a big business," "it is bad for the players," and so on. Such round phrases thudding against the reader's brain are unlikely to convince him, though they may well render him unconscious.

15   If you want the reader to believe that college football is bad for the players, you have to do more than say so. You have to display the evil. Take your roommate, Alfred Simkins, the second-string center. Picture poor old Alfy coming home from football practice every evening, bruised and aching, agonizingly tired, scarcely able to shovel the mashed potatoes into his mouth. Let us see him staggering up to the room, getting out his econ textbook, peering desperately at it with his good eye, falling asleep and failing the test in the morning. Let us share his unbearable tension as Saturday draws near. Will he fail, be demoted, lose his monthly allowance, be forced to return to the coal mines? And if he succeeds, what will be his reward? Perhaps a slight ripple of applause when the third-string center replaces him, a moment of elation in the locker room if the team wins, or despair if it loses. What will he look back on when he graduates from college? Toil and torn ligaments. And what will be his future? He is not good enough for pro football, and he is too obscure and weak in econ to suceed in stocks and bonds. College football is tearing the heart from Alfy Simkins and, when it finishes with him, will callously toss aside the shattered hulk.

16   This is no doubt a weak enough argument for the abolition of college football, but it is a sight better than saying, in three or four variations, that college football (in your opinion) is bad for the players.

17   Look at the work of any professional writer and notice how constantly he is moving from the generality, the abstract statement, to the concrete example, the facts and figures, the illustration. If he is writing on juvenile delinquency, he does not just tell you that juveniles are (it seems to him) delinquent and that (in his opinion) something should be done about it. He shows you juveniles being delinquent, tearing up movie theatres in Buffalo, stabbing high school principals in Dallas, smoking marijuana in

Palo Alto. And more than likely he is moving toward some specific remedy, not just a general wringing of the hands.

18   It is no doubt possible to be *too* concrete, too illustrative or anecdotal, but few inexperienced writers err this way. For most the soundest advice is to be seeking always for the picture, to be always turning general remarks into seeable examples. Don't say, "Sororities teach girls the social graces." Say, "Sorority life teaches a girl how to carry on a conversation while pouring tea, without sloshing the tea into the saucer." Don't say, "I like certain kinds of popular music very much." Say, "Whenever I hear Gerber Spinklittle play 'Mississippi Man' on the trombone, my socks creep up my ankles."

Get Rid of Obvious Padding

19   The student toiling away at his weekly English theme is too often tormented by a figure: five hundred words. How, he asks himself, is he to achieve this staggering total? Obviously by never using one word when he can somehow work in ten.

20   He is therefore seldom content with a plain statement like "Fast driving is dangerous." This has only four words in it. He talks thought, and the sentence becomes:

> In my opinion, fast driving is dangerous.

Better, but he can do better still;

> In my opinion, fast driving would seem to be rather dangerous.

If he is really adept, it may come out:

> In my humble opinion, though I do not claim to be an expert on this complicated subject, fast driving, in most circumstances, would seem to be rather dangerous in many respects, or at least so it would seem to me.

Thus four words have been turned into forty, and not an iota of content has been added.

21   Now this is a way to go about reaching five hundred words, and if you are content with a "D" grade, it is as good a way as any. But if you aim higher, you must work differently. Instead of stuffing your sentences with straw, you must try steadily to get rid of the padding, to make your sentences lean and tough. If you are really working at it, your first draft will greatly exceed the required total, and then you will work it down, thus:

> It is thought in some quarters that fraternities do not contribute as much as might be expected to campus life.

> Some people think that fraternities contribute little to campus life.

> The average doctor who practices in small towns or in the country must toil night and day to heal the sick.

> Most country doctors work long hours.

When I was a little girl, I suffered from shyness and embarrassment in the presence of others.

I was a shy little girl.

It is absolutely necessary for the person employed as a marine fireman to give the matter of steam pressure his undivided attention at all times.

The fireman has to keep his eye on the steam gauge.

22   You may ask how you can arrive at five hundred words at this rate. Simply. You dig up more real content. Instead of taking a couple of obvious points off the surface of the topic and then circling warily around them for six paragraphs, you work in and explore, figure out the details. You illustrate. You say that fast driving is dangerous, and then you prove it. How long does it take to stop a car at forty and at eighty? How far can you see at night? What happens when a tire blows? What happens in a head-on collision at fifty miles an hour? Pretty soon your paper will be full of broken glass and blood and headless torsos, and reaching five hundred words will not really be a problem.

Excerpts from "How to Say Nothing in Five Hundred Words" from *Understanding English* by Paul Roberts. Reprinted by permission of Harper & Row Publishers, Inc.

A Nobel Prize scientist wins $340,000 for 11 years of research. Meanwhile, the Rambos and bimbos of the country make millions.
So much for education.

Jeanne Jennings, Los Angeles Times

REACT . . .

to the reading selection.

◇ WRITING JOURNAL ENTRY

In your writing journal, write your reaction to "How to Say Nothing in Five Hundred Words." Discuss (1) how you felt while reading it, (2) what you learned that might help you with your own writing, (3) what questions or problems you want to raise in class, and (4) anything else you want to say about it.

◆ TEXTBOOK ENTRY

A. Understanding the Content

In the blanks provided, write your answers to the following questions. Refer to the reading selection for answers when you need to.

1. The subject or topic of this essay is _____

2. The author's main idea (thesis) about the subject is _____

_____

_____

3. What is the meaning of Roberts's heading "Nothing About Something"? How does the sample student essay on college football provide an example of what he means? _____

_____

_____

_____

4. Why does Roberts suggest that you "Take the Less Usual Side" (paragraphs 10–13)? _____

_____

_____

_____

5. Summarize paragraph 10 in one sentence. _____

_____

_____

_____

6. What does Roberts mean by "Slip Out of Abstraction"? _____

_____

_____

_____

7.   What is Roberts's point in paragraph 18? _____

_____

_____

_____

8.   What is the main idea of paragraphs 19–22? _____

_____

_____

_____

B. Noticing Writing Techniques and Style

9.   Roberts had a particular *audience* in mind for his essay. To whom was he

writing? _____ How do you know? _____

_____

_____

_____

10.   Authors usually reveal an *attitude* about their topic, which is expressed by using a certain *tone*. A tone, just like a tone of voice, can be serious, pleasant, humorous, sarcastic, nasty, ironic, or biased in order to get the reader to react to the thesis. What do you think is Roberts's attitude toward his audience?

_____

What words or phrases does Roberts use to give you this impression?_____

_____

_____

11.   The first four paragraphs of Roberts's essay are used as a kind of anecdote or story that shows the way some students go about completing a freshman composition assignment. How does the student essay serve as an example of the

points about essay writing that Roberts discusses? _____

_____

_____

_____

12.   Based on Roberts's attitude and tone, explain why you would or would not
       want him as an English instructor. _____

       _____

       _____

       _____

       _____

> After hiring the young man, the employer gave him a broom. "Your first job," he said, "will be to sweep out the office."
> "But," the youth protested, "I'm a college graduate."
> "Very well," replied the boss, "hand me the broom, and I'll show you how."
>
> *Masonic Bulletin*

PLAN . . .
an essay on some aspect of learning.

When assigned to write an essay, some students frequently wait until a day or two before it is due, then suddenly panic, causing cloudy thinking. Some students begin by writing on the given topic until they fill a page or two, just as Roberts describes in his essay, hoping that what they have written will be acceptable. A few may scratch their heads and decide to be absent the day the assignment is due. And still others may sit with pen and paper (or in front of their word processors) waiting impatiently to be zapped by divine inspiration. To avoid such usually drastic approaches, try the following three-step approach *before* writing a first draft. Each step will be discussed more fully later, but for now, just read them carefully.

Step 1: Select a topic that is neither too broad nor too narrow by using exploration techniques that help you discover what you know and can say about the subject. Always look for a way to turn the assignment into something you can handle.

Step 2: Write a working thesis based on the ideas gained from the exploration of the topic assigned.

Step 3: Analyze and organize the ideas by putting together those that are similar; then rearrange the ideas in the order you will use them in your essay.

These three steps, if done correctly, will get you started in the right direction. Here is more about each step.

STEP 1: Selecting and Exploring a Topic: Brainstorming

There are several ways to explore a topic in order to find the best way to approach it and to make sure that you know enough about it. Each one will be covered thoroughly as we move from unit to unit. For now, learn about **brainstorming**.

One way to think through a topic before writing about it is to brainstorm. Brainstorming requires listing as many ideas as possible about the topic exactly as they come to mind. The trick is not to judge the value of an idea during your brainstorming session. Sometimes, the crazier the idea the better because it could lead to an interesting or unusual approach to the topic assigned. Brainstorming can be done alone or in small groups. Here's how it works.

If, for example, the topic *education* is assigned, the first obvious thing to do is to narrow it down. As a topic, education is much too broad. Books have been written about education, so the topic has to be narrowed to something manageable in a 500-word essay. A good way to begin is to write the word *education* at the top of a blank page and jot down whatever ideas come to mind about education. Every idea is acceptable. Don't judge any of the ideas, as this will slow down the thinking process.

The following is a brainstorming list on education done by a student named Lisa Benton:

Education

grades	textbooks
teachers	money for tuition
formal education	what makes a good teacher
street-wise education	importance of college
grade school	Mr. Wrinkle, UGH!
school levels	cheating on tests
lousy counselors	junior colleges
vocational schools	

The list contains a variety of thoughts. At this point Lisa has several options. One might be to look over the list and see what items would be usable for an essay. Although some of them are still too broad, there are several possible topics here: how to get money for tuition, what makes a good teacher, the importance of college, Mr. Wrinkle, and cheating on tests. These are certainly narrower in scope than the other items.

Most of the items left from which to choose are fairly typical, the sort of ideas most of us might think about; however, chances are no one else would write about Mr. Wrinkle. Following the advice Roberts gives to avoid the obvious and take the less usual side, Lisa decided to write about something she knew and for which she had some feeling: Mr. Wrinkle.

Her next step was to do some more brainstorming on Mr. Wrinkle. Here is her list:

Mr. Wrinkle

hard teacher
always scratching his chin
doesn't believe in giving A's
the course makes me miss lunch
talks as if we know more than we do
uses too many big words
often comes to class late
gives too many essay-writing assignments
walks around the room too much
never looks students in the eye
I didn't take enough English in high school
doesn't have a friendly attitude toward students

When she was finished, Lisa noticed that all but two of the items on the list were negative remarks about Mr. Wrinkle. Draw a line through the two items that don't relate to him.

The two items that aren't needed are "the course makes me miss lunch" and "I didn't take enough English." The rest of the list all deals with Mr. Wrinkle and reveals why Lisa reacted with an "ugh!" to his name on her brainstorming list. Now she not only has narrowed the topic to something she can handle and knows well but also has ideas to use when she starts her first draft.

◆ WRITING JOURNAL ENTRY

Before going on to Step 2, try brainstorming for about three minutes on one of the following topics or on a topic already assigned to you. The list you develop will be useful when you are assigned your next essay. When you are finished, go on to Step 2.

1. my favorite teacher
2. learning a foreign language
3. writing essays
4. the grading system
5. learning about myself
6. what being on the streets teaches
7. learning a trade
8. what I need to learn
9. why I want to go to college
10. (Pick your own topic related to learning.)

STEP 2: Writing a Working Thesis

A thesis, remember, is what an author wants to say about a subject. A **working thesis** is one that is used to help begin a first draft. It is not one that a writer has to stick with; it's primarily a guide to follow so that information needed to develop the topic won't be left out. A working thesis, as does a final version, contains key words that guide the writer and lets the reader understand the point being made in the essay.

Here are some examples of the difference between a topic and a thesis:

Topic: How Some Instructors Use Grades Against Students

Possible Working Thesis Statements:

1. Some instructors use grades to punish students.
2. Some teachers at our school take advantage of their power by using grades to punish students.
3. Instructors can keep students from advancing to other courses by giving them poor grades.
4. Teachers who grade by the curve harm some students.

Notice that in all of these statements a claim is being made that some instructors use grades unfairly. In all cases, it would be necessary to prove this claim by providing examples that support it. As a writer proceeds to prove this claim, it may be that the working thesis may have to be modified or changed completely. But by using a working thesis, a writer will be able to control the writing rather than rambling all over the place.

Here is another example:

Topic: The Qualities Necessary for a Good Teacher

Possible Working Thesis Statements:

1. The most important qualities a good teacher should have are a thorough understanding of the subject being taught, a variety of teaching methods, and a concern for the students' needs.
2. There are only two qualities necessary for good teaching: a love for the subject being taught and a willingness to help students learn.

The first thesis statement mentions three qualities, each of which would have to be developed within the essay. The second thesis statement presents two qualities that need development. In both cases, they provide the writer with a plan, a direction to pursue. Notice, too, that thesis statements are complete sentences.

In Step 1, Lisa brainstormed on education and discovered a topic she wanted to write about: Mr. Wrinkle. She then brainstormed some more and discovered the things she wanted to say about Mr. Wrinkle. Since all of the items listed are fairly negative, her thesis had to reflect a negative attitude toward him. In this case, Lisa's working thesis was Mr. Wrinkle "bugs" me. Although the working thesis was stated too informally to be used in her final draft, it helped her control what she wanted to say about him. Here, then, is what she now had to help her write her essay:

Working Thesis: Mr. Wrinkle "bugs" me.

Why? hard teacher
always scratching his chin
doesn't believe in giving A's
talks as if we know more than we do
uses too many big words
often comes to class late
gives too many essay-writing assignments
walks around the room too much
never looks students in the eye.

The next step is to organize these ideas. But before going on to Step 3, do the following activities to make certain you understand Step 2.

◆ TEXTBOOK ENTRY

Following is a list of some statements. Place a check mark by the ones you feel are good thesis statements, those that are neither too narrow nor too broad for a 500-word essay.

_____ 1. The most important human qualities cannot be graded.
_____ 2. Learning a foreign language should be required of all college students.
_____ 3. There are advantages to the credit–no credit system over the letter grade system.
_____ 4. Textbooks are boring.
_____ 5. The history of American universities.

The first three could be used as thesis statements for short essays. The first one requires an explanation and discussion of the important human qualities that can't be graded. The second one requires support for the argument that foreign language courses should be a college requirement. The third one requires that the credit–no credit grading system be shown as advantageous over the letter grade system.

Number 4 is too broad. It implies that *all* textbooks are boring. (Obviously, this textbook proves the statement is false, right?) Unless someone is familiar with all textbooks and can prove this opinion, it is a very weak statement. It needs to be narrowed to something such as, "My psychology textbook is boring," and then to show why. Of course, in the process of proving it, the writer might discover "boring" is the wrong word. It might be changed to "difficult to read" or "assumes I know more than I do about the subject." Still, it serves as a working thesis.

Number 5 is not a thesis statement; it's a topic. What about the history of American universities? There is no point to be made. Besides, the topic is much too broad for a short essay. More brainstorming would be required to narrow it down.

Look now at the brainstorming list you completed in your writing journal after reading Step 1 (page 24). In the following space, write the topic you picked and then write a working thesis that would cover all the items you have listed for that subject.

Possible essay topic: _____

Working thesis statement: _____

_____

_____

STEP 3: Analyzing and Organizing the Brainstorming List

The next step is to analyze and organize the brainstorming list so that the items are arranged in a usable way. A brainstorming list usually produces a list of items that are both general and specific, so it becomes necessary to sort the items into some type of category. For instance, in Lisa's list, "hard teacher" is a general statement. The items "gives too many essay-writing assignments" and "never gives A's" are specific examples of the more general statement, "hard teacher."

In the case of the working thesis, "Mr. Wrinkle bugs me," here is the way Lisa rearranged her brainstorming list:

General statement: *hard teacher*

Specifics: — *gives too many essay-writing assignments*
— *never gives A's*

General statement: doesn't have a friendly attitude toward students

Specifics: — uses too many big words
— talks as if we know more than we do
— comes to class late

After looking at the last three items on her list, Lisa realized they were all specific mannerisms that annoyed her, so she categorized them as follows:

General statement: annoying personal mannerisms

Specifics: — always scratching chin
— walks around the room too much
— never looks students in the eye

The list of brainstorming items now appears in three general categories: hard teacher, attitudes toward students, and annoying personal mannerisms. Each of these categories can now be developed into three separate paragraphs. The first draft will probably be a five-paragraph essay based on the following organization:

Opening paragraph:
    Introduction to Mr. Wrinkle
    Thesis statement containing three categories
        difficult teacher (key supporting point)
        attitudes toward students (key supporting point)
        personal mannerisms (key supporting point)

Second paragraph:
    Difficult teacher (key supporting point)
        gives too many essay-writing assignments (supporting detail)
        never gives A's (supporting detail)

Third paragraph:
    Attitude toward students (key supporting point)
        uses too many big words (supporting detail)
        talks as if we know more than we do (supporting detail)
        comes to class late (supporting detail)

Fourth paragraph:
   Personal mannerisms (key supporting point)
      always scratches chin (supporting detail)
      walks around the room too much (supporting detail)
      never looks students in the eye (supporting detail)

Fifth paragraph:
   Conclusion of some type to be determined later

An essay can easily be written by following this organization. It may not be the final organizational pattern, but it serves as a good start. Naturally, a different organizational pattern could be used, placing paragraph 4 where paragraph 2 is, and so on. But the basic idea of planning before trying to write a first draft helps to narrow a topic, develop a working thesis, and plan an organization of the supporting ideas.

At this point, it's time to look again at the thesis. By combining the three major categories of the Wrinkle outline, a tighter thesis than the original "Mr. Wrinkle bugs me" can be formed. Lisa changed her thesis to read, "Mr. Wrinkle is a difficult teacher whose attitudes toward students and personal mannerisms caused me to dislike his class." This statement is more to the point and served as a guide for her first draft. Chances are that without going through the various prewriting stages, writer's cramp would have set in long before a sense of direction was found.

As mentioned earlier, the writing process is not orderly. There are times when you may know a subject so well that you can sit down and write a first draft without going through the planning process just described. But more often than not, the three planning steps will save time by getting you started in the right direction.

◆ WRITING JOURNAL ENTRY

Return now to your brainstorming list in your journal. Try rearranging your list of ideas in a way similar to the Mr. Wrinkle example. Look for general and specific statements. You may need to come up with general statements for specifics on your list, or you may need to brainstorm some more for specifics to list under your general statements. Then, at the top of a new page in your journal, write a new thesis statement if necessary to fit your organizational plan and organize your key points and supporting details, as shown in the Mr. Wrinkle example. This is the plan you will follow when assigned to write an essay. Your instructor may want to see your organizational plan.

Practice in Organizing and Planning

If you or your instructor feel you need more practice on organizing and planning activities, go to page 286.

WRITE . . .

a first draft on some aspect of learning.

Before directing you to begin a first draft for an essay, this section will present useful information on (1) the nutshell statement and (2) writing paragraphs with topic sentences.

The Nutshell Statement

A good way to discover if you are ready to put all your prewriting activities into essay form is to write a nutshell statement. A nutshell statement is a one-paragraph statement that includes (1) the *purpose* of your essay, (2) the *audience* to whom you are writing, and (3) a *summary* of your supporting points.

For instance, the following is a possible nutshell statement for the topic Mr. Wrinkle:

> The purpose of my essay is to show why I did not care for Mr. Wrinkle as a teacher. My audience will be other students thinking of taking his class. I will support my essay with examples of his attitudes toward students, his personal mannerisms that bothered me, and I will discuss what makes him a difficult teacher.

With this nutshell, a sense of direction for a first essay draft is set.

Of course, another direction could be established with a nutshell statement such as the following:

> The purpose of my essay is to discuss how learning can be difficult when instructors are not aware of their class presence. My audience will be students, teachers, and anyone interested in education. I will support my purpose by using Mr. Wrinkle as an example of what teachers should not be like, giving examples of his attitudes, mannerisms, and methods.

Notice the difference in purpose and audience. The first nutshell statement focuses on why the author didn't care for Mr. Wrinkle and was aimed at an audience of fellow students who might be considering taking his class. The second nutshell statement focuses on how learning can be difficult when instructors aren't aware of their mannerisms and is geared toward an audience of students, teachers, and others interested in education. The key points and supporting details contained in the organized list can be used for either nutshell statement.

◇ TEXTBOOK ENTRY

In the blanks given, write a nutshell statement for the thesis and brainstorming list you developed in the **Plan** section.

The purpose of my essay is _____

_____

My audience is _____

_____

I will support my thesis by _____

_____

_____

Paragraphs and Topic Sentences

Every essay consists of units of thought called paragraphs. Most, but not all, paragraphs contain a *topic sentence*, which is the sentence in the paragraph that states what the paragraph is all about. The topic sentence is the most general statement and contains key words or phrases that need further support or development in the paragraph.

In a way, the paragraph is a mini-essay. The topic sentence functions as the thesis does in an essay. The rest of the sentences in the paragraph function as the supporting paragraphs in an essay.

Frequently, writers place the topic sentence at the beginning of the paragraph, but it can appear anywhere within the paragraph. Some paragraphs contain no topic sentence but rather imply or suggest the main point through details or description. Here is an example of a paragraph with a topic sentence at the beginning:

> Around the country, high-school guidance counselors are under more pressure than ever before. One adviser at an affluent private school tells me that parents are "acting crazier than ever" and are putting more pressure on their kids to get into the most selective colleges. Some parents are even encouraging their children to submit applications to as many as 15 to 20 highly selective colleges, no matter what

their prospects are. Forget about putting the poor kid in the position of receiving 20 rejection letters. The counselor is then placed in an awkward position, stuck between parents' desires and student ability. (G. Gary Ripple, "Gold-Plating Our Students." *Newsweek* 4 Apr. 1988: 9)

The first sentence is more general, stating that high-school guidance counselors are under pressure. The topic sentence, then, lets us know what the subject of the paragraph is (high-school guidance counselors) and what point the writer wants to make (they are under more pressure than before). Each of the other sentences are more specific and provide details that show why the guidance counselors are under pressure. The author's writing plan may have looked something like this:

Paragraph's main idea or key point: High-school guidance counselors are under more pressure today.

Supporting details:

1. Parents putting pressure on their kids to get into best colleges.
2. Some parents encourage 15–20 application submissions.
3. Student will receive many rejection letters.
4. Counselor placed in awkward position.

All of the supporting details are examples of the key word in the topic sentence: *pressure*.

Read the following paragraph, looking for the key words in the topic sentence and the supporting details.

A telephone company attempting to recruit workers finds 86% of applicants fail the entry test. A steelworker misorders $1 million in parts because he cannot read well. An insurance clerk who doesn't understand decimals pays a claimant $2,200 instead of $22. A congressional study shows most high school juniors cannot write a simple letter seeking a summer job. Illiteracy caused by poor education has become an economic time bomb, threatening both the quality of the American work force and the nation's ability to compete on world markets. ("U.S. Seen Facing a Literacy Crisis." *Los Angeles Times* 20 Mar. 1988: IV, 1)

In this case the topic sentence is the last one. The first four sentences are examples of the effects of illiteracy on the American work force. These examples support the key words and phrases in the topic sentences: *illiteracy, threatening, work force, ability to compete.* A planning outline for writing this paragraph might have looked like this:

Supporting details:

1. 86% of telephone company applicants fail test.
2. $1 million error in parts order by poor reader.
3. Insurance clerk doesn't know decimals causing $2,200 error.
4. Most high-school juniors can't write letter for summer job.

Paragraph's main idea or key point: Illiteracy is threatening both America's work force and ability to compete on world markets.

In this example, all of the supporting points lead up to the topic sentence.

As you read this next paragraph, look for the key words in the topic sentence and the supporting details.

> Readers may read as slowly or as rapidly as they wish; if they do not understand something, they can stop and reread it. Clearly, then, readers are in control of their pace and pleasure. They can accelerate their pace when the reading is easy, and they can slow down when the reading is tough or entertaining. They can stop and reflect for a few moments, knowing that what they read will be there when they come back to the book. (Adam Ribb, "Reading vs. Television." *Wall Street Journal* 4 Apr. 1988: 4)

Here the topic sentence is the second sentence. A writing plan might look something similar to this:

Supporting detail:

1. Readers may read slowly or rapidly as desired.
2. They can stop and reread if they don't understand.

Paragraph's main idea or key point: Readers are in control of their reading speed and pleasure.

Supporting detail:

3. Accelerate pace when easy reading; slow down when tough.
4. Can stop and reflect, knowing the book will be there when ready.

Notice that four major points are made, all having to do with the key words: *readers in control, pace, pleasure.*

Here is one last example. Again, look for the topic sentence and supporting details.

> The story is told of an exam in the Harvard philosophy class taught by William James that called for an essay on comparative values in philosophy. Gertrude Stein was in the class and turned in a one-sentence essay—"I don't feel much like writing about philosophy today"—and received a top grade. Several students who submitted full papers but who received lesser grades questioned James on his grading of Stein's answer. "One of the prime values of philosophy is honesty," he replied. "She demonstrated it." (Norman Cousins, "Schoolyard Blues." *Los Angeles Times Magazine* 6 Oct. 1985: 42)

There is no topic sentence in the paragraph. In this case, the paragraph is used by the author as an example of some point he is making. Since we don't have the whole essay here, we can't relate the paragraph's point to his thesis. However, we can make some inferences and guess at the main idea. The story or anecdote deals with grading essay exams, in particular the way William James graded his students in his philosophy class. Based on the way he graded Stein's one-sentence essay, we can infer or guess that James was against grading on a curve, that he treated his students as individuals, and that he tried to apply his course content to his own grading philosophy. Still, there is no clear statement that can be called a topic sentence.

Generally, it is not a good idea for beginning writers to write paragraphs without a topic sentence. Such a paragraph could run the risk of not being organized. However, if a paragraph such as the preceding example fits into the context of a paragraph that comes before or after, it is acceptable.

◆ TEXTBOOK ENTRY

Part A.   As with a thesis statement, a topic sentence should be neither too broad nor too narrow. It should contain not only the main idea of the paragraph, but also key words or phrases that control what can and can't be said in the paragraph. In the blanks provided, write your comments regarding the following possible topic sentences. State whether they are too broad, too narrow, and what key words or phrases would need to be developed. The first one has been done for you.

1.   Lisa has been in college two years.

    too narrow

    _____

2.   Ms. Garcia is a good teacher.

    _____

    _____

3.   Jake learned three important things about going into business.

    _____

    _____

4.   The time has come to rethink what education is and how it relates to the needs of society.

    _____

    _____

5.   Never challenging the rules brings with it at least two potential dangers.

    _____

    _____

6.   Happiness is going to college.

    _____

    _____

7. When Japanese teenagers finish the twelfth grade, they have the equivalent of three to four more years of school than U.S. high-school graduates.

_____

_____

8. Only 6 percent of U.S. high-school students study calculus.

_____

_____

Part B.   Read the following paragraphs. Then, using the space provided, identify the number of the topic sentence and make an outline for each paragraph. The first one has been done for you.

A.   (1) When we have anxieties that we feel we can do nothing about, we sometimes fool ourselves with different kinds of defenses. (2) One of the most common defenses is to rationalize by offering an incorrect reason for what happened. (3) Another defense is to project onto someone else the motives or faults causing our anxieties. (4) Still another defense against anxiety is to resort to fantasy or daydreaming.

1.   Which is the topic sentence? _____*1*_____

2.   Paragraph's main idea: *to show the different kinds of defenses we sometimes use to combat anxieties we feel we can't control*

Supporting details: *(1) one defense is to rationalize by offering an incorrect reason*
(2) another is to project motives onto someone else
(3) another is to resort to fantasy or daydreaming

B.   (1) The U.S. Department of Education released a 111-page report, "Japanese Education Today," showing how seriously academics are taken in the country that many experts believe does the best at providing quality education for the masses. (2) Most Japanese high-school students don't date, drive cars, hold part-time jobs, or even do household chores. (3) They study. (4) Success in formal education is considered largely synonymous with success in life. (5) Japanese society is education-minded to an extraordinary degree.

1.   Which is the topic sentence? _____

2.   Paragraph's main idea: _____

_____

_____

Supporting details: _____

_____

_____

_____

_____

C. (1) Invariably newspaper and magazine articles on Asian-American success cite an importance of family. (2) Asian children seek to honor their parents. (3) I could say the same thing about Mexican children. (4) Mexican-American children seek to honor their parents. (5) But whereas in one culture to honor one's parents means doing well in public, in another culture honoring one's parents may mean staying closer to home, not getting "too much education." (Richard Rodriguez, "Asians: A Class by Themselves." *Los Angeles Times* 11 Oct. 1987)

1. Which is the topic sentence? _____

2. Paragraph's main idea: _____

_____

_____

Supporting details: _____

_____

_____

_____

_____

D. (1) College is both an intellectual and an emotional experience. (2) You must learn to fit into the academic world and to mature socially and emotionally at the same time. (3) You must learn to deal with freedom and responsibility; there is no way to separate the two. (4) For some students it is the educational program (learning) that is the big problem. (5) For others it is maturing in a new climate of freedom that causes the stress. (6) But for most students, it is the combination that bounces them. (E. Chapman, *So You're a College Freshman.* SRA 1967: 4–5)

1. Which is the topic sentence? _____

2. Paragraph's main idea: _____

_____

_____

Supporting details: _____

_____

_____

_____

_____

_____

The next several units will present more information about paragraph development. As you develop your skill in writing paragraphs, you'll learn how and where to place topic sentences.

Practice with Topic Sentences

If you or your instructor feel you need more practice with topic sentences, go to page 291.

◆ WRITING JOURNAL ENTRY

Return to your rearranged brainstorming plan in your journal. Turn each one of your major headings or sections into a working topic sentence you can use when you begin your first draft. These will be working topic sentences that can be changed later if necessary. If you notice that the supporting items or ideas listed under the major headings are too broad, you may need to brainstorm again or rethink that section of your organizational plan.

REWRITE . . .
your first drafts.

Rewriting requires at least three steps: revising, editing, and proofreading. Revising requires looking at the essay as a whole, editing requires close attention to each sentence, and proofreading requires close attention to such fine details as checking for typographical errors on the final draft. Each unit will provide new information or reinforcement of each of these three steps.

Keep in mind that these three activities can occur at any time. It is not uncommon for writers to think they have completed a final draft only to discover during the proofreading stage that an entire paragraph needs to be revised or that during the revision stage a punctuation or spelling error needs to be corrected. Rewriting is the heart of good writing.

Many students think there is something wrong with them because they make so many false starts or take so much time to write an acceptable essay. Don't be discouraged. Professional writers don't sit down and quickly dash off what you read. All you see is the final draft that has been revised and edited by not only the writer but a professional editor as well. You don't see all the thrown-away pages, the scratched-up manuscripts, and the frustration the writer went through to make what you read seem easy. Good writing is hard work.

Revising

If you know word parts, you know that *revise* means "to look at" or "see again" (*re* = "again"; *vis* = "see" or "look"). Once that first draft is complete, it's necessary to look at it again, with fresh eyes if possible. When you have finished your first draft, put it aside for a day; then come back to it with new energy.

Get in the habit of checking your organizational pattern to see if ideas move from one point to the next; this often means that you have to rearrange sentences or whole paragraphs. You may need to "cut and paste," meaning you literally cut out parts of your paper from your draft and paste them at a better position in the essay. (If you use a word processor, moving text around is quite easy and saves much retyping.)

Also check to make certain you have developed what you want to say with enough examples; sometimes this step requires more writing or even deleting what doesn't fit. The length of a paragraph can vary, depending on what needs to be said at the point it is being used in the essay. Sometimes a one-sentence paragraph is forceful, creating a desired effect. Other times a paragraph may run quite long. But length isn't important; full development of the topic sentence is. Unless you are writing short paragraphs for a deliberate effect, it could be they are underdeveloped. If paragraphs become too long, it could be they lack clarity and coherence.

The following is an example of a first draft of a supporting paragraph from an essay on earning college credits through the Electronic University Network.

> Universities and colleges participating in the Electronic University Network (EUN) offer a variety of credit, noncredit, undergraduate, and graduate courses. Special credit courses are also given through EUN from time to time.

After looking carefully at this paragraph, the author realized she did not develop her two points. Both sentences in her original paragraph required more development. She revised to this:

> Universities and colleges participating in the Electronic University Network (EUN) offer a variety of credit, noncredit, undergraduate, and graduate courses. For instance, you can complete either your AA or BA degree in liberal arts and business through Thomas A. Edison College or earn an MBA degree from John F.

Kennedy University. For those seeking to advance their knowledge and abilities in narrower subjects, both institutions mentioned offer certificate programs in accounting, finance, information management, and other specialties.

Special credit courses are also given through EUN from time to time. For example, Bank Street College of Education offers courses in methods in computer applications in the classroom for teachers, as well as courses in starting and managing your own business and principles of accounting.

Notice that examples were provided as a way to develop and support the topic sentences of both paragraphs.

How Revision Works

The revision process can best be illustrated by examining the various drafts of the introductory paragraph in Lisa's essay on Mr. Wrinkle.

Mr. Wrinkle was my high-school biology teacher. I did not like his science class very much. I did not learn very much and I think he's a difficult teacher. His personal mannerisms and his attitude toward students leave a lot to be desired.

As a first draft, this at least got Lisa writing about her topic and thinking about her thesis statement. But after reading it aloud, she realized several things:

◆ It sounded flat and uninteresting.
◆ She wondered what audience would be interested in her essay.
◆ She wondered if it sounded like she was going to discuss the class or the teacher.
◆ She used "I did not" and "very much" twice, close together.

Notice the changes in her second draft:

Have you ever had a teacher that was so bad that you will remember him or her forever? A teacher that had so many personal quirks that you paid more attention to him than to the subject? A teacher who made you wonder why they taught since they had poor attitudes toward the students? If so, then maybe you had Mr. Wrinkle.

In this version, Lisa uses the question technique, aiming questions at an audience who also might have had bad experiences with teachers. The emphasis on the

class has been dropped, with everything now pertaining to Mr. Wrinkle. She
liked this draft, so she turned it in.

Here is what her instructor said:

---

who for people,
that for things

sentence
fragments

shift from
singular to
plural

Have you ever had a teacher ~~that~~ *who* was so bad that
you will remember him or her forever? A teacher ~~that~~ *who*
had so many personal quirks that you paid more attention
to him than to the subject? (A) teacher who made you
wonder why they taught since (they) had poor attitudes
toward the students? If so, then maybe you had Mr.
Wrinkle.

Your use of questions helps bring in your
readers and helps them to focus on teachers.
Also, your questions, taken together, imply
negative feelings on your part regarding
Mr. Wrinkle. Still, the opening lacks "punch."
Try another opening, perhaps using an
anecdote.

At first, Lisa was upset. She thought she had written a good opening. But
after thinking about the instructor's comments, she tried again. After tossing
aside a few more approaches, Lisa finally decided that an anecdote based on her
real feelings was the best way to begin her essay. This is what she submitted:

All through the tenth grade, I itched to be in the eleventh
because only juniors and seniors could take science lab courses. The
idea of peering at test tubes bubbling with chemical mixtures, being
surrounded by weird electrical devices snapping lightening-like bolts,

and combining chemicals to create foul smells appealed to me. Even the thought of dissecting frogs intrigued me. The time finally came. But after two days with my teacher, Mr. Wrinkle, I was ready to dissect him! Not only was he a difficult teacher, but his personal mannerisms and attitudes toward students ruined the class for me.

Lisa's time spent on revision was worth it. Here is what her instructor wrote on her paper:

good specifics

All through the tenth grade, I itched to be in the eleventh because only juniors and seniors could take science lab courses. The idea of peering at test tubes

vivid description

bubbling with chemical mixtures, being surrounded by weird electrical devices snapping lightening-like bolts, and combining chemicals to create foul smells appealed to me. Even the thought of dissecting frogs intrigued me. The time finally came. But after two days with my teacher,

sets a strong tone

Mr. Wrinkle, I was ready to dissect him! Not only was he a difficult teacher, but his personal mannerisms and attitudes toward students ruined the class for me.

Much better, Lisa! Your use of specifics and the description of your expectations shifts the focus of your disappointment in the class to Mr. Wrinkle himself. Clear thesis.

Revision often means taking a totally different approach from your first drafts before getting at the best you can offer. It takes time, but that is why you are here—to spend time developing your reading, writing, and thinking skills.

Editing

Editing requires forgetting the content for a moment and looking at each individual sentence. By the time you are ready to edit, you know the content of your essay very well. For this reason, it is advisable to put your draft aside for at least an hour or two. As with revision, a day away from it is even better.

It helps during the editing stage to look at each sentence by starting with the last one in the essay. Read it aloud to hear how it sounds and to make certain it makes sense. Make any necessary changes in wording or punctuation. Rewrite it if necessary. Then move on to the second to the last sentence and do the same with it. Work your way to the beginning of the essay, a sentence at a time.

It is usually helpful to get another student or two in the class to read your paper to you and then comment on it. Although you don't have to make any changes suggested, you should consider what you are told. By sharing your essays, you will discover how various readers react to your writing.

At this early stage in the course, you may not be able to edit as efficiently as you'd like. But as you learn more about grammar and mechanics, you will find your editing ability improves.

The Essay Form

As you work through the text you will learn more specific techniques for editing. But in addition to the specifics, it is important to know what form your essay should take before turning it in to your instructor.

The type of essay generally required from freshman college students has three basic parts: (1) the introductory paragraph, (2) the supporting paragraphs, and (3) the concluding paragraph. Usually, college essays run around 500 words or so, but the length of an essay really depends on the thesis. A broad thesis will require more supporting points, resulting in more words; a narrower thesis will require less. However, think less in terms of length and more in terms of what you need to say to support whatever the topic and thesis require. Remember Paul Roberts's comments on how to say nothing in 500 words?

With the organizational plan of the Mr. Wrinkle outline as an example, the essay form will look something like the following:

Introductory paragraph:	1. Should create reader interest in Mr. Wrinkle. 2. Should state or hint at the thesis. 3. Should be indented five spaces from the left margin.

↓

Supporting paragraph:	1. Should discuss only one of the three key supporting points about Mr. Wrinkle. 2. Should have a topic sentence that controls what will be said about the one key point. 3. Should contain all of the supporting details for the key point of the paragraph. 4. Should be indented five spaces.

↓

Supporting paragraph:	1. Should discuss one of the three key supporting points about Mr. Wrinkle. 2. Should have a topic sentence that controls what will be said about that key point. 3. Should contain all of the supporting details for the key point of the paragraph. 4. Should be indented five spaces.

↓

Supporting paragraph:	1. Should discuss one of the three supporting points about Mr. Wrinkle. 2. Should have a topic sentence that controls what will be said about that key point. 3. Should contain all of the supporting details for the key point of the paragraph. 4. Should be indented five spaces.

↓

Concluding paragraph:	1. Should draw together all that has been said by summarizing or drawing a conclusion. 2. Final statement should be strong. 3. Should be indented five spaces.

Following a planning outline makes it fairly easy to write a rough draft. Of course, if new ideas occur while writing, and if those ideas help support the thesis, they should be added in the appropriate place. The planning outline is only a working model to follow and ensures an organized first draft. However, never force an outline into an essay if it doesn't seem to be working. Remember, writing is not always a step-by-step process. It may be necessary to return to a brainstorming session while in the middle of writing a first draft.

The first draft of an essay is an attempt to put, into an essay form, the ideas that have been gathered and arranged. In all probability, it will require revision and editing. Don't attempt to make a first draft the final one. Don't be too worried about mechanics, grammar, or punctuation at this stage. Attention to these things comes later.

As an aside, if you have access to a word processor or the opportunity to learn how to use word processing, do so. Using a word processor is an excellent way to save time writing drafts and revising. It allows you to make mistakes without having to erase, waste paper, or get writer's cramp copying things over and over. It allows more time to be spent on thinking and organizing.

Proofreading

Proofreading is the last step before turning in your final draft. At this point in the writing process you are satisfied with your content, organization, and style. Now you check your paper for any typographical errors, misspelled words, and punctuation errors. If you find some mistakes, don't recopy your essay. If you have double-spaced each line, you will have room to insert any changes in spelling, to insert an omitted word or punctuation mark, or to capitalize a letter if needed.

Most of the proofreading marks you will need appear on the inside cover of this book. However, more information about proofreading marks will be discussed in a later unit.

◆ TEXTBOOK ENTRY

In the spaces provided, state what needs to be done to develop the following first-draft paragraphs.

1.   Many corporate executives are complaining that college students are not taking the right classes. They are specializing too early in their schooling and should take other classes.

_____

_____

_____

2. Happiness is going to college. It's freedom. It's exhilarating. You are treated more like an adult. But sometimes freedom is a two-edged sword.

_____

_____

_____

Practice in Revising

If you or your instructor feel you need more practice in revision, go to page 322.

◆ WRITING JOURNAL ENTRY

Return to the first draft of the essay you previously based on your brainstorming list. Revise the entire first draft, paying particular attention to your introductory paragraph. Use the following checklist.

_____ 1. Does your opening paragraph reveal the subject or topic of your essay?
_____ 2. Does your opening paragraph contain a thesis or hint at your views or feelings toward your topic?
_____ 3. Does your opening paragraph use a method that draws the interest of your readers?
_____ 4. Did you write about a topic you know or have feeling for?
_____ 5. Did you avoid the obvious and take a fresh approach to your topic?
_____ 6. Did you share your essay with someone else before turning it in?

If you are satisfied that you have done your best, turn in a final draft to your instructor. Otherwise, try another revision or another subject.

UNIT 2

PEANUTS by Charles M. Schulz

*Words are like sunbeams—the more they are condensed,
the deeper they burn.*

Robert Southey

THINK . . .

about language.

◆ WRITING JOURNAL ENTRY

When we think of language we usually think of the words people use to communicate with one another. But we also hear such phrases as "the language of love," "music—the universal language," "sign language," "body language," and so on. In your journal, write about some aspect of language that has nothing to do with words.

◆ TEXTBOOK ENTRY

In the spaces provided, answer the following questions. Give some thought to your responses before you write.

1.   Define *language* as you think of it. _____

_____

_____

_____

2.   Educators are always saying that a better command of language will contribute

to a better way of life. Explain your opinion. _____

_____

_____

_____

3.   Do you feel that you should know more about your language than you do?

Explain. _____

_____

_____

_____

4.   What other language would you like to be able to speak besides your own?

_____ Why? _____

_____

_____

_____

5.   Are your answers to the last three questions honest or have you written what you thought an instructor would want to hear? _____

_____

THINK ABOUT IT . . .

We are so accustomed to think of English as an inseparable adjunct to the English people that we are likely to forget that it has been the language of England for a comparatively short period in the world's history. Since its introduction in the island about the middle of the fifth century, it has had a career extending through only 1,500 years. The evolution of English in the 1,500 years of its existence in England has been an unbroken one. Within this development, however, it is possible to recognize three main periods. The period from 450 to 1150 is known as Old English. From 1150 to 1500 the language is known as Middle English. The language since 1500 is called Modern English.

Old English [around the year 597]
Đā wæs æfter manigum dagum þæt sē cyning cōm tō þǣm ēalande, and hēt him ūte setl gewyrcean

Translation
Then it was after many days that the king came to the island and commanded (them) in the open air a seat to make him

Middle English [Kentish, 1340]
Þis boc is dan Michelis of Northgate, y-write an englis of his oȝene hand. þet hatte: Ayenbyte of inwyt. And is of þe bochouse of saynt Austines of Canterberi . . .

Translation
This book is Dan Michel's of Northgate, written in English with his own hand. It is called Remorse of Conscience and belongs to the library of St. Augustine's at Canterbury . . .

Middle English [London, c. 1387]
Whan that Aprille with his shoures sote
The droghte of Marche hath perced to the rote,
And bathed every veyne in swich licour
Of which vertu engendred is the flour

Translation
When April's sweet showers
Pierce to the root the dryness of March,
And bathe every vein with that liquid
Which creates the flower

Modern English [Shakespeare, 1603]
Goes the King hence today?
(Macbeth)

Translation
Is the King leaving today?

Modern English [Los Angeles, 1988]
That's a grody hat, man. Drop some billies on something more viscious. Bag your face, man, for sure.

Translation
That's a terrible hat. Spend some money for a better one. I disagree.

Adapted from Albert C. Baugh and Thomas Cable, *A History of the English Language*, 3rd ed. Englewood Cliffs, N.J.: Prentice-Hall, 1978.

6.   Do you own a good dictionary? _____

7.   Do you own a good thesaurus, a dictionary of synonyms and antonyms? _____
     If not, think about buying the latest editions of *The American Heritage Dictionary* and *The Merriam-Webster Thesaurus* or ask your instructor for recommendations.

READ . . .

about language as a symbol of humankind.

A thesis, remember, is the main idea or point that authors want to make about their subjects. The subject of the following essay concerns written language as a means of communicating. As you read it, look for the author's thesis. But first, prepare to read by doing the following:

1.   Read the title of the essay. In your own words, explain what you think it

     means. _____

     _____

     _____

     _____

2.   Read only the first paragraph and then answer these questions:

     a. Who is the man in the paragraph? _____

     _____

     b. What do you think you will learn from reading this essay? _____

     _____

     _____

3.   The meaning an author intends may be lost if the reader does not understand the author's use of certain words and phrases. Make sure that you understand the following words. The number after the word is the number of the paragraph where the word appears:
     a. *profound* (4) = far beyond the superficial; far-reaching.
     b. *pictographs* (5) = pictures that relate familiar objects in a meaningful way

    c. *ideograms* (5) = a character or symbol representing an idea or thing without using words

    d. *syllabic* (6) = having to do with signs representing sounds

    e. *embodied* (7) = made or included as part of

    f. *electromagnetic* (7) = a series of electric charges in motion

    g. *exobiologists* (8) = those who study extraterrestrial biology

    h. *interstellar* (9) = between stars and planets

4. Now read the essay. Underline what you think are key points to remember, and write notes and questions in the margin as an aid to better reading.

SYMBOLS OF HUMANKIND

Don Lago

1   Many thousands of years ago, a man quietly resting on a log reached down and picked up a stick and with it began scratching upon the sand at his feet. He moved the stick slowly back and forth and up and down, carefully guiding it through curves and straight lines. He gazed upon what he had made, and a gentle satisfaction lighted his face.

2   Other people noticed this man drawing on the sand. They gazed upon the figures he had made, and though they at once recognized the shapes of familiar things such as fish or birds or humans, they took a bit longer to realize what the man had meant to say by arranging these familiar shapes in this particular way. Understanding what he had done, they nodded or smiled in recognition.

3   This small band of humans didn't realize what they were beginning. The images these people left in the sand would soon be swept away by the wind, but their new idea would slowly grow until it had remade the human species. These people had discovered writing.

4   Writing, early people would learn, could contain much more information than human memory could and contain it more accurately. It could carry thoughts much farther than mere sounds could—farther in distance and in time. Profound thoughts born in a single mind could spread and endure.

5   The first written messages were simply pictures relating familiar objects in some meaningful way—pictographs. Yet there were no images for much that was important in human life. What, for instance, was the image for sorrow or bravery? So from pictographs humans developed ideograms to represent more abstract ideas. An eye flowing with tears could represent sorrow, and a man with the head of a lion might be bravery.

6   The next leap occurred when the figures became independent of things or ideas and came to stand for spoken sounds. Written figures were free to lose all resemblance to actual objects. Some societies developed syllabic systems of writing in which several hundred signs corresponded to several hundred spoken sounds. Others discovered the much simpler alphabetic system, in which a handful of signs represented the basic sounds the human voice can make.

7   At first, ideas flowed only slightly faster when written than they had through speech. But as technologies evolved, humans embodied their thoughts in new ways: through the printing press, in Morse code, in electromagnetic waves bouncing through the atmosphere and in the binary language of computers.

8   Today, when the Earth is covered with a swarming interchange of ideas, we are even trying to send our thoughts beyond our planet to other minds in the Universe.

Our first efforts at sending our thoughts beyond Earth have taken a very ancient form: pictographs. The first messages, on plaques aboard Pioneer spacecraft launched in 1972 and 1973, featured a simple line drawing of two humans, one male and one female, the male holding up his hand in greeting. Behind them was an outline of the Pioneer spacecraft, from which the size of the humans could be judged. The plaque also included the "address" of the two human figures: a picture of the solar system, with a spacecraft emerging from the third planet. Most exobiologists believe that when other civilizations attempt to communicate with us they too will use pictures.

9   All the accomplishments since humans first scribbled in the sand have led us back to where we began. Written language only works when two individuals know what the symbols mean. We can only return to the simplest form of symbol available and work from there. In interstellar communication, we are at the same stage our ancestors were when they used sticks to trace a few simple images in the sand.

10   We still hold their sticks in our hands and draw pictures with them. But the stick is no longer made of wood; over the ages that piece of wood has been transformed into a massive radio telescope. And we no longer scratch on sand; now we write our thoughts onto the emptiness of space itself.

"Symbols of Mankind" originally published in *Science Digest*, March, 1981. Reprinted by permission.

REACT . . .
to the reading selection.

◇ WRITING JOURNAL ENTRY

In your writing journal, write a one-paragraph summary of what you learned from reading "Symbols of Humankind." To do so, first make a list of all of the informational items you learned. Next, organize the list. Then write a topic sentence that permits you to discuss what you learned. Last, put it all together in paragraph form. Your instructor may want to see the results.

◇ TEXTBOOK ENTRY

A. Understanding the Content

In the spaces provided, write your answers to the following questions. Refer to the reading selection for answers when you need to.

1.   The subject or topic of the reading is _____

2.   The thesis or main idea about the subject is _____

_____

_____

3. What did early people learn were the advantages to writing? _____

_____

_____

4. In what language is the message on the plaque aboard the spacecraft Pioneer? _____

5. After pictographs and ideograms, what was the next major leap in the development of written language? _____

_____

6. Summarize paragraph 9 in one sentence. _____

_____

7. In paragraph 10, what is meant by "the stick is no longer made of wood"?

_____

_____

B. Noticing Writing Techniques and Styles

8. Explain why the title of this selection does or does not fit its contents.

_____

_____

9. How do the two opening paragraphs help get the readers' interest?

_____

_____

10. To what audience do you think the author is writing and what choice of words helps indicate his audience? _____

_____

_____

11. Look at each paragraph and decide with what time period they deal. Does the essay follow a chronological or time sequence? Explain. _____

_____

_____

12. In what paragraph does the author begin to use the first person plural, *we*? Why does he not use it earlier? _____

13. Describe the author's overall tone. Does he simply present his information matter-of-factly or does he have some feeling toward his point? _____

WHAT DO YOU THINK?

Rosalie Maggio, writing in the Minneapolis *Star Tribune*, says that our "rich and varied language has everything we need to express ourselves." The problem is that "exclusive language has helped perpetrate racism, anti-Semitism, and abuses against Native Americans, Asians, gays, disabled persons, poor people, and individuals of both sexes. All that is required is an understanding of the powerful damage done by exclusive language and a commitment not to be a part of it."

PLAN . . .
an essay on some aspect of language.

STEP 1: Selecting and Exploring a Topic: Freewriting

The last unit introduced the brainstorming method as a way to select and narrow a topic for an essay. This unit deals with another method called freewriting. In *Writing Without Teachers*, Peter Elbow states that the most effective way he knows for people to improve their writing is to do freewriting exercises at least three times a week. His idea is to begin writing for 10 to 20 minutes without stopping, writing quickly without worrying about what comes out on paper. The point is to capture all thoughts on paper as they come into your head. It's a bit like trying to tape-record thoughts on paper. There is no worry about organization, spelling, punctuation, or word choice. If all that comes to mind is "I can't think of anything to say," that's what you write until another thought comes. It's not likely that there is never a thought in your head.

Freewriting can help overcome "writer's block." When the blank page just seems to stare back, start writing anything that comes to mind, whether or not it makes sense. Freewriting frequently breaks writer's block with the simple act of putting words on paper, even if the outcome has nothing to do with the subject assigned.

Look at this example, just part of student Al Escobar's ten-minute free-writing:

> The teacher said to freewrite on language but I'm not sure I even know what freewriting is. How can it help me. why am I doing this what am I doing in this class and what do I know about language anyway I don't know what to say about language and it feels weird not putting in punctuation sometimes what am I supposed to say say say oh say can you see this is silly so I am freewriting huh. I need a new thought. Interesting article about the history of English we read but it was a little dry. read more like a damn whoop - textbook than an essay, but that's college I wonder if I could write about obscene language. What makes obscene language bad? Maybe I should read more from that book it was from or maybe I should write about foul language, or sports language or foreign language, god, I have a Spanish test tomorrow. Interesting though how many words in Spanish are now part of English. I need a topic I can sink my teeth into, sink my teeth into, that's a funny bunch of words. Maybe I could write about — what are they called? figures of speech..... yeah strange figures of speech.

Notice that there is no order in this example and sometimes no punctuation. Mistakes such as these are permissible in freewriting, which is called just that because it frees the mind. Freewriting allows you to think openly and honestly without having to consider grammar, spelling, awkward phrases, or style. It allows the mind to think without interference.

Most important, however, is that there are some essay ideas on language in the freewriting. Al started out in no particular direction, but gradually in a short space he came up with some possible topics: writing about obscene language, reading more about language, the language of sports, foreign language, the influence of Spanish on English, and strange figures of speech.

THE WIZARD OF ID   by Brant parker and Johnny hart

By permission of John Hart and Field Enterprises, Inc.

◆ WRITING JOURNAL ENTRY

Now try some freewriting. Pick one of the following freewriting suggestions. In your journal, freewrite for about ten minutes. Review the description of freewriting before you start. This activity may be the basis for your new essay. When you have finished, return to the **Textbook Entry** that follows.

Freewriting Suggestions

1. My favorite words
2. Words that are overused; clichés
3. Computerese: the new language
4. The need for a universal language
5. The importance of written language
6. The language of . . . (music, animals, politics, science, religion, sports, etc.)
7. Sign language
8. The need for dictionaries
9. The difference in language used with friends, with family, and at work
10. The pros and cons of bilingual education
11. Why colleges should (not) require learning a foreign language
12. Sending messages to outer space

Don't in any way feel limited by these suggestions for possible topics. Your only restriction is to write an essay on some aspect of language. (Unless, of course, your instructor assigns another topic.) By looking over the preceding items you can see what a wide range there is. Remember, make the topic your own by writing about what *you* know. Freewriting and brainstorming are ways to help you discover what you know about a topic.

If you use a word processor, try turning the monitor light down so you can't see as you freewrite. After you have finished, turn the light up and read what you wrote. Doing so prevents you from seeing typing mistakes that you may be tempted to correct, causing an interruption in your flow of thoughts.

◆ TEXTBOOK ENTRY

Look over your freewriting. In the following spaces, write any possible topics for an essay on language that came from your freewriting.

_____

_____

_____

Once some ideas appear, you may want to freewrite some more or you may want to combine freewriting with brainstorming. For instance, after some ideas appeared from his freewriting, Al decided to brainstorm on strange figures of speech in English. Here is what he listed:

Strange Figures of Speech

sink my teeth into
bad taste in mouth
spoon-fed
died on the vine
warmed-over ideas
half-baked ideas
stupid ideas
back on your feet
old hat
take the rough edges off
head and shoulders above
little white lie
take my chances
ace in the hole
smooth her feathers
stand pat
play your cards right

Since Al came up with many examples of figures of speech, he decided he had enough to try writing an essay about them. But his problem was what to say about these figures of speech.

STEP 2: Writing a Working Thesis

Al's next step, of course, was to think of a working thesis that would provide some reason for writing about all these figures of speech. Since the one thing all the figures of speech had in common was that they seemed peculiar, he decided on the following working thesis to get him started:

> We have some odd ways of expressing ourselves in the English language.

This working thesis contains the phrase "odd ways of expressing ourselves," which is based on his brainstorming and provides Al with some sense of direction.

STEP 3: Analyzing and Organizing Your Ideas

The last step before writing a first draft is to analyze and organize the list of ideas. After trying various approaches, Al noticed that some of the figures of speech had to do with food, some with body parts, and some with gambling. To organize better, he numbered the items on his list in the order he thought of them and then began to categorize them by number into the three groups. Here is what he ended with:

Strange Figures of Speech

1. sink my teeth into	1. sink my teeth into
2. bad taste in my mouth	2. bad taste in my mouth
3. spoon-fed	3. spoon-fed
4. died on the vine	5. warmed-over thoughts
5. warmed-over ideas	6. half-baked ideas
6. half-baked ideas	— smells fishy
7. stupid ideas	} food related
8. back on your feet	8. back on your feet
9. old hat	11. head and shoulders above
10. take the rough edges off	15. led by the nose
11. head and shoulders above	— eyes popped out of his head
12. little white lie	— starry eyed
13. take my chances	} body parts
14. ace in the hole	13. take my chances
15. led by the nose	14. ace in the hole
16. stand pat	16. stand pat
17. play your cards right	17. play your cards right
	— luck of the draw
	— up the ante
	} gambling

Al formed three basic groups and discarded items that didn't fit. Notice, too, that as he was organizing, he thought of five expressions—the ones unnumbered—that don't appear on his original list. That is very typical and can happen at any time during the writing process.

◇ WRITING JOURNAL ENTRY

Pick one of the possible topics you wrote in the preceding **Textbook Entry**. In your journal, brainstorm on that topic to see if you have enough ideas and support for an essay. Analyze your list of ideas and organize them into some type of outline or plan you can follow. Add any new ideas that may occur to you. Pick another topic if you don't have enough support. Return here when you have finished.

◇ TEXTBOOK ENTRY

You'll remember from the last unit that a working thesis is a guide, a way to organize your thoughts about a topic. What follows are a few thesis statements. Circle what you think are the key words in the statement that would help a writer focus on what to include in an essay. If you believe a thesis statement is too broad or too narrow, write your response in the blank after it and give the reason for your opinion.

1.   All advertising claims are ridiculous when you look more closely at them.

     _____

     _____

     _____

2.   Parents should make a special effort to teach their children new vocabulary, even in the high-school years. _____

     _____

     _____

3.   Four-letter words can hurt. _____

     _____

     _____

4.   Immigrants who come to this country should be required to take English until they can pass a proficiency test. _____

     _____

     _____

5. Almost every profession has its own jargon, but one of the most colorful uses of language exists among jazz musicians. _____

_____

_____

Compare your remarks with these. The key words in Statement 1 are "all" and "ridiculous." But to cover "all" advertising claims would be too broad a task. It would be best in a short essay to concentrate on a few ads or a few words that are ridiculous in their claims. Statement 2 is probably workable; changes might be necessary after a first draft, but the key words here, "special effort," "new vocabulary," "even high school," are a good focus for a start. Statement 3 is useful; examples of four-letter words that hurt people when used would make a good essay. Statement 4 is also workable at this point; the key words "proficiency test" and "required" are argumentative points, and the author would have to show why this idea is beneficial to the immigrants. Statement 5 is also workable. The thesis acknowledges that there are many professional jargons but that the writer is going to zero in on one: that used by jazz musicians.

Using what you listed in your writing journal entry, write a possible working thesis that could be used to help plan your essay.

Possible working thesis: _____

_____

_____

WRITE . . .
a first draft on some aspect of language.

The Nutshell Statement

Writing a nutshell statement can give a sense of direction for a first draft. Here is what Al wrote before writing his first draft:

> The purpose of my essay is to call attention to some of the strange everyday expressions used in English that we take for granted. My audience will be adults interested in language usage. I will support my thesis by providing examples of figures of speech from three groups, those that have something to do with food, with body parts, and with gambling.

Although Al's nutshell statement may not reflect his final draft, he used it successfully to start writing his essay.

Before beginning a first draft for an essay, write a nutshell statement for the thesis and organizational plan you wrote in your journal.

The purpose of my essay is _____

_____

My audience is _____

_____

I will support my thesis by _____

_____

_____

Introductory Paragraphs

An introductory or opening paragraph to an essay is important. It should do three things: one, give a statement about the subject or topic; two, state or suggest a thesis or point of view about the subject; and three, convince your readers it is worth their time to read the rest of the essay by drawing their interest. Whenever you write an introductory paragraph, keep these goals in mind.

There is no one way to begin an opening paragraph to an essay. In fact, you should attempt to be as original as you can, provided you accomplish the three things mentioned. Authors use several methods for opening essays. The following are some of them. Each one will be discussed more fully later.

Method 1. Ask the reader a question that will interest or irritate him or her.
Method 2. Use a short anecdote or brief incident that interests the reader in the subject.
Method 3. Use a quotation that is related to your topic and that either agrees or disagrees with the essay's thesis.
Method 4. Briefly state the supporting detail that will be developed in the essay.
Method 5. Appeal to the reader by indicating the importance of the topic.
Method 6. Combine two or more of these methods into one or two paragraphs.

These methods are used frequently in various ways, but they are not the only means. Once you learn how to handle these devices you will probably find your own methods, depending on the topic of the essay being written. Just keep in mind that the purpose of an introductory paragraph is to give a statement about the topic, to give or hint at your thesis or viewpoint about the subject, and to convince your readers it is worth their time to read the essay by engaging their interest. Notice how these different methods work as introductions to essays on food.

1. Ask the reader a question that will interest or irritate him or her. The question can be one that does not have an easy answer or one that you intend to answer for the reader in the essay. If the subject is controversial, the question may even irritate the reader enough so that he or she will want to find out what you have to say. The following is an example of how an author uses the questioning technique in an attempt to get the reader's interest.

> Encouraging tourism in this country would help bring down our national deficit. In 1984 alone, foreign visitors spent $13.8 billion. But chances are we won't get many more visitors to come than we already do. Why? Because most foreigners speak little or no English. It's a problem even if they come in groups. What if their guides get sick or they oversleep and miss their group's day trip, or they want to sample America's sights and sounds alone? Where even in our largest cities, will they find the police, doctors, shopkeepers, postal clerks, waiters, hotel staff, cabbies, bus drivers, bank tellers, and just plain passers-by who can speak even non-exotic languages such as French, Italian, Portuguese, or German? (E. B. Glick, "English-Only: New Handicap in World Trade." *Los Angeles Times* 17 May 1988)

Notice how the questions are used to establish the subject of the average U.S. citizen's general inability to speak anything but English as being a handicap to bringing in more tourism, which he suggests might be a possible way to reduce the federal deficit.

2. Use a short anecdote or brief incident that draws the reader into the subject. Often a reader is attracted to an essay because of a story or incident an author relates in the opening. The reader wants to see what the story has to do with the subject. For example,

> Sometimes I have a student who is really good right from the beginning. I'm thinking of one in particular. The air was electric when he read, and he was often shaking. The writing process split him open; he was able to tell about being fourteen years old in a mental hospital, about walking the streets of Minneapolis tripping on LSD, about sitting next to the dead body of his brother in San Francisco. He said he had wanted to write for years. People told him he could be a writer, but anytime he sat down to write he couldn't connect the words on paper with the event or his feelings. (Natalie Goldberg, *Writing Down the Bones.* Boston: Shambala, 1986. 36)

Here the author grabs our interest by telling us about a former student, how desperately he wanted to write, but how difficult it was for him. As readers, we are curious. Did he ever learn to "connect words on paper"? We want to read on to find out.

3. Use a quotation that is related to your topic and that either agrees or disagrees with the essay's thesis. Using a famous quotation or quoting the words of others can be a useful way to open an essay. Make sure, of course, that the quotation fits the point you are making and that it fits your tone.

> Our high officials have recently found ways to rewrite history. Former President Jimmy Carter has termed his aborted helicopter raid on Iran "an incomplete success." Ronald Reagan refuses to call the MX weapon what it is, a "missile experi-

mental," preferring to call it "the peacekeeper." And after the invasion of the tiny island of Grenada, he told reporters, "Your frequent use of the word 'invasion' is wrong. It was a rescue mission." And Admiral Wesley McDonald, trying to avoid admitting that the Navy had not known exactly what was happening on the island just before the U.S. landing, took a deep breath and declared, "We are not micro-managing Grenada intelligencewise until about that time frame." By changing the language that describes their actions, a government can implicitly deny those actions. (Adapted from Otto Freidrich, "Of Words That Ravage, Pillage, Spoil." *Time* 16 Nov. 1981)

By using quotations from government officials, the author provides examples that reflect his subject and thesis, which is stated in the last sentence.

4. Briefly state the supporting detail that will be developed in the essay.   Using this device means getting right to the point by giving a brief, overall view of what will be said in more detail. Notice how the author immediately sets up his subject and thesis, establishing the three major points of the essay:

> We have three fairly distinct meanings of the word style. Style as personal idio-syncrasy; style as technique of exposition; style as the highest achievement in litera-ture. The opportunities for confusion are great. (J. Middleton Murray, *The Problem of Style*)

The three distinct meanings are stated, alerting us that each will be discussed in the essay more fully in relation to his thesis, which is that such distinctions can cause confusion. This approach can be rather flat if not done correctly and aimed toward the right audience. However, this method is one you usually want to use when writing essay exams because it gets right to the point the instructor wants addressed.

5. Appeal to the reader by indicating the importance of the topic.   If you think your audience may not be interested in your subject, or if you are going to present a viewpoint that is controversial, it is sometimes effective to appeal to your reader by stressing the importance of your subject. Notice how the following example states the importance and need for everyone to support bilingual education:

> Bilingual education is the most important educational innovation ever launched in this country on behalf of Hispanics. Hispanics are quick to point out that there can be no qualifying or compromising on this. As a concept as well as a program, bilingual education has served ethnolinguistic people well. . . . Thus, it should surprise no one that Hispanics tend to view any and all attempts to cut back or to discontinue bilingual education as anti-Hispanic actions. (Tomas A. Arciniega, "Bilingual Education in the Eighties." *Educational Research Quarterly* Fall 1981)

Of course, you may disagree with the author, but he makes some very strong statements regarding the importance to Hispanics of bilingual education.

6. Combine two or more methods into one or two opening paragraphs.   Frequently, more than one of the methods for writing introductory paragraphs are combined, as in this example:

Although experienced writers may do all kinds of revision almost as they write, they are apt first to try reducing the number of words. The Victorian writer Walter Pater said, "All art doth consist in the removal of surplusage." The secret is in knowing which words are the surplus words. To make this discussion of reduction easier, I've divided the reduction routine into three subroutines: greater reductions, lesser reductions, and micro-reductions. (Adapted from Theodore A. Rees Cheney, *Getting the Words Right*. Cincinnati: Writer's Digest Books, 1983. 2–3)

Here we see a combination of using a quotation and briefly stating the supporting detail. The quotation is used to back up the idea that part of revision requires reducing the number of words written. To show how this can be done, the author will present three "reduction routines."

These methods, remember, are not the only ones for writing introductory paragraphs, but they should serve as models for you to use if you need help in getting started. Feel free to try your own approaches.

One last word about an introductory paragraph. Often the last paragraph you write is the introductory paragraph. You may find that once you have finished your first draft, what you originally wrote as an opening no longer fits everything you've said and needs to be rewritten. Therefore, many writers start their early drafts by first writing supporting paragraphs, deliberately postponing the introductory paragraph.

◇ TEXTBOOK ENTRY

See how well you understand the workings of introductory paragraphs. Read the following paragraphs; in the spaces provided after each, write which introductory paragraph method is used, what the topic of the essay is, and, if possible, what the thesis of the essay probably is. You may not be able to tell in all cases, but guess when you are in doubt.

1. Clichés, said Dr. Lois DeBakey, "are the language of thoughtlessness," and indeed they are. They are poor, tired, but comfortable and familiar cubbyholes to which we retreat when imagination fails us. All of us recognize clichés. They fall like casual dandruff on the fabric of our prose. They are weary, stale, flat, and unprofitable. If we consider all the uses of our words, surely we can find something better than the bromide—for a bromide by definition is a sedative. Bromides put us to sleep. (James J. Kilpatrick, "Clichés," *The Writer's Art*. Kansas City, Mo.: Andrews, McMeel & Parker, 1984)

Paragraph method used: _____

Probable topic of essay: _____

Probable thesis: _____

2. "Feminism" has almost become a dirty word in America. A word that used to stand for equal rights for women now carries a negative connotation. The question

is why? (Tammy K. Daley, "When a Good Word Takes on a Negative Meaning." *Newsweek* 12 Jan. 1987: 9)

Paragraph method used: _____

Probable topic of essay: _____

Probable thesis: _____

---

3.   We were talking, a group of us at a party, about a new book remarkable for its ferocious obscenity. "I couldn't read it," someone said. "All those dirty words." At that, an indignant young woman fixed the speaker with a withering glance and announced, "There are no dirty words—only dirty minds." This extreme position, accepting any kind of language, however gross or violent, is not uncommon today. (Joyce Brothers, "What 'Dirty Words' Really Mean." *Good Housekeeping* May 1978)

Paragraph method used: _____

Probable topic of essay: _____

Probable thesis: _____

---

4.   I hear of something called "bilingual education"—a scheme proposed in the late 1960s by Hispanic-American social activists, later endorsed by a congressional vote. It is a program that seeks to permit non-English speaking children (many from lower class homes) to use their "family language" as the language of school. I hear them, and am forced to say no. It is not possible for a child, any child, ever to use his family's language in school. Not to understand this is to misunderstand the public uses of schooling and to trivialize the nature of intimate life. (Richard Rodriguez, "Aria: A Memoir of a Bilingual Childhood," *Hunger of Memory.* Boston: David R. Bodine, 1982)

Paragraph method used: _____

Probable topic of essay: _____

Probable thesis: _____

---

5.   There are at least six different methods a writer can use to develop an introductory paragraph for an essay: one, ask a question; two, use an anecdote or story; three, use a quotation; four, give a brief overview of your subject; five, stress the importance of the topic; or six, use a combination of these methods. Let's examine each method more closely.

Paragraph method used: _____

Probable topic of essay: _____

Probable thesis: _____

Mistakes to Avoid

Opening paragraphs should draw the interest of your readers, not turn them away. The following are some common mistakes made by many beginning writers that you should definitely try to avoid when writing. Read them carefully.

1. Not getting to the point quickly enough. Usually, this happens because the writer doesn't know his or her thesis.
2. Using quotations that have been used so often they are stale expressions or clichés that lack any punch.
3. Announcing the essay's purpose with tiresome phrases such as "In my essay, I would like to deal with . . ." or "This paper will attempt to discuss. . . ."
4. Apologizing for writing about the subject by stating, "I really don't know much about . . . but I think. . . ." or "My intention was to write about . . . but I. . . ."
5. Relying on the title of the paper to say what should be stated in the opening paragraph. For instance, in writing about a book or essay, some students use the title of the book or essay as their title and then begin with "This book is one everybody should read." A safe bet is not to title your essay until you have finished writing it and to make sure it reflects your thesis. Never use the title of a book, play, essay, or poem as your title.
6. Using dictionary definitions. "According to the dictionary, love means. . . ." If you are going to write about love, define it in your own way.
7. Stating the obvious. "The telephone has made life easy for us" or "Religious issues can create strong controversies among people."

Remember, an opening paragraph should

a. Contain a statement about the subject or topic.
b. State or hint at your thesis (this isn't always necessary, but do it until you feel more competent as a writer).
c. Convince readers your essay is worth reading.
d. Never contain any of the common mistakes just listed.

Sometimes it's best *not* to begin with the introductory paragraph. Try writing the second paragraph or a section of the essay that you know needs to be developed. Often the last paragraph you write will be your introductory one because once you have written more deeply into your topic, it may be that your opening needs to be rearranged to fit all the support you came up with. Remember, an outline is not something you have to stick to; it's merely an organizer of ideas to serve as a guide, and it may need to change as you write.

According to Cleveland Amory, writing in *The Animal's Voice* (Vol. 1, No. 1), we have used language to pigeonhole and bully the finned, furred, and feathered creatures we share the earth with. A person can be as greedy as a pig or as dumb as an ox and so forth—all of which amounts to a bad rap for these mute constituents of the wild kingdom. "As for man," Amory concludes, "he doesn't even consider himself an animal—which, considering the way he considers them, is probably, all things considered, the most considerate thing about him."

Practice in Writing Introductory Paragraphs

If you or your instructor feel you need more practice in writing introductory paragraphs, go to page 266.

◆ WRITING JOURNAL ENTRY

Write in your journal a first draft for the thesis and organizational plan you have been working on. When you have finished with your first draft, look carefully at your introductory paragraph, making certain you have applied to it what you have learned here.

REWRITE . . .

your first drafts.

Revise for Clarity

In his book, *Getting the Words Right,* Theodore Cheney states,

> The beginner [writer] is so accustomed to having a teacher or a supervisor rip his work to shreds that he tries to compose perfect prose, paragraph by paragraph, sentence by sentence. This self-censorship at the moment of conception can result in a boring, unpersuasive, and ineffective piece. . . . Established writers avoid this problem by allowing the words to flow and afterward revising, revising, and revising yet again before sending their work out into the world. If professionals must do this, new writers can hardly expect to expose their first drafts to the people who count. (Cincinnati: Writer's Digest Books, 1983. 8)

Interestingly enough, Cheney's entire book deals with the revision process, because revision *is* writing. As Cheney or any other professional writer will tell you, get your ideas on paper first; then worry about making those ideas sound better.

Do you think the author of the following letter to a government agency bothered to revise it? Is she communicating her needs?

> Dear Sir:
>   Please help me. My husband had his project cut off 2 weaks ago and I haven't had no relief since than. Both sides of my parents are poor and I can't expect nothing from them, as my mother has been in bed for one year, with the same doctor, and won't change. Please send me my husband's form to fill out. I can't get any pay. I have six children, can you tell me why this is?

What does this woman want? How would you help her if you received this letter? The woman got her ideas on paper but obviously failed to revise for clarity.

Revision calls for closer attention to organization, clarity of thought, paragraph development, and consideration of the reader.

Read the first draft of Al's introductory paragraph for his essay on figurative language and then answer the questions that follow.

STRANGE EXPRESSIONS IN ENGLISH

Language is something we generally take for granted. Many figures of speach have made their way into English. We use and here these expressions so often that we don't even think about there meaning. Its' interesting that literal definitions of certain words can mean something entirely different when used as metaphorical expressions. Metaphors are comparisons or attempts to describe or compare things that can't be taken at their literal meaning.

---

1. Does the opening paragraph get your interest? Explain. _____

_____

2. How clear is the subject and thesis? _____

_____

3. What suggestions for revision would you make to Al? _____

_____

_____

When Al looked over his draft, he noticed some misspelled and misused words, but since he felt he needed to do some massive revision, he didn't bother with them. He decided to rewrite his opening paragraph, which seemed dry, uninteresting, and unfocused. He felt he wasn't grabbing the attention of his audience and wasn't sure he even had a clear thesis.

After several revisions, Al wrote this:

MEANINGFUL OR MEANINGLESS METAPHORS

Do you generally get *all fired up*, do a *bang-up job*, and *crank out* good work? Or does your boss *put the damper on* and demand that you *take off the rough edges*? Do you usually *generate* new

> ideas? Or have you *run out of gas?* Do you *produce good work* for your boss as your *intellectual productivity* increases? Or does your work need to be *honed down* and *refined?* Are you paid *chicken feed* or are you *a big wheel* who is paid *astronomical wages?* Somewhere along the line, metaphorical expressions like these have become a part of our everyday use of language. When you stop to think about what some of these metaphors are really saying, they are rather funny.

1. What is your impression of Al's revision? _____

    _____

    _____

2. What method does Al use in his introductory paragraph to get readers interested? Is it effective? _____

    _____

    _____

3. What changes do you notice that improved the introduction? _____

    _____

    _____

    _____

Al's use of questions that contain some of the metaphorical expressions he wants to write about help draw his reader's interest. Based on his last sentence, we expect as readers that he will reveal for us some of the funny expressions that we have come to take for granted. It is certainly a better opening than his first version.

◆ WRITING JOURNAL ENTRY

Apply the following revision checklist to your essay draft. Make any corrections or changes you think will strengthen your essay.

_____ 1. Read it aloud to hear your choice of words. How does it sound? Are your word choices appropriate for your intended audience? Is your tone appropriate for the topic?

_____ 2. Do you move easily from one major point to the next? Have you provided enough support for each point? Are your paragraphs in the right order? Do you need to rearrange them?

_____ 3. Is your thesis or point clear? Is it too broad or too narrow? What could be cut? What needs to be added?

_____ 4. Are you being honest? Are you writing about something you have some feeling for and interest in? Have you made the topic your own?

_____ 5. Do you conclude your essay or does it just stop?

_____ 6. Will your audience enjoy reading what you've said and how you've said it? What would make it better?

Edit for Correct Word Choice

Once you have applied the revision checklist to your essay and made any changes required, it's time to edit sentence by sentence what you have written. One editing task is to check to see if you've used the correct words.

IT'S KEY, IT'S THICK, IT'S LIVE

**Translation: It's Cool, It's Great, It's Happening.
A Lexicon of Common College Slang**

Ape: A hot Betty (see "Betty")

Bail: To leave, give up, bail out, usually accompanied by the word "dude," e.g., "Let's bail, dude."

Beer Goggles: To be wearing these is to be subject to alcohol-impaired vision, thus making choices you will probably regret later. (Especially related to scamming. See "Scam.")

Betty: A hot chick. You wish you could meet one.

Body Splat, Beef: To fall down, especially dramatically and embarrassingly

Bout: To reject, ignore, blow off

BT, GT: Bad trip and good trip, meaning you're having a bad time or a good time

Bustin' Out: An energy burst, to come up with something new and tricky

Chud: A pinhead, a geek

Crib: To sleep, or the place where you live

Flail: To mess up, to blow it

Flow: To share or give. E.g., Santa flows presents at Christmas time.

Jelling: When you're spacing out or doing nothing

Jibbs: Little particles of stuff. E.g., "You've got some food jibbs on your teeth."

Key: Cool

Live: It's hot, it's happening, it's where you want to be

Lop: A squid, misfit, geek

Minor: Bad, bogus

Nectar: Very, very good

Railin': Messing up, being a loser

Rank: Bad, real bad

Scam: To try to meet a member of the opposite sex while having lustful intentions

Sickest: The best

Skank: Something icky, nasty. Or a person with low morals

Spoon, Spoony: A clueless, airhead girl

Starfished: To be passed-out drunk and spread-eagled

Toast: You're finished, washed up. You're toast.

Wedge: To eat, or some tasty food. I.e., "Nilla wafers are wedge; I wedge Nilla wafers."

Yoach: A hippy-ish, granola-eating, natural-essence person

—*Mary Eppen*

"It's Key, It's Thick, It's Live" Reprinted courtesy of the Santa Barbara Independent, Inc., 1988.

Using the correct words at the proper time in your essay is as important as proper sentence and paragraph control. If you want your ideas clearly expressed, you must make certain you are using the words that best state or explain those thoughts. And if your word choice and usage are not appropriate for the type of essay you are writing, your essay will seem elementary or unsophisticated, thereby causing a reader to lose respect for your ideas. Here are some pointers to help you edit for correct word choice.

1. Be aware of what your audience needs.   What words to use can often be decided on the basis of your audience. For instance, the essay "Symbols of Mankind," which you read earlier in this unit, appeared in *Science Digest*. Readers of that publication are interested in science, so the author's use of such words as *exobiologists*, *binary language*, *massive radio telescope*, and *electromagnetic waves* are appropriate. If he had been writing for a nonscientific audience, the author probably would have used simpler terms or perhaps explained them in his essay. Although you should never "write down" to your audience by using less forceful words, make certain the ones you use are appropriate for the reader.

2. Make certain you have accurately said what you mean.   What we mean and what is said are sometimes different. For instance, notice what is said and what was probably meant in the following newspaper headlines:

> Orioles Beat Rangers as Pitcher Relieves Himself (*Las Vegas Sun*, 30 July 1983)
> Teacher Strikes Idle Kids (*Las Vegas Sun*, 1 Sep. 1983)
> Utah Girl Does Well in Dog Show (*Salt Lake Tribune*, 30 Dec. 1981)
> Sisters Reunited After 18 Years in Checkout Line at Supermarket (*Arkansas Democrat*, 29 Sept. 1983)

To avoid such confusion, check your sentences to make certain your words are placed in the correct position.

3. Avoid using slang or informal language in formal essays by using standard English. Although it may be "key" to call someone a "skank," "chud," "lop," or "spoony," especially if they are "scamming" on "beer goggles," don't "flail" in a "body splat" and be "toast" by using such language in your essays. (See boxed insert for translation.)

Standard English is that language which educated people accept as proper. It is the language used in business letters, technical reports, reputable magazines and newspapers, and textbooks like this one. As long as you stick to standard English, you will be on safe ground. Informal words and phrases such as "nerd," "he blew it," "klutz," "airhead," "bad vibes," and "get your act together" should be avoided. Just don't get too formal and stuffy by writing something like "One should always hold one's cup with one's small finger slightly extended."

4. Use figures of speech with caution, avoiding cliché figures of speech.   When we say that someone made a killing on the stock market, we don't mean it literally; we mean a profit was made. When someone is caught red-handed, it means there is no doubt of the guilt. These figures of speech were once fresh, but they have been used so often they are now clichés. Although fresh figures of speech can be descriptive and make your writing lively, worn-out ones lessen the effectiveness of your ideas. Most of the figures of speech in Al's brainstorming list are clichés, overused and good ones to avoid. However, if you can come up with your own figure of speech or feel that a particular figure of speech is appropriate, use it. (See Unit 8 for more on figurative language.)

5. Look for commonly confused words.   Many words can cause confusion in correct usage. Here is a list of some of the more troublesome ones. As you edit your essays, check to see if you have used the following words accurately.

> *accept* and *except: Accept* means "to receive" or "to say yes to an invitation." *Except* means "to exclude" or "with the exclusion of something."
>
> She will *accept* the award at the banquet.
>
> All the words *except* this one are on the list.
>
> *advice* and *advise: Advice* is a noun. *Advise* is a verb meaning "to give or offer solutions."
>
> The counselor gave me poor *advice.*
>
> The counselor *advised* me to take the class.
>
> *affect* and *effect: Affect* means "to influence." *Effect* means "to achieve or cause something" if used as a verb and means "the result of something" if used as a noun.
>
> The new law will *affect* many of us.
>
> The doctors *effected* the new changes in the law.
>
> The *effect* of the medicine is still not known.
>
> *all right* and *alright: All right* is the correct spelling for a term meaning "everything is correct" or "all is well." *Alright* is not accepted as correct spelling for *all right.*
>
> My answers were *all right.*
>
> He's not *all right* in the head. (informal)
>
> *a lot:* Usually, these two words are incorrectly spelled *alot.* Avoid using *a lot.*
>
> *already* and *all ready: Already* refers to time and means "before or by the time being discussed." *All ready* means "prepared."
>
> They had *already* arrived before we got there.
>
> They were *all ready* to leave by noon.
>
> *among* and *between*: *Among* is used only when referring to three or more. *Between* is used only when referring to two.
>
> We had no more than five dollars *among* us. (three or more)
>
> We had no more than five dollars *between* us. (two persons)
>
> *anyways* and *anywheres:* Both words are incorrect; the correct forms are *anyway* and *anywhere.*

bad and *badly:* *Bad* is used with nouns and with verbs that refer to the five senses—*feel, smell, look, taste,* and *hear. Badly* is used after most other verbs.

It was a *bad* mistake. (used to modify a noun)

He feels *bad.* (used after a verb referring to a sense)

He spells *badly.* (used after most verbs *not* referring to senses)

When Doris A. Stokes applied for a VISA credit card from Citibank over the telephone, the bank employee asked Stokes if she wanted a second card for another member of her family. Stokes replied, "Maybe later."

When her credit card finally arrived, so did one for Maybe Later.

---

bad, worse, and *worst:* Each of the three refers to different degrees of "badness."

It was a *bad* accident. (positive)

It was *worse* than your accident. (comparative)

It was the *worst* accident of all. (superlative)

can and *may:* *Can* is a verb referring to the ability or ableness to perform. *May* is used to request permission. Often, *can* is used incorrectly.

I *can* go with you. (ability to go)

May I go with you? (requesting permission)

can't hardly: An improper use of the term *can hardly.*

She *can hardly* see through the windshield.

choose and *chose:* *Choose* means "to pick or select." *Chose* is the past tense of *choose.*

Choose one from the box.

She *chose* one yesterday.

could of, should of, and *would of:* These are improper phrases meaning *could have, should have,* and *would have.* Often, the improper *could of* comes from the sound of the contraction *could've,* meaning *could have.*

Mark *could have* won if he had tried harder.

Mark *should have* won, but the referee was unfair.

Mark *would have* won if the referee had seen the foul.

different from: Do not say, "Different than."

Her country's politics are *different from* ours.

etc.: This is a Latin abbreviation meaning "other things." It is best to avoid using the term. Think of other things to list rather than using *etc.,* which often means, "I can't think of anything more to list."

fast, faster, and *fastest:* Each of the three refers to different degrees of speed.

His car is very *fast.* (positive)

His car is *faster* than mine. (comparative)

His car is the *fastest* of all. (superlative)

◆ TEXTBOOK ENTRY

Underline the correct word within parentheses in the following sentences.

1. How did the new medicine (affect, effect) him?
2. Don't worry, it will be (alright, all right).
3. They are (all ready, already) to leave.
4. Just (among, between) us three, who is the winner?
5. The man's wife feels (bad, badly).
6. (Can, May) your daughter go with us?

Following are some more commonly confused words you should carefully look over.

here and *hear: Here* is an adverb. *Hear* is a verb. (It has the word *ear* in it; ear = hear.)

Here is the car I want to buy.

Do you *hear* that beautiful music?

infer and *imply:* To *imply* means that an author or speaker is suggesting some idea or meaning he or she is not stating outwardly. *Infer* is what the reader or listener does when he or she reaches a conclusion based on supplied evidence or information.

The author *implies* that the Mafia controls the market.

On the basis of what the author says, I *infer* that the Mafia controls the market.

irregardless: This is incorrect for *regardless.*

He will resign *regardless* of what you do.

is when and *is where:* These are both awkward phrases and should not be used.

Incorrect: Spring *is when* the leaves and buds begin to appear on the plants.

Better: Spring *is* the season when leaves and buds begin to appear on the plants.

its and *it's: Its* is possessive, just as *his, hers, yours,* and *ours.* No apostrophe for forming the possessive case in a pronoun is needed. *It's* is the contraction for *it is* and nothing else.

Its cage is near the window. (possessive)

It's a nice cage. (contraction)

kind of and ***sort of:*** Both these phrases are informal and should not be used in formal writing.

Informal: Her hair was *kind of* messy.

Formal: Her hair was rather messy.

Informal: He was *sort of* late.

Formal: He was somewhat late.

lose and ***loose:*** *Lose* means no longer to have or know where something is. *Loose* means to set free or to free from restraint.

Did you *lose* your scarf?

He let the dog *loose* from its leash.

shone and ***shown:*** *Shone* is the past tense of the verb *to shine*. *Shown* is the past participle of the verb *to show*.

The sun *shone* brilliantly on the water.

We were *shown* through the house.

stationary and ***stationery:*** *Stationary* means not movable or not moving. *Stationery* means writing paper and envelopes. (Keep in mind that paper ends in *er* and so does *stationery*.)

The cash register is *stationary*.

The clerk used blue *stationery*.

their*, *there*,** and ***they're: *Their* is the possessive pronoun. *There* is an adverb. *They're* is the contraction of *they are*.

I went to *their* house.

I went *there* last night.

They're good friends of mine.

to*, *too*,** and ***two: *To* is a preposition. *Too* is an adverb meaning also or implying more than what is needed, as in "*too* much food." *Two* is the spelling for the number.

They danced *to* the music.

We danced to the music, *too*. We danced *too* much.

We danced to the music until *two* in the morning.

who*, *which*,** and ***that: *Who* is used to refer to humans. *Which* refers to nonhumans. *That* introduces only restrictive clauses.

Sara is the one *who* hired me.

The books, *which* she sells in the other store, are expensive.

The book *that* I bought is expensive.

who's and *whose:* *Who's* refers to the contraction *who is.* *Whose* is the possessive case of *who.*

Who's going with me?

Whose coat is this?

◆ TEXTBOOK ENTRY

Underline the correct word within parentheses in the following sentences.

1. The writer (infers, implies) that the truth will never be known.
2. I am going (irregardless, regardless) of what you say.
3. (Its, It's) impossible to tell from this information.
4. He likes his collars to be (lose, loose).
5. The (stationary, stationery) had a faint touch of perfume.
6. Let's all go (there, they're, their) with them.
7. I can't go because (there, they're, their) is (to, too, two) much to do.

Practice in Correct Word Choice

If you or your instructor feel you need more practice in correct word choice and usage, go to page 295.

◆ WRITING JOURNAL ENTRY

Return to your essay draft and edit carefully, looking for any improper word choice or usage.

Proofread

Proofing requires looking for misspelled words, typographical errors, punctuation errors, spacing problems, page numbering, and in general anything that needs to be cleaned up. Using the proofreading marks that appear on the inside cover of this book, correct what you think is necessary in the following passage. There should be three paragraphs when you've finished.

I am pleesed to know that dialects are not an endangered species. The add charm, wit and perspective to the language. A dialect is to English as a fun-house mirror is to our image of ourselves. How I would miss Ozark, in which *frash* means *fresh*, as in "Them eggs ain't frash"; *oral* means oil, as in "Your cyar needs two quarts of oral," and *rah cheer* means right here, asin "He was borned rah cheer in this town."Jimmy carter's election gave us a renewed awareness of the inflections of the Southern plains: *bone*, as in "bone and braid in Georgia"; *cayut,* a domestic feline, and *cram*, a felony or misdemeanor.But the most charming of dialects is Hawaiian pidgin. It is a mixture of Hawaiian, english, portugese, Japanese, Samoan, Tongan, teen slang and genius—satirical, graphic and lyrical:

> 1st beachboy: "Otsamatah you?"

> 2nd beachboy: "Otsomatah *you*?"

> 1st beachboy: "Otsomatah *me*? *You* otsomatah?"

Compare what you marked with the following, as it appeared in the final version:

I am pleased to know that dialects are not an endangered species. They add charm, wit and perspective to the language. A dialect is to English as a fun-house mirror is to our image of ourselves. How I would miss Ozark, in which *frash* means *fresh*, as in "Them eggs ain't frash"; *oral* means oil, as in "Your cyar needs two quarts of oral," and *rah cheer* means right here, as in "He was borned rah cheer in this town."

Jimmy Carter's election gave us a renewed awareness of the inflections of the Southern plains: *bone,* as in "bone and braid in Georgia"; *cayut,* a domestic feline, and *cram*, a felony or misdemeanor.

But the most charming of dialects is Hawaiian pidgin. It is a mixture of Hawaiian, English, Portuguese, Japanese, Samoan, Tongan, teen slang and genius—satirical, graphic and lyrical:

> 1st beachboy: "Otsamatah you?"

> 2nd beachboy: "Otsomatah *you*?"

> 1st beachboy: "Otsomatah *me*? *You* otsomatah?"

(From Jack Smith, "Talks of the Town," *Los Angeles Times Magazine,* November 30, 1986.)

Practice in Revising

If you or your instructor feel you need more practice in revision, go to page 322.

◆ WRITING JOURNAL ENTRY

After you have finished your final draft, use the following checklist before turning in your essay to your instructor.

_____ 1. Read it aloud to hear your choice of words. How does it sound? Are your word choices appropriate for your intended audience? Is your tone appropriate for the topic?

_____ 2. Does your introductory paragraph create an interest in your topic? Does it hint or state your topic and thesis?

_____ 3. Do you move easily from one major point to the next? Have you provided enough support for each point? Are your paragraphs in the right order? Do you need to rearrange them?

_____ 4. Is your thesis or point clear? Is it too broad or too narrow? What could be cut? What needs to be added?

_____ 5. Do you conclude your essay or does it just stop?

_____ 6. Did you proofread carefully, looking for typing errors? Did you use the dictionary to check any spelling you doubt?

_____ 7. Will your audience enjoy reading what you've said and how you've said it? What would make it better?

_____ 8. Has someone read your essay aloud to you so you can hear how it sounds and get his or her opinion?

If you are satisfied you have done the best you can, turn in your essay to your instructor. Otherwise, keep revising or change the topic to something you can handle.

UNIT 3

PEANUTS by Charles M. Schulz

To Do Is to Be.

Socrates

To Be Is to Do.

Plato

Do Be Do Be Do.

Sinatra

THINK . . .

about self-awareness.

THINK ABOUT IT . . .

Self-knowledge is the beginning of wisdom.

Socrates

◆ WRITING JOURNAL ENTRY

In your writing journal, make two separate entries. In one, write what you think people would say about you if they were writing a biography entry for an encyclopedia. What facts about your life would they include? What kind of person would they say you were? What qualities would they say you had? What will people remember about you? Don't be afraid to exaggerate a bit.

In another entry, write your own entry, one that describes the you that no one else knows. Discuss your secret desires, your unfulfilled ambitions, the person you wanted to be but never were, the places you wanted to go but never got to, your greatest source of satisfaction that others may not know about.

◆ TEXTBOOK ENTRY

Read the following paragraphs and answer the questions that follow them. Think carefully before writing your responses.

A.   All the philosophers and wise men of the ages tell us that individuals are rare. Yet the curious thing is that virtually all people consider themselves individuals. . . . We are not individuals automatically. Rather we become individuals by our willingness to realize our potential and our effort to be "self-aware, self-critical, self-enhancing." (Vincent Ryan Ruggiero, *The Art of Thinking*. New York: Harper & Row, 1984. 37)

1.   What does the author mean? _That we are all (you have to work at being a unique individuals — but it is something individual.) we grow to become over a period of time._

2.   Explain why you agree or disagree with the statement. _____

_____

_____

3. What is your definition of an individual? *An individual is any person who has their own opinions.*

4. Name some people you consider individuals who fit your definition. *myself, my mom, basically anyone*

5. Are you an individual? *yes* Why? *Because I have my own opinions and I am not always told what to do or what to think.*

B. Acknowledge the influences that have shaped your thinking. Say to yourself, "My mind is full of other people's ideas and attitudes, which I received uncritically and accepted because I was young and trusting. Many of those ideas and attitudes are now hardened into principles and convictions. Yet some of them are surely erroneous or unworthy." (Vincent Ryan Ruggiero, *The Art of Thinking.* New York: Harper & Row, 1984. 37)

1. What does the author mean?

2. Do you agree or disagree? Why?

3. Name at least one person you especially admire and who has had some influence on you. *my grandmother*

4. Have you knowingly or unknowingly accepted that person's views on religion, race, nationality, marriage, or life-style? If not, where did you get your present beliefs? *Knowingly - because my mother & sister have given me several points of views (marriage)(religion)*

C. You may say that it is more satisfactory to help another than to think about yourself. What is the difference? It is still self-concern. If it gives you greater satisfaction to help others, you are concerned about what will give you greater satisfaction. . . . Why not say, "What I really want is satisfaction, whether in sex, or in helping others, or in becoming a great saint, scientist or politician"? It is the same process, isn't it? Satisfaction in all sorts of ways, subtle and obvious, is what we want. . . . What we are really seeking is a satisfaction in which there is no dissatisfaction at all. (J. Krishnamurti, *Freedom From the Known.* New York: Harper & Row, 1969. 39–40)

1. What does the author mean? _____

   _____

   _____

2. Explain why you agree or disagree. _____

   _____

   _____

3. What satisfaction are you seeking? _____

   _____

   _____

   _____

D.   Every stage of your life involves growth and change and decision-making and adjustment, sometimes pleasant, sometimes painful. What makes the college years unique is not their freedom from human problems, but the opportunity they offer you to devote your time and energy to becoming the person you want to be. The maintenance of a sense of balance and order in living—a healthy emotional climate—is essential for achieving success in college. It is through living each day realistically that you can best maintain your emotional health. (Walter Pauk, *How to Study in College*, 2nd ed., Boston: Houghton Mifflin, 1974. 11)

1. What does the author mean? _____

   _____

   _____

2. Explain why you agree or disagree. _____

   _____

   _____

3. How can attending college help you become the kind of person you want to

   be? _____

   _____

   _____

   _____

4. Are you living each day realistically? What does that mean to you? _____

   _____

   _____

   _____

WHAT DO YOU THINK?

Confronting Problems

What most high school and many college students need to learn is not how to avoid problems but how to confront them. They need to learn that frequently what they perceive as a "problem" in understanding a text is not a sign of their inability to read but the result of their authentic engagement in the reading process—a process that requires them not to retreat from a difficult text with the excuse that they haven't been taught what they need to know to understand it, but to give their attention back to the text and to the additional thought and frustration that may be necessary before they can figure out the author's meaning. To be unable to figure it out is not an occasion to doubt one's literacy but for recognizing a literary problem—one that remains to be worked out by the literate reader. Often, the difference between a student and a literary critic is that what the student encounters as a reading problem, and sees as evidence of his/her own insufficiency, is for the critic an occasion for an essay on a problem in reading a particular text. It is our willingness to confront such problems and our courage in working them out—not our defenses against having them—that define and exemplify our literacy and represent the mode of disciplined attention which we are responsible for passing on.

Sheridan Blaw

Journal of Reading 25.2 (1981):105

READ . . .
about obtaining self-awareness.

Many people and forces help shape who we are or who we think we are. Our parents, our friends, our teachers, the television and movies we watch, the music we listen to, the newspapers and magazines we read, the advertisements of the media—these and many other factors influence us, sometimes without our awareness. The following selection presents a personal awakening to an influence that had gone unnoticed before.

Before you read it closely, read the title and the first paragraph. Then answer the following questions.

1.   What do you think is the thesis or main point of this reading selection?

_____

_____

2.   What do you expect to learn from reading this selection? _____

_____

_____

_____

3.   The meaning an author intends may be lost if the reader does not understand
     the author's use of certain words and phrases. Make sure you understand the
     following words before you read. The number after the word is the number of
     the paragraph where the word appears.
     a. *spartan* (1) = bare; simple; austere
     b. *emulsified* (2) = made into a liquid in which the two ingredients don't mix
         well
     c. *discreet* (2) = attempting to go unnoticed; not calling attention to
     d. *complacency* (3) = self-satisfaction
     e. *bridled* (4) = an abrupt reaction, in this case showing resentment
     f. *precludes* (6) = prevents
     g. *meticulous* (6) = extremely precise
     h. *femme fatale* (9) = seductive woman
     i. *pantomimes* (9) = communicates through gestures and facial expressions

Now read carefully. Practice underlining and marking key points.

THE LIES WE PERSIST IN TELLING OURSELVES

Linda Weltner

1   "Not me," I thought, adding my two cents to a conversation about advertising
and its powerful effect upon consumers. As I straightened out the bathroom to the
pleasant chatter of the radio talk-show host and his guest, I surveyed the spartan inte-
rior of my medicine cabinet and mentally patted myself on the back.

2   There was one container of body lotion (dandelion blossoms and comfrey root
naturally emulsified), two containers of talcum powder (his, antifungal; hers, deli-
ciously scented), one bottle of cologne (unopened), eight plastic cylinders of prescribed
drugs, dental floss, deodorant, a thermometer, and no more than a half-dozen assorted
jars and tubes. A toothbrush and toothpaste sat by the side of the sink. Shampoo and
conditioner waited at the bathtub's edge. There was a small tray with a few discreet
cosmetics on a small wooden chest, and inside the drawers, the staples of every woman's existence. I allowed myself a moment of self-satisfaction. Clearly, I was not the
type to be taken in by empty promises.

3   "Most people think that other people are fooled by advertising." The radio voice was hell bent on challenging my complacency. "I rarely meet anyone who doesn't believe that he or she is the exception. It's an almost universal self-deception."

4   I bridled, like a squirrel unjustly accused of hoarding acorns, but if I had stocked no more than I needed, why did I suddenly feel uneasy and unmasked? The bathroom, with its old fashioned fixtures and plain white tile, seemed on the verge of revealing something I did not want to know about myself.

5   I looked at the contents of the medicine cabinet again. Though it was at least a year old, the bottle of body lotion was almost full. All but two shakes of the talcum powder were still stored beneath its silvery cap. My container of make-up foundation had been more than half full when I replaced it with another brand; the half dozen eye-shadow pencils had still been sharp when I brought home jars of color to take their place. For some reason, I bought body lotion for a woman who never used it, and routinely purchased make-up for a woman who rarely wore any. The tip of the iceberg was poking out of my medicine cabinet, and I suspected I would find evidence of it everywhere I looked. As I wandered from room to room, it was easy to see its outline taking shape. The house was full of things I had purchased not for me, but for the woman I would like to be.

6   There were electric hair curlers and an electric curling iron, purchased for some lady with perfectly groomed hair, then stored in a closet because my nature precludes any procedure that takes more than five minutes from start to finish. There were 25 shades of nail polish and two sets of manicure tools for some lady with meticulously cared for finger nails, even though my own nails look like tiny patchwork quilts hours after the polish dries. What use is all this equipment to a lady who can go without filing a broken nail for days, and who only remembers the gardening gloves after the weeding (and the damage) is done?

7   I bought the conscientious housekeeper I will never be four large cans of floor wax, a shoe box full of shoe polish and three kinds of metal polish. I bought the perfect homemaker in my mind six popover pans and an elaborate Jello mold she has never used. I bought the thinner me packets of chicken broth, cottage cheese, and low calorie salad dressing. She never ate them. And the healthier me will not take her vitamins every morning, no matter how many bottles I bring home from the health food store.

8   These multiple personalities are the real consumers. I know a woman who buys silk blouses for some secret self, but reaches for a T-shirt every morning, and at a yard sale, I met a woman with 10 hats for sale, none of which she had ever worn. If I am any example, she was likely to spend the money she made from the hats on more of them.

9   The tireless homemaker in me promises she will make popovers; the femme fatale pantomimes how sweet smelling her skin will be after le bain. The orderly housekeeper whispers how much energy she has for waxing floors and the well-coiffed woman swears she will be a delight to her hairdresser. They are the women in me who are swayed by commercials, the ones who absorb the messages of the women's magazines. These infinitely perfectible beings are the ones with great expectations, and they always come shopping with me. It turns out that the empty promises I believe are the ones I keep making to myself.

10   I am slowly coming to the conclusion that it is not advertising's false assurances that ensnare us. Hidden behind the price tags of all the products we buy and never use are the lies we persist in telling ourselves.

"The Lies We Persist in Telling Ourselves" Reprinted by permission. Linda Weltner is the author of *No Place Like Home: Rooms and Reflections from One Family's Life*.

REACT . . .

to the reading selection.

◆ WRITING JOURNAL ENTRY

Think about some of the products you buy, such as cosmetics, perfumes, after-shave lotion, clothes with name brands on them, and so on. Why do you buy them? What do they add to you as a person? What do they say about you as a person? In your journal, freewrite on this subject for five to ten minutes.
Think about the people who have influenced you? Teachers, clergy, and other authorities figures.

◆ TEXTBOOK ENTRY

A. Understanding the Content

In the spaces provided, write your answers to the following questions. Refer to the reading selection for answers when you need to do so.

1. The subject or topic of the reading selection is *self-awareness*

2. The thesis or main idea about the subject is *10 para*

3. What is the "universal self-deception" that Weltner did not want to acknowledge? *3 para.*

4. What does Weltner mean when she says, "The house was full of things I had purchased not for me, but for the woman I would like to be"? _____

5. Does Weltner blame advertising for her purchases? Explain. *para. 10*

B. Noticing Writing Techniques and Styles

6. What introductory paragraph method does Weltner use? _____

_____

7. Where do you think the thesis is best stated, or is it implied? _____

_____

8. How do the first four paragraphs work together as a unit? What is their major

    function? _____

_____

_____

9. Why does Weltner repeat phrases such as "for some lady," "for a woman who
    never used it," "the conscientious housekeeper," "the perfect homemaker"?

    Is this an effective method? _____

10. Discuss the effectiveness of the last paragraph. _____

_____

_____

11. To what audience is the author writing? How do you know? _____

_____

_____

PLAN . . .

an essay on some aspect of self-awareness.

STEP 1: Selecting and Exploring a Topic: Clustering

As ways to select and narrow a topic for an essay, you have learned how to
brainstorm and freewrite. This unit deals with still another method: **clustering**.

In *Writing the Natural Way*, Gabriele Rico says about getting started on a
writing assignment:

> Too many of us get stuck because we *think* we should know where to start and
> which ideas to develop. When we find we don't, we become anxious and either
> force things or quit. We forget to wonder, leaving ourselves open to what might
> come. Wondering means it's acceptable not to know, and it is the natural state at
> the beginning of all creative acts, as recent brain research shows.

Though we cannot force the birth of an idea, we can do the next best thing: we can cluster, thus calling on the pattern-seeking Design mind and bypassing the critical censorship of the Sign mind, which relieves the familiar anxiety about what to say and where to start and opens us to the freedom of expression we knew in childhood.

By Sign mind, Rico means the left side of the brain largely occupied with rational, logical, and critical thought. In contrast, the Design mind, or right side of the brain, thinks in complex images, designing patterns instead of clear-cut signs. Rico has discovered that clustering allows us to tap, for writing, the side of the brain that we normally do not use. In turn, clustering can help us overcome writer's block and get in touch with thought that provides us with a fresh perspective and insight on a subject.

So, what is clustering? The best way to understand is to follow these steps on a blank sheet of paper:

1. In the middle of the page write *fear* and draw a circle around it, thus:

2. What thoughts or words come to mind as you think of the word *fear?* Without being judgmental, write each word or thought that comes to mind, circle it, and draw a connecting line to *fear* so that it begins to look somewhat like this:

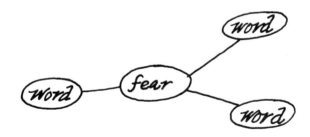

Use arrows to indicate the direction of any words or thoughts that seem related.

3. At first, some writers feel foolish or judgmental and allow the Sign mind to think a word or connection is silly or nonsensical, but ignore those thoughts and allow your creative side to dominate.

4. Allow yourself three or four minutes to create some type of pattern by clustering your words and thoughts together with circles, lines, and arrows. You may have a pattern like the one on the next page when finished.

5. Don't force anything; let the clustering happen naturally; even doodle if necessary by looking over your circled words and drawing connecting arrows to similar groups or thoughts.

6. When you are through clustering, look over your circled words and connections. There will be one group of clustered words or phrases that you like or feel the urge to write about. Don't try to write about everything in your cluster, only the strongest group or set.

7. Take ten minutes to write about whatever cluster set you have selected to deal with. When finished, spend a few minutes reviewing and changing what you wrote in order to improve it. Usually, you will have a good nucleus for an essay on a topic you may have never considered before.

Here is an example of one student's cluster and ten-minute writing.

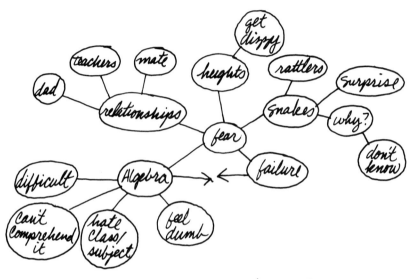

Funny, I immediately thought of snakes when I wrote down fear. When I was 13-14, I used to catch snakes for fun. Even copperheads. No fear then. But now that I'm older I've developed a fear of snakes, especially rattlesnakes. Even pictures of them disturb me. Why? The idea of them even ruins hikes I take. I'm always on guard, afraid I'll be surprised by one.

Notice that the writing focused on only one part of the cluster, the part about snakes. The clustering brought up a fear that the student might not have considered as a possible topic for an essay on fears. At this point, the student is ready to pursue as a possible essay topic the fear of snakes. Of course, it's possible that there is no more to say about snakes, or that the student isn't really interested in saying more. That's fine. In that case, a possible topic has quickly been eliminated and another branch of the cluster can be pursued.

Here is another example, the way a student clustered on the word *change:*

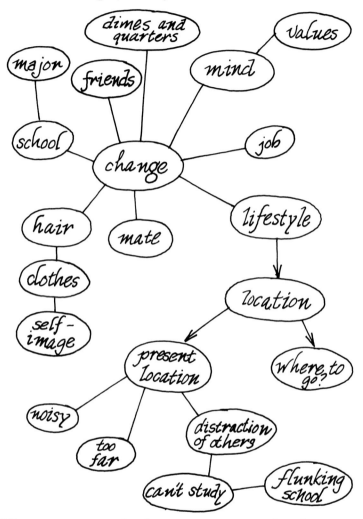

The following is an example of a ten-minute writing based on the preceding sample cluster:

> Interesting word—change. It can be the tangible stuff I feel in my pockets or the intangible change of friends or mates. I need a change. Where I live now is too distracting. I party too much. Most of the people I hang out with don't seem to care whether they do well in school. I do, I just realized. I'm going to have to make a move and find a better place to live, somewhere more quiet and conducive to studying or I'm going to flunk out of school!

Notice that the ten-minute writing is focused on the cluster group that has to do with change of life-style and location. All the other items are not mentioned. At the time the writer was jotting down these words and thoughts, they were not evaluated or thought to be right or wrong. The thoughts just popped up while clustering. But very soon a cluster group moved from the unconscious mind to the conscious. The writer discovered a topic that needs to be considered seriously.

◆ TEXTBOOK ENTRY

What follows is a partly drawn cluster with the word *self* circled in the middle. Key words have been supplied in the outer circles as a way to help you try clustering. Normally, you don't draw circles before clustering, but for practice fill in as many circles as you can, feeling free to add circles and arrows where appropriate.

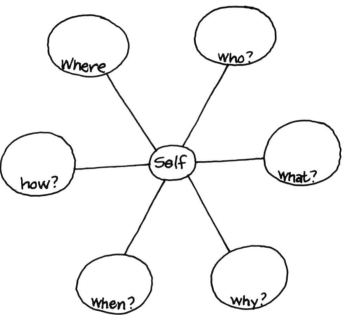

Following is another partly drawn cluster around the word *pressure*. Try filling in the circles already drawn and extending them to more circles where you can.

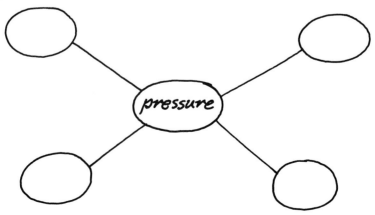

◆ WRITING JOURNAL ENTRY

In your writing journal, pick at least three of the following words and do a clustering, with a ten-minute writing follow-up on each one.

1. goals   4. adjusting   7. awareness
2. stress   5. parents   8. defenses
3. happiness   6. influences   9. anxieties

Go to Step 2 when finished.

STEP 2: Writing a Working Thesis

Look back at the student cluster and ten-minute writing on the word *fear*. Two possible working theses might be these: *My fear of snakes keeps me from enjoying hiking,* or *For some reason, I have developed a fear of snakes.* If, however, the student feels these statements are too restrictive for an essay, another look at the cluster group might provide an idea for a different topic, such as the fear of failing algebra, or perhaps the student might want to do more clustering this time on the fear of relationships. After more clustering a clearer topic and thesis might appear.

   Now look back at the sample ten-minute writing on the cluster for *change*. In the space given, write what you think might be a working thesis for an essay that would continue to discuss that topic.

_____

_____

_____

   There is no right answer, of course, but the focus is on the need for a change in living location. A working thesis might be this: *I need to move from where I now live or I may flunk school;* or *If I don't do something about changing my present living conditions, I may not pass my courses.*

   Look at each of the three clusterings and ten-minute writings that you did in your journal. Pick one that you feel may lead to an essay topic. In the following space, write a possible working thesis. If you have trouble with one, try one of your other clusterings.

Possible working thesis: _____

_____

_____

STEP 3: Analyzing and Organizing Your Cluster Group

Clustering already sets up some sort of organizational pattern. With the sample clustering on *change,* a direction took place. Many of the clustered items were ignored, as they should be, and the focus on changing living conditions took over.

The following are the items from that part of the cluster set:

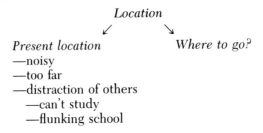

Location

Present location
—noisy
—too far
—distraction of others
  —can't study
  —flunking school

Where to go?

There may be enough order here for the writer to begin a first draft, but chances are some more brainstorming or clustering might produce more ideas and possible solutions. The subject "where to go?" needs more thought. The possibility of staying where the writer lives but changing study hours or studying somewhere else needs to be considered. These things can all be explored through any of the three planning methods: brainstorming, freewriting, and clustering.

FEIFFER®

◆ WRITING JOURNAL ENTRY

Look again now at your selected cluster and working thesis. Are you ready for a first draft, or do you need to explore some areas more thoroughly? You may need to try more clustering, brainstorming, or freewriting. Analyze your list of ideas and organize them into some type of outline or plan you can follow. Add any new ideas that may occur to you.

If you have given clustering a good try and you can't seem to find from this approach a suitable topic for an essay on self-awareness, return to the **Think** section at the beginning of this unit and see if there is a possible topic in one of your responses to the paragraph questions. However, make certain you have given clustering a fair chance.

Go to the **Write** section when you have finished.

WRITE . . .
a first draft on some aspect of self-awareness.

The Nutshell Statement

In the following space, write a nutshell statement for your proposed essay before you begin your first draft. Remember, this is only a guide to get you started.

The purpose of my essay is _to make people more aware of different causes of stress,_

My audience is _general public_

I will support my thesis by _explaining some of the different causes of stress + possible solutions_

Writing Paragraphs by Using Examples and Illustrations

As you know, a topic sentence requires support, and the type of support is often determined by the way the topic sentence is phrased. Look at this topic sentence:

Some words are loaded with good associations.

It's reasonable to assume that if the writer wants to support this topic sentence, examples of some words must follow. The following is the whole paragraph:

Some words are loaded with good associations. Such words as *home, happiness, contentment, tenderness, baby,* and *mother* generally bring out favorable feelings or connotations. The word *mother,* for example, makes most people think of home, love, safety, care, food, and the like.

The writer supported the main idea by giving examples that illustrate words loaded with good associations. Notice also that the phrase "for example" makes it clear that examples are being given.

Here's another example of a paragraph that uses illustration and example:

> The easiest way to achieve honesty in your writing is just to be yourself. Don't glut your prose with literary references that are new to you, so that you'll appear learned when you are not. Don't try to be hip when you are square. Don't try to bulldoze your way into a personal writing style that simply is not you. Don't try to write like Hunter Thompson or Erma Bombeck if such styles don't come easily to you. Try to write like you. Don't use the thesaurus to find words you never saw before; use it to find words you do know. That's honesty. (Gary Provost, "The 7 Beacons of Excellent Writing." *Writer's Digest*, Mar. 1984)

An outline of the paragraph looks like this:

Main idea: The easiest way to achieve honesty in writing is to be yourself.

Supporting point:

1. Don't use literary references that you don't know.
2. Don't try to be hip if square.
3. Don't bulldoze.
4. Don't write like someone you're not.
   a. Hunter Thompson
   b. Erma Bombeck
5. Don't use the thesaurus to find new words; use it to find words you know.
6. Try to write like you.

Notice how the author gives as many examples as possible to show how to achieve honesty in writing.

The following is still another example (which is what this paragraph is!):

> A major part of our self-image is shaped by the work we do. Consider how we describe ourselves: "I'm just a janitor." "I'm only a housewife." "I'm a senior vice-president of the company." "I'm out of work just now." "I'm the boss here." Both our friends and fellow workers refer to us by our jobs (teacher, student, lawyer, doctor, pilot) and by what we do, not our roles as parents, children, or lovers.

Main idea: The work we do shapes a major part of our self-image.

Examples:

1. Consider our self-description.
   a. just a janitor
   b. only a housewife
   c. senior vice-president
   d. out of work
   e. the boss
2. Friends and fellow workers refer to us by our jobs.
   a. teacher
   b. student

    c. lawyer
    d. doctor
    e. pilot
  3. Not referred to by our roles as parents, children, or lovers.

Perhaps by looking at paragraphs in this way, you can see both the prewriting stage (the thinking and organizing that went into planning the paragraph) and the end product, the paragraph itself.

Sometimes a paragraph may be developed by more than one method or pattern. Notice how the following paragraph uses description, but the description used serves as an example of what happened when one student didn't stick to his study schedule:

> Here, for example, is what happened to one student whose schedule was to read English literature from seven until ten o'clock. Determined to do his reading on schedule, he sat down at his desk promptly at seven. First, he discovered that his pencil was out of lead and needed a refill before he could make any notes. Walking across the hall to the room of a friend to see if he had some lead, he found an interesting discussion going on about the merits of Fords versus Chevrolets. Becoming absorbed in this, it was some time before he remembered that he was supposed to be studying English. Starting back to his room, he recalled that there was a good TV program on. With the aid of a little wishful thinking, he convinced himself that he could be studying while watching TV in the lounge. Next, with his attention divided between the TV and the book, he found himself daydreaming about the weekend coming up. And so it went. Ten o'clock came, time to go out for a bite to eat—and still no work done.

An outline for writing this paragraph might have looked something like this:

Main idea: Here is an example of what happened to a student who didn't stick to his study schedule even though determined.

Examples:
  1. Went across hall to refill pencil with lead.
  2. Got stopped in hall by his interest in conversation about cars.
  3. Remembered there was a good TV program on.
  4. Tried to study while watching TV in lounge.
  5. Started daydreaming about the weekend.
  6. At ten o'clock went out to eat.
  7. No studying done.

These are just the bare ideas. The descriptive touch provided in the paragraph itself makes these examples of being sidetracked more interesting to read about.

◆ TEXTBOOK ENTRY

See how well you understand the use of illustration and examples in paragraph development. Read the following paragraphs and then in the blanks provided fill in the items requested.

A. Some words are what we call "colorful." By this we mean that they are calculated to produce a picture or induce an emotion. They are dressy instead of plain, specific instead of general, loud instead of soft. Thus, in place of "Her heart beat," we may write "Her heart *pounded, throbbed, fluttered, danced.* Instead of "He sat in his chair," we may say, "He *lounged, sprawled, coiled.*"

Main idea: _____

_____

_____

Supporting points:

    1. _____

    2. _____

    3. _____

    4. _____

        a. _____

        b. _____

Your wording and ordering may be different, but, basically, this is one way you might have outlined the paragraph:

Main idea: Some words are colorful.

Supporting points:

    1. produce a picture or emotion
    2. dressy instead of plain
    3. specific instead of general
    4. loud instead of soft
        a. *beat* vs. *pounded, throbbed, fluttered*
        b. *sat* vs. *lounged, sprawled, coiled*

This paragraph has examples within examples to help the reader understand what colorful words are.

B. Another common defense is to project to someone else the motives or faults that lie within the person. If, for example, a student has a strong desire to cheat on an examination but is unwilling to admit it to himself because he knows it is wrong, he may be unduly suspicious of others and accuse them of cheating when they are innocent. Or, if he feels like being nasty to other people and yet knows that this is not right, he may accuse other people of being nasty to him when in fact they have not been.

Main idea: _____

_____

_____

Supporting examples: _____

_____

_____

_____

_____

C.   A man may get angry at his boss but knows he shouldn't blow off at him, so he comes home and bawls out his wife. A little girl, finding her newborn brother the center of attention, would like to attack the brother, but knows she will be punished for this. So she tears up her doll. A student who is mad at the instructor may come back to the dorm and get in an argument with his roommate. These are all examples of displacement that can take place quite unconsciously.

Main idea: _____

_____

_____

Supporting examples: _____

_____

_____

_____

_____

Practices in Using Illustration and Example

If you or your instructor feel you need more practice with this method of paragraph development, go to page 269.

◆ WRITING JOURNAL ENTRY

1. Pick any one of the following topic sentences and in your journal write a paragraph for each that uses examples or illustrations to support it.
   a. The contents of my bathroom medicine chest reveal my secret desires.
   b. We need to conform at times.
   c. Some words should be banned from use.
   d. Adjusting to college has not been easy for me.
   e. I'm not the same person I was a year ago.
2. Look back over your nutshell statement and organizational plan for an essay on self-awareness. Write a first draft based on your notes. Try to include at least one paragraph that is supported by illustration or examples if possible.

REWRITE . . .
your first drafts.

Revise by Using Transitional Devices

One way to move smoothly from idea to idea and paragraph to paragraph is through the use of *transitional devices. Transition* refers to moving from one idea to another. For your essay to read smoothly, you need to use *transitional words* or *expressions* that enable your reader to move smoothly from one idea to the next, both between sentences and between one paragraph and the other. Doing so will give your reader the feeling of a unified or cohesive essay.

Notice how the following sentence with a transitional expression reads more smoothly than the sentences without any.

With transitional expression: I like going to the movies, *but* I can't afford to go very often.

Without transitional expression: I like going to the movies. I can't afford to go very often.

In the example without the transitional word *but*, the two sentences seem abrupt and unrelated. One sentence deals with liking to go to the movies; the other one deals with not being able to afford to go often. But when the two sentences are used as one, with the transitional word *but*, the two ideas are linked together smoothly.

Here is another example:

With transitional expression: John said he was going to the game *even though* his mother said he couldn't go.

Without transitional expression: John said he was going to the game. His mother said he couldn't go.

Again, notice how the transitional expression *even though* gives the two thoughts a smoother connection. You could, of course, change the sentence with the transitional expression coming first, such as *Even though his mother said he couldn't go, John said he was going to the game.* The meaning has not changed, but the sentence is more sophisticated and more coherent than two separate sentences.

Transitional words and expressions are often necessary within paragraphs to make clear the arrangement of the ideas being expressed. Notice the use of transitional words in the following example.

In (summary,) Commager states that there are at least six common characteristics of the American. (First) is his carelessness regarding manners, dress, food, social relationships, education, and politics. (Second,) his generousness or openhandedness in giving to churches, schools, hospitals, and the like. (Third) is the American's self-indulgence regarding comfort and luxury. (Still another) characteristic is his sentimentality toward his children, his alma mater, his history. (Fifth) is his gregariousness or friendliness. (And last) is his quest for materialism.

Transitional aids

The author's use of the circled words helps the reader by announcing that a summary is coming and then by identifying each of the six characteristics.

Here is another example of useful transitions at work. Circle what you think are transitional devices.

Instructors have a limited amount of time. Therefore you ought to try to get help from your instructors immediately before or after the regularly scheduled class hours. Be brief and businesslike.

However, don't let this advice discourage you from raising legitimate and interesting questions with your instructor. If there is an important point she hasn't made clear, don't hesitate to ask her to straighten you out. Don't shy away, either, from asking questions that interest you or questions about the implications of the things you learn in a course. She, on the other hand, is pretty sure to enjoy and to profit from your genuine expression of interest in her course.

The use of *therefore* makes an easy transition from the first sentence to the second. The word *however* in the second paragraph makes a smooth transition from the first paragraph to the second, alerting us to the fact that there will be a change in the point made earlier. And the phrase *on the other hand* in the last sentence takes us from the suggestions for the student to the probable reaction of the teacher.

A list of transitional words and expressions appears on the next page. Take a moment to look them over. When you revise your essay, try to use the appropriate words.

USEFUL TRANSITIONAL WORDS AND EXPRESSIONS

1. To tell your reader more of the same idea is coming:
   also, additionally, in addition, and, besides, equally important, further, furthermore, moreover, next, finally
2. To show sequence of events:
   first, second, third, and so forth, next, then, last, finally, after, afterward, previously
3. To show time relationships:
   first, second, third, and so forth, meanwhile, soon, soon after, afterward, later, after a few days, after a while, immediately, yesterday, today, tomorrow
4. To show a place or position:
   adjacent to, above, across, beyond, below, under, on the opposite side, to the left, to the right, in the background, in the foreground, nearby, close at hand
5. To compare things:
   like, likewise, similarly, in the same manner, also
6. To contrast things:
   however, nevertheless, but, yet, on the contrary, although, at the same time, even so, even though, conversely, on the other hand, still
7. To draw a conclusion:
   therefore, thus, consequently, as a result, finally, accordingly, as a consequence, in conclusion, due to, for these reasons, because of
8. To emphasize a point:
   to repeat, in fact, truly, again, indeed, to this end, with this in mind, for this purpose
9. To emphasize an example:
   for example, for instance, a case in point, as an illustration
10. To summarize a point:
   to sum up, in summary, this, in brief, in short, as I have said, in conclusion, therefore, consequently, as has been noted, in any event, to conclude, as a result

◆ TEXTBOOK ENTRY

Part A: Read the following passage and circle all of the transitional words and expressions. Be able to explain the function of each as explained in the list of "Useful Transitional Words and Expressions."

Defense mechanisms, when used to excess, have two major weaknesses. First, they don't solve the problem that made us use them. Consequently, if a problem is serious, using a defense mechanism merely puts the problem on hold and will probably return at some point in the future. Second, defense mechanisms may not protect us in new and unusual situations when the problem rises again. For example, a student may rationalize her poor performance on weekly quizzes by giving excuses about poor teaching, a difficult textbook, or unfair tests, thus feeling she is not to blame. However, when final exam time comes, such defenses no longer work. As a consequence, she may become so anxious about failing the test that she can't study. Likewise, she may be so anxious that she can't think clearly during the test. In short, the defense mechanisms that helped her feel better after doing poorly on the quizzes failed to deal with the larger problem.

Part B: Write a short paragraph using at least five transitional words or expressions: _____

_____

_____

_____

_____

_____

_____

Practice in Using Transitional Devices

If you or your instructor feel you need more practice with transitions, go to page 298.

Edit for Fragments, Run-ons, and Comma Splices

Among the common errors found in sentence development are sentence fragments, run-on sentences (sometimes called fused sentences), and comma splices. Each of these improper sentence formations is explained in what follows.

Sentence Fragments (frag)

Sentence fragments are incomplete sentences. They are just fragments or pieces of sentences. Usually, sentence fragments are incomplete because the subject or the verb of the sentence is missing. Sometimes a sentence fragment is created by the wrong punctuation. Still other times, a fragment is created because of a missing object. The following are some examples.

1. Examples of Fragments Caused by a Missing Subject

The subject of a sentence is that part of a sentence *about* which something is said. For instance, in the sentence "The man sat on a chair," *man* is the subject. If the subject were left out it would read "Sat on a chair" and thus be a fragment.

    a. Everyone enjoyed her cake. Made it yesterday afternoon. (Notice that the second sentence needs the subject "She." Otherwise, we don't know who [subject] made the cake yesterday.)

    b. During half time, the football team was "chewed out" by the coach. Listened uncomfortably. (The second sentence needs the subject "They." Without the subject, we don't know who listened carefully.)

This type of fragment is usually caused by carelessness in writing or by assuming your reader knows whom you are talking about. Remember, every sentence must have a subject unless it is a command, where the "you" is implied, such as

Go to the store for me. ("You" is understood.)

Hurry downstairs! ("You" is understood.)

Drop dead! ("You" is understood.)

2. Examples of Sentence Fragments Caused by a Missing Verb

The verb (often called predicate) of a sentence is the word or words that say something about the subject. In the sentence "The man sat on a chair," *sat* is the verb because it tells what the subject is doing. If the sentence read "The man on a chair," it would be a fragment.

   a. Around the corner, Jack and his dog. (What did Jack and his dog do? There's no verb to tell us.)
   b. The man who came to the house. (What did the man who came to the house do? There is no verb to tell us.)
   c. A famous author with many books to his credit. (Again, there is no verb to tell us what the author is doing.)

These examples all fail to tell us what the subject of the sentence is doing. Verbs, besides describing a subject, also tell us what is happening. Notice the connections from fragments to complete sentences.

   a. Around the corner, Jack and his dog *stopped* at a fireplug.
   b. The man who came to the house was *selling* real estate.
   c. A famous author with many books to his credit *gave* a lecture at school.

3. Examples of Sentence Fragments Caused by the Wrong Punctuation

Notice in the following sentences how incorrect punctuation causes sentence fragments.

Wrong: He ran into a tree. Because he was sleepy.

Right: He ran into a tree because he was sleepy.

Or: Because he was sleepy, he ran into a tree.

Wrong: If I arrive late. I will get more demerits.

Right: If I arrive late, I will get more demerits.

Wrong: I will get more demerits. If I arrive late.

Right: I will get more demerits if I arrive late.

Wrong: While I was gone. The house was robbed.

Right: While I was gone, the house was robbed.

Or: The house was robbed while I was gone.

4. Examples of Sentence Fragment "Cliff-hangers"

Many sentence fragments are like "cliff-hanger" stories or movies that don't have clear or understandable endings and leave you "hanging in the air" about what happened. These types of sentence fragments are dependent clauses, which means they are dependent on a more complete statement to complete the thought. Notice the following examples.

    a. After the party was over. (What happened after the party?)
    b. Until I arrive home. ("Until I arrive home . . ." where? what?)
    c. If John wants to go. ("If" what?)
    d. Because the end of the project is nearing completion. ("Because" what?)
    e. While the teacher talked about verbs. (What happened while the teacher talked?)

Also notice in the preceding sentences that they would be complete and not fragments if the first word were omitted. But with cliff-hanger words they are all dependent on something more for a complete thought. Beginning sentences with cliff-hanger words can cause fragments unless you complete the whole thought of the sentence.

The following are some cliff-hanger words. If you use them in sentences, check to make certain you have written a complete thought.

after	because	although
until	unless	that
if	where	what
since	when	how
while	as	before
rather	inasmuch as	with

Correct any of the following sentence fragments by writing complete sentences.

1. If you never go to school. _____

    _____

2. Because I thought I saw you there. _____

    _____

3. As we all left together. _____

    _____

4. Unless you think we should drive separate cars. _____

    _____

5. Until the bell rang. _____

    _____

Run-on or Fused Sentences (r.o. or fs)

A run-on or fused sentence is created when a writer fails to use correct punctuation and capitalization between two or more independent sentences. In other words, the sentences "run-on" together, or else they are "fused" together by improper punctuation. Notice the following examples.

Wrong: My mother is coming home tomorrow I'm going to meet her.

Right: My mother is coming home tomorrow. I'm going to meet her.

Wrong: Hemingway wrote *The Old Man and the Sea* he won the Pulitzer Prize for it.

Right: Hemingway wrote *The Old Man and the Sea*. He won the Pulitzer Prize for it.

Wrong: Mike pushed his bike up the hill Carl rode his.

Right: Mike pushed his bike up the hill. Carl rode his.

Or: Mike pushed his bike up the hill; however, Carl rode his. (Note the use of a semicolon and a transitional word.)

Wrong: He enjoys watching them practice he thinks they are good players.

Right: He enjoys watching them practice. He thinks they are good players.

Or: He enjoys watching them practice because he thinks they are good players. (Note the use of the transitional word rather than punctuation.)

The main thing to remember about run-on sentences is that they confuse your reader by not providing the proper pause for thought control. Correct punctuation or transitional devices will help you avoid writing run-on sentences.

Correct any run-on or fused sentences.

1. I went to the theater I sat in the last row.

2. Her name is Sally she was raised in Missouri.

3. I waited in line a long time it made me very impatient.

4. Because of his voice, he was asked to be the announcer on the program for next week.

5. John came to take Gayle to the movies she had already left, however.

Comma Splices (cs)

To splice means "to link" or "join together." Comma splices are created when a writer splices or attempts to link two sentences together with a comma. In other words, two completely different sentences or complete thoughts are connected with a comma rather than with the correct punctuation. Notice the following examples.

Wrong: We packed all our luggage, then we were on our way.

Right: We packed all our luggage. Then we were on our way.

Wrong: Highway 5 is a very busy road, thousands of trucks, cars, and motorcycles use it every day.

Right: Highway 5 is a very busy road. Thousands of trucks, cars, and motorcycles use it every day.

Wrong: Because of the publicity, my friends and I went to see the play, I didn't care for it though.

Right: Because of the publicity, my friends and I went to see the play. I didn't care for it though.

Correct the following comma splices.

1.   I spoke to the district attorney, he remembered the case clearly.

2.   Two distinct reasons can be presented for your actions, one is the concern for grades, the other is your misconception regarding what learning is.

3.   I see no reason to wait any longer, let's go on into the theater.

4.   She actually thought she had won, by the time she learned differently it was too late.

◆ TEXTBOOK ENTRY

Look over each of the following sentences. In the spaces provided, explain what is wrong with the sentence; then write it correctly. You may have to add some of your own words.

1.   Around the back of the house near the swing set.

Error: _____

Corrected: _____

_____

2.   Because of the man who drove the truck.

Error: _____

Corrected: _____

_____

3.   Heather was happy. Because finals were over.

Error: _____

Corrected: _____

_____

4.   Walking across the campus. Mr. Smythe tripped and fell he couldn't get up without help.

Error: _____

Corrected: _____

_____

5.   Joey stood by the fence looking at the players he wanted to be out there with them.

Error: _____

Corrected: _____

_____

6.   No one will deny that what others think is very important to us, we all try to show people our best side.

Error: _____

Corrected: _____

_____

Practices in Writing Correct Sentences

If you or your instructor feel that you need more practice in understanding fragments, run-ons, and comma splices, go to page 299.

Proofread

Using the proofreading marks found inside the cover of this book, make the necessary corrections that should be made on this portion of a student essay before it is turned in.

> When children make believe or pretend to be a storekeeper, cowboy, or teacher, they project themselves through imagination into anothers role. They realize how it feels to be that person and view themselves thru the eyes of the pretend personality. Studies show that adults also are known to role play in different situations they try to become what they wish they were by wearing clothes that they think help create the role they want to play. Carefully worded advertisement come-ons, such as "You've got the look, the the Jordache look," cause many people to believe they can change who they are. They aren't buying the clothes, their buying the image the advertisements produce.

Compare your markings with these:

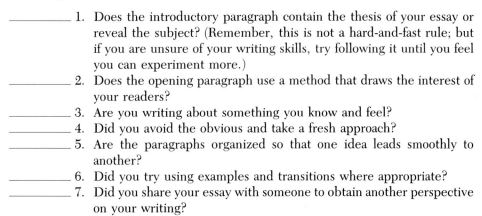

When children make believe or pretend to be a storekeeper, cowboy, or teacher, they project themselves through imagination ① into another's role. They realize how it feels to be that person and ② view themselves thru the eyes of the pretend personality. Studies show that adults also are known to role play in different situations ③ they try to become what they wish they were by wearing clothes that they think help create the role they want to play. Carefully worded advertisement come-ons, such as "You've got the look, the ④ the Jordache look," cause many people to believe they can change ⑤ who they are. They aren't buying the clothes, they're buying the image ⑥ the advertisements produce.

① possessive case   ④ delete
② spelling   ⑤ C.S.
③ run-on   ⑥ spelling

If you discover as many mistakes on your essay as you see here, type it over. A messy-looking paper isn't going to endear you to your instructor.

At this point, you should have the first draft of an essay dealing with some aspect of self-awareness. Before turning in your work, check your draft for the following:

_____ 1. Does the introductory paragraph contain the thesis of your essay or reveal the subject? (Remember, this is not a hard-and-fast rule; but if you are unsure of your writing skills, try following it until you feel you can experiment more.)

_____ 2. Does the opening paragraph use a method that draws the interest of your readers?

_____ 3. Are you writing about something you know and feel?

_____ 4. Did you avoid the obvious and take a fresh approach?

_____ 5. Are the paragraphs organized so that one idea leads smoothly to another?

_____ 6. Did you try using examples and transitions where appropriate?

_____ 7. Did you share your essay with someone to obtain another perspective on your writing?

If you are satisfied you have done the best you can, give your essay to your instructor.

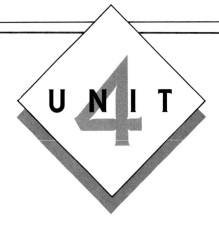

UNIT 4

THE FAMILY CIRCUS ®   **By Bil Keane**

12-2

"Thinking is when the picture is in your head
with the sound turned off."

Brains well prepared are the monuments
Where knowledge is most surely engraved.

Jean Jacques Rousseau

THINK . . .
about thinking.

◇ WRITING JOURNAL ENTRY

Pretend that you are a third-grade teacher. Your students are having trouble answering a problem you put on the board. You tell them to think hard about the answer. One of your students sincerely asks, "How do you think hard?" In your journal, write how you would answer this student.

◇ TEXTBOOK ENTRY

In the spaces provided, answer the following questions.

1. Circle the following words that you think help define the word *think*.

    believe   understand   imagine
    reflect   digest   weigh
    reason   realize   ponder
    contemplate   dream   meditate

2. What one word do you think best defines *think?* _____

    Why? _____

    _____

    _____

3. Explain why you think that intelligence and thinking are or are not related.

    _____

    _____

    _____

4. When was the first time you remember being taught how to think? _____

    _____

    _____

5. How do you go about thinking through a problem or a decision? _____

    _____

    _____

6.   Do you regularly take time, like you might for exercise, to just sit and think?

_____

Why? _____

_____

7.   Do you think these questions are stupid? _____

Explain. _____

_____

8.   Read the following paragraphs and answer the questions.

A.   We believe that almost anything is more important than thinking. . . . It is easy to understand the causes of this prejudice against thinking. One problem is that to most of us, thinking looks suspiciously like loafing. Homo sapiens in deep thought is an uninspiring sight. He leans back in his chair, props up his feet, puffs on his pipe and stares into space. He gives every appearance of wasting time; he reminds us more of Dagwood and Beetle Bailey than of Shakespeare and Einstein. We wish he would get up and *do* something; mow the lawn, maybe, or wash the car. Our resentment is natural.

But thinking is far different from laziness. Thinking is one of the most productive activities a human being can undertake. Every beautiful and useful thing we have created—including democratic government and freedom of religion—exists because somebody took the time and effort to think of it. (Carolyn Kane, "Thinking: A Neglected Art" *Newsweek* 17 Apr. 1981: 4)

1.   What is the author's point? _____

_____

_____

2.   Explain why you agree or disagree. _____

_____

_____

B.   Our schools and our culture do not particularly foster the ability [to think]. Too often they emphasize acquiring facts, following standard procedures and being right. This is learning and reacting but not thinking. Such schooling prepares us poorly for coping with the real world. (Paul McCready, "The Floating Needle." *Science Digest* Mar. 1983: 21)

1.   What is the author's point? _____

_____

_____

2. Explain why you agree or disagree. _____

_____

_____

C.   Highly intelligent people often turn out to be poor thinkers for reasons that we call the "intelligence trap." For example, a highly intelligent person can take up a position on a subject and then use his or her thinking to defend that position very well. That person may do such a good job that he or she never sees any need to explore other possible alternatives. Someone who is less able to defend a point of view may end up doing more exploring. (Edward de Bono, "Clear Thinking. . . ." *U.S. News & World Report* 2 Dec. 1985)

1.   What is the author's point? _____

_____

_____

2.   Explain why you agree or disagree? _____

_____

_____

THINK ABOUT IT . . .

Male/Female Thinking Styles

   At birth there are basic differences between male and female brains. The female cortex is more fully developed. The sound of the human voice elicits more left-brain activity in infant girls than in infant boys, accounting in part for the earlier development in females of language. Baby girls have larger connectors between the brain's hemispheres and thus integrate information more skillfully. This flexibility bestows greater verbal and intuitive skills. Male infants lack this ready communication between the brain's lobes; therefore, messages are routed and rerouted to the right brain, producing larger right hemispheres. This size advantage accounts for males having greater spatial and physical abilities and explains why they may become more highly lateralized and skilled in specific areas.

   Some researchers claim that these differences can be attributed to socialization, and without doubt, cultural expectations do play a major role. Physical differences also play a major role, and it is not clear which came first. Perhaps this agreement between neurosurgeon Karl Pribram and researcher Diane McGuinness forms an acceptable premise: "Women and men are different from the very beginning; what needs to be made equal is the value placed upon these differences."

   From Jacquelyn Wonder and Priscilla Donovan, *Whole Brain Thinking*. New York: Wm. Morrow, 1984, p. 24.

READ . . .

about creative thinking.

The following reading selection draws much of its content from Dr. Edward de Bono's book *The Learn-to-Think Coursebook*. Recently, de Bono and other researchers have come to believe that people need to be taught thinking skills. Growing information seems to verify that creative or dull thinking has less to do with the amount of intelligence you have and more with how you use it.

Before reading closely, take a moment to read the title, the opening paragraph, and the first sentence of each paragraph. Then come back and answer the following questions.

1.   What do you think is the thesis or main idea of this reading selection?

_____

_____

_____

2.   What do you expect to learn from reading this selection? _____

_____

_____

_____

3.   The meaning an author intends may be lost if the reader does not understand the author's use of certain words and phrases. Make sure that you understand the following words before you read. The number after the word is the number of the paragraph where the word appears.
   a.   *theory of relativity* (2) = the theory, introduced by Albert Einstein, which views space and time as not separate but seen to form a four-dimensional continuum called space-time
   b.   *gray matter* (3) = a reference to the brain, more specifically, intelligence
   c.   *spheres* (4) = a domain or area of power
   d.   *spatial* (4) = relating to space
   e.   *linguistic* (4) = the nature and structure of human speech
   f.   *cotton gin* (5) = a machine used for separating cotton fibers from the seed
   g.   *Shaker* (5) = a member of a religious group practicing communal living and celibacy
   h.   *analogy* (6) = showing likeness between two things that otherwise are dissimilar
   i.   *prioritize* (7) = arrange in order of importance

Now carefully read the selection. Practice your marking and note-taking skills.

CREATING CREATIVITY

Health Net News

1   Creativity doesn't always start in a laboratory or end with an acceptance speech for the Nobel Prize. According to Dr. Edward de Bono, a professor at Cambridge University in England and author of *The Learn-to-Think Coursebook*, genius lies in creatively solving the problems of everyday life.

2   When you come to think about it, he's right. Sure, it takes a tremendous amount of creativity to come up with the theory of relativity. But it also takes an impressive amount of the same to stop flies from getting into the house without boarding up the windows. Or, to store the lifetime of junk that filled a four-bedroom house in your new one-bedroom condo. Or, to retain your sanity when your teenage son gets his driver's license.

3   Although people used to believe creativity was reserved for geniuses, scientists now think that anyone can be creative. According to recent studies, the difference between creative and dull thinking lies not so much in the quality of your gray matter, but the way in which you use it.

4   Or, should we say, the ways in which you use it. Howard E. Gardner of Harvard University theorizes that people have at least seven distinct intellectual capacities. The logical-mathematical mode dominates adult thinking, but the other existing spheres are musical, spatial, linguistic, sensitivity of bodily sensations, self-understanding, and the understanding of others. In Gardner's view, creative people are those able to shift fluidly from one type of intelligence to another until a problem is solved.

5   Many experts now believe that this fluidity of thinking—this creativity—can be taught. In workshops, different techniques designed to free up and combine intellectual capacities are presented. Some of these techniques are:

♦ *The use of analogies to spur the solutions*—In fact, many of the most ingenious inventions came from using nature or the human body as a role model. Eli Whitney watched a cat trying to catch a chicken through a fence and, with this combing action as an inspiration, came up with the cotton gin.

♦ *Synergy, combining existing factors in a new way to improve a process or method of organization*—A Shaker woman, Sister Tabatha Babbett, watched two men sawing wood with a straight blade while she was at her spinning wheel. She combined these two ideas and invented the circular saw blade.

♦ *Associations, combining a random piece of information with the problem to come up with new ideas*— Reconciling the two concepts will force you to think about the problem in new ways. A greeting card company that selected the word "shrink" from the dictionary ended up with a new product line: a series of small greeting cards to be slipped into lunchboxes or shirt pockets.

6   Even if you aren't trying to build a better mousetrap, you can use these techniques successfully. The next time you're frustrated in your attempt to make a home repair, look for some analogies in nature. When you're trying to create more time in your crowded life, try combining various activities in an unusual way to see what happens.

7   Perhaps you should also try Edward de Bono's seven-step system to creative thinking. These basic tools have been used by people from all walks of life—from executives at big corporations to government officials in the United States and Sweden:

1. Think about a problem without limiting your vision. Most of us hear a new idea or solution, react instinctively, then use our intellect to justify this viewpoint. Be broadminded; consider the pros, cons, and even neutral points of any solution.
2. Brainstorm to gather all factors that affect a decision. If, for example, you are considering moving to a new town, you will undoubtedly assess its school system and tax base. But don't forget about such quality-of-life factors as garbage collection, movie theaters, even a local leash law.
3. Look at the short- and long-term consequences of a decision. Sometimes analyzing short-term effects will help uncover longer-term possibilities.
4. Try to understand all your reasons—your overt and hidden goals—for doing something in a particular way. Defining goals can yield creative solutions. De Bono tells of a grandmother whose toddler grandson screamed every time she confined him in a playpen to keep him away from her knitting. Then she realized she wanted to save her yarn, not restrict the child. She creatively solved the problem by freeing the child and climbing into the playpen herself.
5. Analyze and prioritize all your considerations. Often we do what feels most important only to later realize that hidden emotional factors obscured what was really important.
6. If still not satisfied, use creativity techniques to come up with alternatives. Use some of the ones already listed. Fantasize about what you would like to have happen and work backwards. Or, think about the exact opposite of what normally comes to mind and go from there.
7. When you are looking for a creative solution to a conflict with another person, try seeing the situation from her or his point of view. Your thoughts may be surprising; they might also point to a solution. Rather than constantly criticizing your child for pouring and spilling juice, for example, put yourself in her place and realize she is trying to be helpful. Improve your relationship and her self-confidence by suggesting tasks she is able to accomplish.

8   And, when discouraged, remember this comment by Mr. Creativity himself, Albert Einstein: "I know quite certainly that I myself have no special talent. Curiosity, obsession, and dogged endurance, combined with self-criticism, have brought me to my ideas. Especially strong thinking powers, brain muscles, I do not have, or only to a modest degree. Many have far more of those than I without producing anything surprising."

REACT . . .

to the reading selection.

◇ WRITING JOURNAL ENTRY

In your journal, summarize the seven-step system to creative thinking proposed by Edward de Bono.

◇ TEXTBOOK ENTRY

A. Understanding the Content

In the spaces provided, answer the following questions. Refer to the reading selection for answers if needed.

1. The main idea about thinking is _____

    _____

    _____

2. According to Howard E. Gardner's theory, we have at least seven distinct intellectual capacities. What is the most dominant sphere?

    _____

3. What are the other six? _____

    _____

    _____

    _____

    _____

    _____

4. What three techniques are used to teach creative thinking? _____

    _____

    _____

    _____

5. Explain which steps of the de Bono seven-step system to creative thinking might be useful to you? _____

    _____

    _____

    _____

B. Noticing Writing Techniques and Styles

6. Where in the selection is the thesis best stated? _____

    _____

7. What is the function of paragraph 5? _____

    _____

8. How many times does the author use examples to support a point?

    _____

9.   Why is this reading selection more of a report than an essay on the author's own ideas? _____

_____

_____

_____

10.   Explain whether or not the last paragraph is effective. _____

_____

_____

11.   What audience do you think the authors had in mind? _____

_____

_____

A TEST

Your powers of observation are great indicators of your level of creativity. Become more aware of your surroundings and details of everyday activity, say the experts, and you'll increase your creative potential.

Try this exercise in mental athletics on for size: Using only your memory, answer the following questions.

1.   On which side of your shirt are the buttons sewed?
2.   Do the cuffs of your jacket have buttons?
3.   On which side of your mouth do you usually chew?
4.   Which way must you turn the key to unlock your front door?
5.   How many keys are there on your keyring?
6.   How many steps are there in your basement stairway?

PLAN . . .

an essay on some aspect of thinking.

STEP 1: Selecting and Exploring a Topic: PMIs

So far you have learned about brainstorming, freewriting and clustering as methods for selecting and exploring a possible writing topic. This unit deals with the **PMI** process. Developed by Edward de Bono in *Learn to Think*, this thinking operation involves examining a topic by looking for the positive, or plus, points (P); the negative, or minus (M) points; and the interesting (I) points. As de Bono points out, we tend to react to an idea by either liking or disliking it. If we dislike something, it's natural not to look for any positive points. If we like something, we tend not to look for any negative points. We also seldom bother to think about what might be interesting about an idea because of our pro or con reaction.

Rather than just saying we like or dislike an idea, we can do what's called a PMI on it. A PMI means we look at the idea for its positive, negative, and interesting points. By doing so we avoid rejecting a good idea that might seem bad at first, and we can see the disadvantages of an idea that we might like. PMIs can also lead us to other ideas we might not have considered.

Here is what de Bono has to say about PMIs:

> Initially schools should offer a special subject area called thinking. I use the CoRT [Cognitive Research Trust] program, which involves giving children some very simple tools. The first lesson, for example, is what we call the PMI—plus, minus and interesting. We get children to look at the positive side of a question, then the negatives and finally just interesting points about the question.
>
> For instance, in a class demonstration in Australia I said to a group of 30 youngsters: "Would it be a good idea if you were each given $5 a week for going to school?" And 30 out of 30 said that was a great idea; they could buy sweets, chewing gum and so on.
>
> Then I asked them to consider the negatives. They began to give some different views: If they had more money, perhaps the bigger boys might bully them and take the money away. Maybe the school would raise its charge for lunch and parents would give them fewer gifts. By the end of that discussion, 29 of these 30 youngsters had totally changed their minds.
>
> Now, the point is I didn't coach the youngsters on their conclusions. I gave them a simple scanning tool, and as a result of that approach, they changed their initial perception. (*U.S. News & World Report* 12 Feb 1985, 76)

The following is an example of a PMI as suggested in de Bono's book:

Idea:	People should be allowed to work ten hours a day for four days and have the rest of the week free, instead of working eight hours a day for five days.
Plus:	More time for hobby or recreation. Family will have father or mother home more. A savings on transportation costs. Rush hour not as crowded. More flexibility of work shifts for employers. Expansion of leisure industry. More time for workaholics or moonlighters.
Minus:	Quality of work may go down. People would argue over work shifts. Managers would have to spend more time supervising. Mothers would be too tired to cook during workdays. People would detest going to work. People would be too tired after work. More coffee breaks would be needed.
Interesting:	Effects on transportation industry. [buses, trains, etc.] Would people know what to do with their free time? Effect on prime time TV schedule.

Stores might be open later but on fewer days.
Would the use of energy change?
Might lead to a three-day workweek.

As you can see, there is no right or wrong in the PMI. In a way it's a form of brainstorming except it is more controlled. Instead of capturing whatever is on your mind, when you do PMIs you focus on the pluses, the minuses, and then the interesting points for a more controlled thinking process.

◆ TEXTBOOK ENTRY

You try a PMI now. Either do this alone or pair off with someone. For about three minutes, think about the pluses, the minuses, and the interesting points of the following idea. You can write phrases or complete sentences.

Idea: Students should not be admitted to college until they are 22 years old or more.

Plus:

Minus:

Interesting:

Discuss your lists with others in the class. What interesting points came up that you hadn't considered before?   .

◆ WRITING JOURNAL ENTRY

In your journal, practice at least two PMIs, using the following topics or topics of your own. Don't take longer than five minutes on each one. Remember not to evaluate or judge your ideas; just make sure you list them in the proper columns:

1. All households should be restricted to owning only one car.

2. There should be no letter grades used in grading essays in composition classes.

3. All college students should be required to take a course on learning to think.

When you have finished your practices in your journal, return here for more practices.

A topic for an essay on thinking may have already occurred to you. If so, the following suggestions won't be needed. Just go ahead with the planning for an essay. However, if you still don't have any ideas for an essay, try brainstorming, freewriting, clustering, or PMIs on one or more of the following.

1. Define thinking
2. Thinking cap, numbskull, airhead, vacuum brain, spacey, losing your marbles, etc.
3. Intelligence/genius/absent-minded
4. Inspiration vs. perspiration
5. Creative thinking
6. The power of positive thinking
7. Thinking can/cannot be taught
8. Respond to the following statements:
   a. "The contrary is also true."—Groucho Marx
   b. "Yours is not to reason why; yours is but to do or die."
   c. "Behold the turtle. He makes progress only when he sticks his neck out."—James Bryant Conant
   d. "Hundreds of scattered and unrelated facts are dumped into the heads of students; their time and energy are taken up with learning more facts so that there is little time left for thinking."—Erich Fromm
   e. "The chief function of your body is to carry your brain around."—Thomas Edison

Remember, don't feel restricted by any of these ideas for topics. They are intended to stimulate your thinking about the general topic assigned—thinking. Change these ideas to make the assignment yours. Brainstorm, freewrite, do PMIs, or practice a combination until you feel you are ready for Step Two.

STEP 2: Writing a Working Thesis

Before attempting to write a working thesis, let's see how it might be done by using the PMI in Step One (page 116). The idea explored was this: People should be allowed to work ten hours a day for four days a week and have the rest of the week free, instead of working eight hours a day for five days. The three lists from the PMI provide several ways to proceed.

One of the advantages of doing a PMI when you can is that you already have a working thesis when you state the idea you want to explore. The next step is to look over the ideas listed in each of the three lists. If the ideas on the plus side seem best, you change the working thesis to fit. In the case of the sample PMI, for instance, the working thesis for the plus side might read,

> Allowing people to work a ten-hour day, four-day week has *several advantages*.

If you like the minus list best, the working thesis might read,

> Allowing people to work a ten-hour day, four-day week has *several disadvantages*.

Or you might decide to present both views, so the thesis would read,

> There are *both advantages and disadvantages* to allowing people to work a ten-hour day, four-day week.

If the interesting points would make a good essay, a thesis might read,

> Allowing people to work a ten-hour day, four-day week *could have some interesting ramifications*.

Of course, it might be possible that one of the interesting ideas listed needs to be explored more through one of the exploring techniques before a working thesis is found.

A PMI, then, can provide you with several directions for pursuing an essay topic.

◆ TEXTBOOK ENTRY

Take some time now to look over your PMI or list of ideas for an essay on thinking that you should have in your journal. In the following space write a working thesis for your essay.

STEP 3: Analyzing and Organizing the PMI List

A PMI list already contains some organization by its very structure: plus, minus, and interesting points. But before a first draft can be written from a PMI, it needs to be organized a bit more. If, for instance, a writer using the PMI example decides on the following working thesis,

> There are several advantages to allowing people to work a ten-hour day, four-day week.

the plus list will need to be rearranged before a first draft is written. The list might be arranged thus:

♦ Advantages to home life
   —parents home more
   —more time for hobbies, recreation
♦ Advantages in traveling to work
   —save on transportation costs
   —rush hour not as crowded
♦ Advantages at work
   —flexible work shifts
   —more overtime or chances for moonlighting

As you can see, the random list of pluses is now based on the key word in the working thesis: *advantages*.

In the space given, write what you think would be a good thesis for the preceding outline.

_____

_____

If you used the three major headings as a guide, you might have written, *There are three major advantages to allowing people to work a ten-hour day, four-day week.* More specifically, a tighter thesis might be *Allowing people to work a ten-hour day, four-day week is advantageous to home life, traveling to and from work, and working itself.* These theses provide the writer both with a sense of direction and an organization for a first draft.

On the other hand, if the minus points seemed more advantageous than the plus points, a writer would have to organize the minus list somewhat thus:

♦ Disadvantages to employees
   —They would argue over work shifts.
   —They would detest going to work.
   —They would be too tired after long working hours.
♦ Disadvantages to employers
   —Quality of work may go down.
   —Managers would spend more time supervising.
   —More coffee breaks would be needed.

All the disadvantages in the minus list are divided into two categories since some concern the employee and others, the employer.

In the space given, write a possible thesis for the preceding outline.

_____

_____

You might have written something similar to the following:

There are many disadvantages to allowing people to work a ten-hour day, four-day week.

Or:

There are disadvantages to both the employee and the employer in allowing people to work a ten-hour day, four-day week.

These at least allow a writer some direction.

Still another approach is to compare and contrast the pluses and minuses. In that case, the writer would need to write a thesis that allowed both lists of ideas to be used. In the space given, write a possible thesis for an essay that would compare and contrast the two lists.

A good beginning for such a thesis might be *Allowing people to work a ten-hour day, four-day week has both advantages and disadvantages.* (There is more on the use of comparison and contrast as a writing method in the next section of this unit.) Of course, if a writer preferred to use one of the ideas from the interesting list, that particular idea would need to be explored through brainstorming, freewriting, or a PMI.

◆ WRITING JOURNAL ENTRY

In your journal, practice rearranging and organizing your ideas for an essay on thinking. Be aware that you may need to do more exploring before you arrive at an outline or organized list you can use for the first draft. When you feel you have what you need to begin writing, go on to the following **Write** section.

WRITE . . .
a first draft on some aspect of thinking.

The Nutshell Statement

In the space given, write a nutshell statement for the thesis and outline you developed on self-awareness.

The purpose of my essay is _____

_____

_____

My audience is _____

_____

_____

I will support my thesis by _____

_____

_____

_____

Developing Paragraphs by Using Comparison and Contrast

Still another method for developing paragraphs is through the use of comparing and contrasting. To compare is to show similarities or likenesses; to contrast is to show differences. Frequently it is necessary to develop a topic sentence or thesis by comparing and contrasting ideas, people, or things. Read the following topic sentence:

> Crime as presented on television is not what it is in reality.

The sentence tells the reader (and writer) that crime on television and crime in reality are not the same; therefore, the rest of the sentence will need to show how different the two are. Here's the rest of the paragraph. Notice how the contrast is done.

> Crime as presented on television is not what it is in reality. On television, murder, assault, and armed robbery are the most common crimes. In reality, quiet burglaries, clever larcenies, unspectacular auto thefts, and drunkenness are the most common. Video detectives solve 90 percent of their cases. In reality the figure is considerably lower. On television only 7 percent of violence occurs between relatives. In reality this accounts for 25 to 30 percent of interpersonal violence.

In the preceding example, the writer alternates the contrast point by point. Outlined, it looks like this:

    I. Most common crimes
        A. On television
            1. murder
            2. assault
            3. armed robbery

        B. In reality
           1. burglaries
           2. larceny
           3. auto thefts
           4. drunkenness
    II. Video detectives versus real detectives
        A. TV detectives solve 90 percent of their cases
        B. Real detectives solve considerably less
   III. Violence between relatives
        A. On television, only 7 percent
        B. In reality, 25–30 percent

Using the same information, the writer could have structured it this way:

Crime as presented on television is not what it is in reality. On television, murder, assault, and armed robbery are the most common crimes. Video detectives solve 90 percent of their cases. And on television only 7 percent of violence occurs between relatives. In reality quiet burglaries, clever larcenies, unspectacular auto thefts, and drunkenness are the most common crimes; detectives solve considerably fewer crimes, and interpersonal violence runs 25 to 30 percent.

The difference here is that all the television points are mentioned together and then contrasted with real statistics.

The following is a paragraph that both compares and contrasts. See if you can sort through it.

The truth is that career choice for most of us was and will always be somewhat by chance. There is no evidence now or even in the old days of people making systematic job searches, with adequate access to information and with a clear, well-ordered set of job preferences. Far more often, careers are selected through a mixture of luck, contacts, and chance. What is different about choosing careers today is not so much that good jobs and objective information are scarcer than they were a few years ago, but rather that expectations about the satisfaction from work are much higher. We are neither nobler, smarter, nor more ambitious than our parents and grandparents. But we are more aware of how much our work shapes our lives and more ready to put self-fulfillment high on our list of priorities.

In the space given, list what is compared and what is contrasted in the preceding paragraph.

Compared: _____

_____

Contrasted: _____

_____

Although the preceding paragraph is not structured as neatly as the previous example, it does make clear distinctions. The author compares choice in the "old days" with now, claiming that there is no evidence that people are making any more systematic job searches now than before. He also compares us to our parents and grandparents, claiming we are no smarter, nobler, or ambitious than they. The contrast is that our expectations about satisfaction, self-fulfillment, and how work shapes our lives are higher than theirs.

Sometimes it takes two paragraphs to compare and contrast. Notice the following example.

> The Production Phase is most closely associated with creative thinking. The mind produces various conceptions of the problem or issue, various ways of dealing with it, and possible solutions or responses to it. Good thinkers produce both more ideas and better ideas than poor thinkers. More specifically, good thinkers tend to see the problem from many perspectives before choosing any one, to consider many different approaches, and to make every effort to produce possible solutions before turning in a judgment.
>
> In contrast, poor thinkers tend to see the problem from a limited number of perspectives (often just one narrow one), to take the first approach that occurs to them and to judge an idea immediately, or to settle only for a few ideas. Moreover, they are overly cautious in their thinking, unconsciously making their ideas conform to the common, the familiar, the expected.

It's easy to see that the first paragraph presents aspects of good thinkers; the second paragraph begins by stating "In contrast . . ." and then shows the traits of poor thinkers.

The use of *analogy* to compare and contrast is useful. An analogy takes two dissimilar things and shows how they are alike in some respects. For instance, in the following passage, the author makes an analogy between mule-team drivers and those knowledgeable in computers. At first the comparison may seem impossible, but notice how the writer does it:

> There's one thing people considering getting into the computer age should be aware of. Back in the country there used to be men who owned teams of mules who would go from farm to farm offering to hire out their animals, equipment, and services to do almost any job that needed doing. Such men were a breed apart. They were an elite and secretive group—they spoke their own dialect, worked on their own, and kept pretty much to themselves. But they knew mules! And if you could ever get one of them to open up and talk, you could learn more about muling than you had ever dreamed was possible.
>
> Professional computer people and computer enthusiasts are a little like that. They tend to be a bit above us ordinary folks. They speak their own languages and, judging from the books and manuals I've read, absolutely *never* write in a language or style intelligble to those outside their group. Seldom can you get a straight or simple answer to a question about how to do something. But if you can ever find one of those fellows willing to stoop to your level and go with you step by step as you begin using a computer, jump at the chance. In no time at all, you'll be fairly comfortable sitting on the wagon seat and holding the reins. (J. Julius Scott, Jr., "On Mules, Computers, and College Teachers." *Chronicle of Higher Education* 11 May 1983)

In the first paragraph, the author describes mule-team owners, stating that they were "an elite and secretive group . . . a breed apart . . . and spoke their own dialect." In effect, they were different. In the second paragraph, the author says computer people "tend to be a little like that." They too have their own language and seem to be a group of their own. Yet if you could ever get one of them to "open up and talk," you could learn much. The paragraph ends with the analogy of sitting comfortably on a wagon seat and holding the reins with that of being comfortable using a computer.

◆ TEXTBOOK ENTRY

To make sure all of this makes sense, do the following exercises.

A.   Read the paragraph below, and answer the questions that follow:

> Left-handed people have to assert themselves more than right-handed people. Because of this, left-handers are likely to be extreme natural right-brainers. On the other hand, right-handers could be right-brained persons who found adaptation easier than fighting the left-brained system. In 1932, 2 percent of the U.S. population was left-handed; today the estimate is 15 percent. This growth is attributed to the discovery that forcing children to become right-handers often causes stuttering and emotional problems.

1. What is being compared or contrasted? _____

   _____

   _____

2. What is the main idea? _____

   _____

   _____

3. What transitional devices help make the comparison and contrast clear?

   _____

B.   Read the passage below, and answer the questions that follow:

> Aside from competition and standards of work, there's another big difference between high school and college. In high school the work was pretty well laid out for you. Most of it was covered in class, and homework, which was easy for the superior student, could be done mostly in the one or two periods set aside for study. You were graded to a large extent on what you did in class and on day-to-day homework. You might have had a few term papers and long-range assignments to do on your own, but for the most part you were paced by the daily round of classes.

REWRITE . . .

your first drafts.

Revise

At this point, you should have the first draft of an essay dealing with some aspect of thinking. Before learning about other revision strategies, check your first draft for the following:

_____ 1. Does the introductory paragraph use a method that draws the interest of the reader?

_____ 2. Are you writing about something you know and feel?

_____ 3. Did you avoid the obvious and take a fresh approach?

_____ 4. Are the paragraphs organized so that one idea leads smoothly to another? Did you use the appropriate transitional devices?

_____ 5. Are your paragraphs fully developed and coherent?

_____ 6. Did you try using description, examples, and comparison and contrast where appropriate? (Don't try to force your ideas into these patterns; only use them when they are the best way to support the ideas.)

_____ 7. Did you share your essay with someone to obtain another perspective on your writing?

If you are satisfied that you have done the best you can, go on to the next revision strategy.

Avoid Fallacies in Thinking

Showing good, clear-cut reasoning in your essays is just as important as showing good structure and grammar. In fact, it may be even more important because the reason for writing is to communicate your ideas to a reader. Your ideas need to be grounded on reason and logic rather than on fallacies in your argument or thinking.

Fallacies in logical reasoning occur when an argument is based on an incorrect belief or judgment. There are many different types of fallacious reasoning. The most common are described in the following sections so that you can attempt to avoid them in your writing.

1. The Bandwagon Fallacy

The bandwagon fallacy is reasoning based on the premise that "because everyone else is doing it, why shouldn't I?" Following are some examples of bandwagon fallacies in logic:

Councilman A: We'd better pass a law banning nudity on the beach.

Councilman B: Why?

Councilman A: Because all the other cities along the coast are doing so.

Notice that there is no logic given for the need to pass a law against nudity on the beach, only the fact that other cities are doing it.

2. The Circular Reasoning Fallacy

Sometimes circular reasoning is referred to as "begging the question." It means that the argument or point being proved just goes in a circle, using the same words, rather than offering any logical proof. Here is an example to help clarify the definition:

Councilman A: We'd better pass a law banning nudity on the beach.

Councilman B: Why?

Councilman A: Because nudity is immoral.

Councilman B: How do you know?

Councilman A: The best ministers say so.

Councilman B: How do you know who the best ministers are?

Councilman A: They're the ones who feel nudity is immoral.

Notice the fallacious reasoning just goes in a circle. Councilman A wishes to prove that nudity is immoral because the best ministers say so and then claims that the best ministers are the ones who feel nudity is immoral.

3. The Contradiction

A contradiction is a statement or argument opposite or contrary to a previous position held by the same writer. Notice the following example:

Councilman A: We'd better pass a law banning nudity on the beach.

Councilman B: Why?

Councilman A: Because all nudists are weirdos, and they'll give our beaches a bad name.

Councilman B: But the mayor is a nudist.

Councilman A: Well, that's different. He's not in the same category.

Councilman A says that all nudists are "weirdos" but contradicts himself when he discovers the mayor is a nudist. Such reasoning is fallacious.

4. False Analogy or Association

A false analogy is the comparison of two items, ideas, or situations that cannot logically be compared. For example,

Councilman A: We'd better pass a law banning nudity on the beach.

Councilman B: Why?

Councilman A: Nudity will attract the criminal elements to our town.

Councilman A equates nudity with crime and criminals, which does not logically follow, any more than saying that because Jim Smith has a wonderful father, Jim will also make a wonderful father.

◆ TEXTBOOK ENTRY

Identify the type of fallacious reasoning used in each of the following examples.

1. I don't see why everyone is so worried about ecology. Everything will work itself out.

    Type of reasoning: _____

2. I know I've quit smoking, but if I don't smoke this carton of cigarettes my girl gave me, I'll hurt her feelings.

    Type of reasoning: _____

3. Don't vote for him. His father used to be active in the Communist movement back in 1930.

    Type of reasoning: _____

4. "Everybody needs milk, even Sylvester Stallone."

    Type of reasoning: _____

5. All kids love hot dogs; so buy Johnny one, too.

    Type of reasoning: _____

Practice in Recognizing Fallacious Thinking

If you or your instructor feel you need more practice in recognizing fallacious thinking, go to page 319.

Edit for Agreement

Clear writing and clear thinking go hand in hand. Just as there are fallacious types of thinking and arguing, there are fallacious types of sentence structure and grammar. This unit deals with an aspect of writing known as **agreement**. Correct sentences will contain subjects, verbs, and pronouns that are in agreement. This means that singular subjects need singular verbs and singular pronouns will refer to a singular antecedent, that plural subjects need plural verb forms and plural pronouns will refer to plural antecedents.

Here are some rules and examples. When you are ready to edit your near final draft, one thing to look for is the proper agreement of subject and verb.

Agreement of Subject and Verb

1. The rule for proper agreement of subjects and verbs is easy. Singular subjects take singular verbs; plural subjects take plural verbs. However, it is not always easy when you are writing to know which is the singular or plural verb form. Look at the following examples:

    The <u>tree</u> in the yard <u>grows</u> very fast.

    The <u>trees</u> in the yard <u>grow</u> very fast.

Notice that a singular subject (*tree*) takes a singular verb form (*grows*). The plural subject (*trees*) takes a plural verb form (*grow*). Notice, too, that usually an *s* ending on a subject means it is a plural subject. Sometimes, however, this is not always the case, as the following examples show:

The women on our block want to organize a bridge club.

The men went to Las Vegas.

The dog and the cat get along well.

In all the preceding cases, the subjects are plural but do not end with the letter *s*.

2. Sometimes, when writing, we use the wrong verb for the subject because of plural phrases or expressions that come between the subject and the verb. Look at the following examples:

Our television, as well as many other televisions, is not built to last beyond the warranty.

Dr. Gibbons, along with his three nurses, appears regularly on the program.

His sisters, who look very much like his brother, are not here today.

As you can see, the need to match the correct verb form with the subject can become difficult if the subject is not sorted out from the other nouns in the sentence.

3. The following words, when used as subjects, take singular verbs because they are considered singular subjects:

each	anyone	neither
every	anybody	nobody
everyone	anything	nothing
everybody	someone	no one
everything	somebody	another
either	something	

Notice the following examples:

Each of us is concerned with the problem.

Everybody wants her to win.

Nothing is the way it was.

Neither of them wants that to happen.

On the other hand, the following words may be used in either a singular or plural sense, depending upon the context of the sentence:

any   all   more   most   none   some

Notice the following examples:

Some of the stockings are too large.

Some of the wood is wet.

None of us are correct.

None is correct.

4.   Two or more subjects linked by *and* usually take a plural verb even if the individual subject is a singular subject. However, when the words *each* or *every* are used before singular subjects linked by *and*, a singular verb is used.

The principal and the teacher walk home for lunch.

(The principal and teacher together make the plural they. They walk home for lunch.)

My mother, father, and sisters want to come to the play.

(Taken together "they" want to come to the play.)

Each novel and play has to be read by Friday.

Every dog and cat likes to drag garbage from the trash cans.

Also, when two or more subjects are joined by the words *either . . . or, neither . . . nor,* the verb agrees with the subject closest to it.

Either you or Sam buys tickets.

Neither my girlfriend nor my best friends want to go.

5.   Subjects plural in form, such as *pants, clothes, scissors,* and *glasses,* usually take a plural verb. However, subjects that are plural in form but singular in meaning, such as *mathematics, physics, economics, news, athletics, family, group,* and *class,* require singular verb forms. Notice the following examples:

My pants are torn.

Physics is a difficult subject for me.

Athletics is not required at this school.

The group is traveling by bus.

In addition, subjects that state an amount of something, such as *money, weight,* or *time,* require singular verbs.

Twenty-five dollars is too much to pay.

The doctor said four ounces of codeine is far too much.

Five weeks of vacation is ideal for the trip.

6.   The singular verb form is used with the title of any written work, even if the title is plural. It is also always used when a sentence begins with *it.*

Arizona Highways is full of colorful illustrations.

The *Los Angeles Times* is a morning newspaper.

Indians of the Plains tells us a great deal about the history of the Cheyenne.

It is my favorite dish.

It is time for us to do something for her.

◆ TEXTBOOK ENTRY

1. For each of the following sentences, underline the subject with one line and the verb with two lines.

   a. That music is one of my favorites.

   b. In some colleges, males and females live in the same dormitories.

   c. They forgot to meet us there.

   d. My mother fixes television sets.

   e. That television program makes me ill.

2. In the following sentences, underline the correct verb form.

   a. Robert, as well as Jim and Paul, (were, was) late.

   b. The hammer, along with my other tools, (were, was) left in the rain.

   c. The boys, who don't care too much for their sister, (were, was) about to leave without her.

   d. Television repairmen, along with auto mechanics, (has, have) poor reputations on the whole.

   e. The crowd, paying no attention to the speaker, (is, are) starting to get restless.

3. Underline the correct verb form in the following sentences.

   a. Each of the three (has, have) a way to get there.

   b. Neither of them (is going, are going) to get it!

   c. Some of the pants (are, is) damaged.

   d. None of the answers (is, are) correct.

   e. Anyone sensible (is, are) in agreement with me.

4. Underline the correct verb form in the following sentences.

   a. The television and the radio always (break, breaks) down at the wrong times.

   b. Dustin Hoffman and Robert Redford (are, is) my favorite actors.

   c. Either the maps or the tablet (has, have) to be moved.

d. Each record and each album cover (have, has) to be marked.

e. Neither your parents nor mine (wants, want) to go.

5. Underline the correct verb form in the following sentences.

a. The entire family (want, wants) to watch the TV special.

b. Six dollars (is, are) a bargain.

c. Economics (is, are) my favorite subject this semester.

d. The scissors (is, are) not working correctly.

e. His trousers (is, are) frayed at the cuffs.

6. Underline the correct verb in the following sentences.

a. *The Seven Minutes* (deal, deals) with obscenity.

b. It (is, are) the parents who demanded action.

c. *Plutarch's Lives* (tell, tells) us about famous Greeks and Romans.

d. Each one (tell, tells) it in his own way.

e. Neither that book nor these movies (show, shows) the truth.

Agreement of Pronoun and Subject

1. To keep from repeating your subject, you should use pronouns as a substitute. For instance,

   Awkward: The housewives said the housewives' demands on the stores were met.

   Better: The housewives said *their* demands on the stores were met.

   Following is a list of pronouns used to replace subjects. There are more, but this list will stir your memory.

   me, my, mine, myself

   you, he, him, her, she

   they, them, these, this, that, their, its

   we, us, who, which, what

2. A pronoun has to agree in number with the subject or word it is replacing. Notice the following examples:

   The students left their books in the room.

   The professor told us about his personal problems.

   I know that my essay was well written.

   They wanted us to go in their car with them.

3. When the subject of a sentence is one of the words in the following list, a singular pronoun should be used.

someone	everybody	nothing
somebody	everything	person
something	no one	man
everyone	nobody	woman

Following are some examples:

Someone should tell us about his or her own food.

Everyone is responsible for his or her own food.

No one can know what lies in his or her future.

4. When a collective noun such as *family*, *group*, or *class* is used as a singular subject, it requires a singular pronoun. When a collective noun is used as a plural subject, it requires a plural pronoun. Notice the following examples:

The family is having its third picnic this year.

The class will do their own projects rather than a group project.

❖ TEXTBOOK ENTRY

In the following blanks, supply the correct pronouns.

1. Someone left _____ bag here.

2. Everybody should do _____ own "thing."

3. Each person must give _____ report on Tuesday.

4. Anyone can join if _____ wants to do so.

5. The professors decided to take _____ problems to a lawyer.

Practice in Agreement

If you or your instructor feel you need more practice in agreement, go to page 304.

❖ WRITING JOURNAL ENTRY

Return to the last draft on your "thinking" essay. Rewrite and edit by using the following checklist:

_____ 1. Have I fully developed and supported my thesis?
_____ 2. Have I fully developed and supported each paragraph?

_____ 3. Have I used transitional elements to help my reader move from one point to the next?

_____ 4. Have I eliminated any sentence fragments, run-ons, and comma splices?

_____ 5. Have I checked for subject, verb, and pronoun agreement?

_____ 6. Have I checked for any fallacious thinking or reasoning?

Proofread

Using the proofreading marks on the inside cover of this text and applying the above checklist, read, mark, and grade the following student essay. Comment on both the good points and the problems you see with the essay.

LOOKING INSIDE THE BRAIN

Researchers tell us that our brains are split into two hemispheres, left and right. The left brain controls our analytical and linguistic functions, and our right brain is more concerned with visual and intuitive skills. Because of our genes, our life-style, and early training, we tend to use one side of the brain more than another. Now all this may be true, but researchers can't lift a lid on our brains and watch how the brain works as we carry on our activities. So how do they know? How do they conduct research on how the brain works? Unfortunately, one of their best "laboratories" for learning is the study of people who have brain damage.

For example, there is the case of a nun who was beaten badly by a burglar. Her brain's left hemisphere was so badly dmamged that she lost her memory for details, her speech became slurred, her ability to make jusgements was impaired, and she became very emotional at odd moments. When the robber was caught. her attorney would not allow her to testify against her attacker because the nun would probably have hugged the accused when asked to identify him. Her ability to identify the robber was destroyed by the injuries to the left side of her brain, her right brain took over speech and produced emotional, uncritical, childlike language. By studying the extent of the brain damage and by retraining parts of the brain, specialists both used and helped the nun in their exploration of the brain's functions.

In contrast. there is the case of the young woman who underwent brain surgery to remove a large tumor from her right hemisphere. Because of some tissue loss, she could no longer do her job which required sorting and matching. It became difficult for her to make physical movements. She could no longer rmember how to do simple tasks, such as getting in and out of a car, or putting on pantyhose. She had trouble doing any tasks that required step-by-step analysis because the left side of her brain that dealt with speech was unaffected, she was able to work quite well as a telephone operator.

It is sad that people with brain damage must suffer. But the positive side is that researchers have an opportunity to learn more about the brain tht in turn may be helpful to others.

Did you check the following when you marked the student essay?

_____ 1. Does the essay have a thesis? Is it developed fully enough?
_____ 2. Does each paragraph have a topic sentence? Are they fully developed?
_____ 3. Are transitional elements used to move smoothly from one point to the next?
_____ 4. Are the sentences well written? Are there many sentence errors? Is there agreement of subject, verbs, and pronouns?
_____ 5. Is there any fallacious reasoning?
_____ 6. Does the title fit the point of the essay?
_____ 7. Does it appear that the author carefully proofread the paper?

Return now to your own essay and apply this checklist to your own work. When you have done the best you can, turn it in.

"Miss Dugan, will you send someone in here who can distinguish right from wrong?"

Drawing by Dana Fradon; © 1975 The New Yorker Magazine, Inc.

A half truth is a whole lie.

Yiddish Proverb

Truth, the whole truth, and nothing but the truth.

Legal Oath

THINK . . .

about honesty.

◆ WRITING JOURNAL ENTRY

The pressure is on. If you don't get a B on your term paper due next week you'll get a D in the class, making you ineligible for a possible scholarship next year. There's no way you can complete the project in time. A student in the class offers to sell you an A-graded term paper from another teacher's class. In your journal, write what you are going to do, providing as many reasons for your actions as you can.

◆ TEXTBOOK ENTRY

In the spaces provided, answer the following questions.

1. Circle all of the words that help define honesty.

deceptive	truthfulness	fraudulent	devious
frank	straightforward	sincere	duplicity
pretense	ethical	integrity	deceit

2. Should a person always be honest? _____ Explain. _____

_____

_____

_____

3. There is an old saying, "Honesty is the best policy." Explain why you agree or disagree. _____

_____

_____

_____

4. Explain whether or not there are times when lying should be excused. _____

_____

_____

_____

_____

5. List some reasons people lie or are dishonest. to avoid hurting someone's feelings

Age -

_____

_____

_____

6. Explain which of the preceding reasons are excusable. _____

_____

_____

Read the following statements and answer the questions that follow them.

A.   Cheating is now considered to be a major problem in colleges and universities. How to cope with it has become a favorite topic of conversation at faculty meetings and conferences. Several professors say they've dropped the traditional term paper requirement. Why? Many students buy prewritten term papers. And faculty members say they can't track down all the cheaters anymore. "I may be wrong," said one professor wistfully, "but I think the situation has gotten worse in the past few years. I used to catch students making up footnotes. Today they simply buy the whole paper." (Stacia Robbins, "Honesty: Is It Going Out of Style?" *Senior Scholastic* 31 Oct. 1980)

1. What point is the author making? _Cheating is a major problem that is_

getting worse & something needs to be done about it.

_____

2. Do you think that those professors who have dropped the term paper as a course

requirement because of cheating are doing the right thing? _____

Explain. _____

_____

_____

_____

B.   Many educators feel that as students gain confidence in themselves and their abilities, they are less likely to cheat. Surprisingly, some efforts to curb cheating may actually encourage cheating—a person may feel "they don't trust me anyway," and be tempted to "beat the system." Distrust can be dangerous. But so can trust! (Stacia Robbins, "Honesty: Is It Going Out of Style?" *Senior Scholastic* 31 Oct. 1980)

1. Explain why you do or do not agree with the first sentence. _I agree because_

if a student has confidence in his or her ability to complete the assignment

required when he or she is not going to feel the need to cheat.

_____

2. Is "they don't trust me anyway" just an excuse for people who would cheat

anyway? _____ Explain. _____

_____

_____

THINK ABOUT IT . . .

Consider what life would be like if everyone could lie perfectly or if no one could lie at all. . . . If we could never know how someone really felt, and if we knew that we couldn't know, life would be more tenuous. Certain in the knowledge that every show of emotion might be a mere display put on to please, manipulate, or mislead, individuals would be more adrift, attachments less firm. And if we could never lie, if a smile was reliable, never absent when pleasure was felt, and never present without pleasure, life would be rougher than it is, many relationships harder to maintain.

Paul Eckman

Telling Lies: Clues to Deceit in the Marketplace, Politics and Marriage

---

C.   Granted that a public lie on an important matter, once revealed, hurts the speaker, must we therefore conclude that every lie has this effect? What of those who tell a few white lies once in a while? Does lying hurt them in the same way? It is hard to defend such a notion. No one trivial lie undermines the liar's integrity. But the problem for liars is that they tend to see most of their lies in this benevolent light and thus vastly underestimate the risks they run. While no one lie always carries harm for the liar, then, there is *risk* of such harm in most. (Sissela Bok, *Lying.* New York: Pantheon, 1978. 24–25)

1.   What is the author's point? *the liar thinks they are doing*
good, but in reality they are only hurting
themselves + others.

2.   What are the risks liars may run? _____

_____

_____

READ . . .

about speaking the truth.

Ethics refers to a system of moral principles or values based on what is right or good. Honesty is considered a good principle or value in which most people claim they believe, but as the following essay reveals, we don't always speak or act honestly.

Before reading closely, take a moment to read the title, the opening paragraph, the first sentence of each paragraph, and the conclusion. Note the length, and make certain that you have the time to read it now. Then answer the following questions.

1.   What do you think is the thesis or main idea of this reading selection?

_____

_____

_____

2.   What do you think you will learn from reading this essay? _____

_____

_____

_____

3.   The meaning an author intends may be lost if the reader does not understand the author's use of certain words and phrases. Make sure that you understand the following words before you read. The number after the word is the number of the paragraph where the word appears.
     a.   *semantic* (2) = pertaining to meaning in language
     b.   *determinants* (3) = influencing or determining factors
     c.   *expeditious* (3) = to be done with speed
     d.   *uncompromising* (5) = inflexible; not making concessions
     e.   *rampant* (5) = growing or spreading unstopped
     f.   *conducive* (6) = contributing or leading to
     g.   *esoteric* (8) = understood only by a small group
     h.   *eradicate* (8) = get rid of

Now carefully read the essay. Practice your marking and note-taking skills.

TO DECEIVE OR NOT TO DECEIVE?

Leo F. Buscaglia

1   It's said that in the 4th Century B.C., Diogenes went in search of an honest man. With a lamp in broad daylight, he traveled everywhere, so he would have the best possibility of finding him. He didn't.

2   Psychological, philosophical and religious literature is full of warnings that a healthy, lasting relationship must be based upon honesty and truth. It is vital for us to believe that at least those we love and who love us will be truthful and honest with us. How can we survive otherwise? Still, it would be interesting to find if anyone reading these pages could, with integrity, say that they know a completely honest person. We generally disguise our own anxiety about answering this question by indulging in such semantic gymnastics as, "What do you mean by honest?" "How honest?" "Under what circumstances?" "With whom?" "Honest about things that matter?"

These questions suggest that most of us feel that there are many kinds and degrees of honesty.

3   However honesty is defined, the fact remains that dishonesty is one of the prime determinants of failed relationships. It has caused families to separate, lovers to physically harm one another or even kill each other in what are referred to as "crimes of passion," businesses to be dissolved, even governments to crumble, and nations to fight their bloodiest wars. In dealing with truth which might ultimately create even a minor crisis, it seems often more expeditious to tell a lie. "As long as it doesn't hurt anybody," we rationalize.

4   A Louis Harris poll, reported in 1969 in *Time* magazine, revealed that six out of ten individuals in the United States felt that lying was justified at times. One percent of those questioned felt that lying was permissible in any situation, at any time; 58 percent said sometimes; 38 percent said it was never permissible to tell a lie, and three percent dodged the issue *honestly* and said they were not sure. In reality, I don't believe that many of us have thought it through clearly enough to have an opinion. We speak of "nothing but the truth," and lie on our income tax forms. We agree that "honesty is the best policy," but we'd never dream of telling most people, if asked, what we truly think of them. This attitude is certainly not unique among those of us living in the United States. The ancient Greeks were actually schooled in lying and were taught techniques to keep from getting caught. Their great philosopher Socrates was, in essence, put to death for telling the truth because his judges believed that his *truth* would corrupt their youth.

5   Ancient Chinese societies advocated a blend of guiltless dishonesty. Rather than encouraging an uncompromising approach to a truth which might cause pain to others they suggested a type of truth "for kindness' sake." To this day we are still teaching these values. Examples of dishonesty are rampant in almost every sector of society, at every level of interaction. They are to be found in the most casual of relationships as well as in the most complex of international politics. If individuals are not actually engaged in lying, they are indulging in creative half-truths or dodging the issues altogether. Some philosophers and sociologists acknowledge that it is questionable if an individual or a society of any size could actually survive if dedicated to the whole truth. Marcel Eck stated that, "a society in which all truths were blindly exposed would be more like hell than a paradise." "Not to speak the truth," he continued, "is sometimes a duty." It is often rationalized that most people don't want to hear the truth, anyway.

6   Our courts require us to take the oath of justice, "the truth, the whole truth, and nothing but the truth." We then sit by and watch as brilliant lawyers present subtle "versions" of the truth conducive to the welfare of their clients in a particular situation. They are not lying, they say in defense, they are but rearranging and adjusting the facts.

7   Advertisers will blatantly tell us that their product is the very best. They will guarantee us instant relief or pleasure if we use it regularly. They promise to cure our colds, help us fall asleep, lose weight, and find romance, satisfying sex, and everlasting love. Even the most naive of us knows that these are lies, but we hear them so often and become so desensitized to them, that they no longer offend. Some of us even buy the products advertised in the hope that there will be some truth in them.

8   Journalists, who give strong lip service to their dedication to bringing us the truth, often lie to gain access to the truth. Political leaders expound esoteric platforms, promising impossible feats which they assure us they will accomplish if elected. They will balance the budget, eradicate crime, end wars, do away with poverty, and put "a

chicken in every pot." Some even assure us that they will revitalize the family and bring morality back to a decaying society. Even after more than a hundred years of being assured of the American dream of freedom, justice, and equality for all, we still have hope. We are not stupid, just conditioned over the years not to expect the whole truth. Even law enforcement officials sometimes use deceitful methods in order to elicit the truth from a criminal. Physicians speak of protecting us from the truth. Teachers and counselors often feel they must cushion the truth. So much have we come to live with this that it has reached the point where we perceive and accept these behaviors as harmless, trivial, even normal. We speak of them as well-intentioned, and say, "How nice to see you," to people we would rather avoid. "We must get together sometime," we say to individuals we dislike. "What an attractive hairdo!" we exclaim when we wonder if the hair stylist has ever been trained. There are those who express gratitude over unwanted gifts, gush over babies they dislike, and feign delight over conversation that is boring them to death. We write positive letters of recommendation for individuals we are eager to get rid of and hope never to see again.

9   We engage in these untruths, we say, in order to protect others from pain, from harm or to spare the innocent. It is no wonder, then, that we no longer view dishonesty as a negative behavior but rather as a condoned necessary social skill. We continue to encourage deceit. We therefore practice it with a clear conscience and teach the processes to our children as part of their growing to sophisticated maturity.

10   I have seen situations where children, not yet schooled in deception, have told grownups what they see as truth, and are straightaway sent to their rooms or the principal's office. Then, in these same situations, we teach, with a straight face, that honesty is the best policy. When children are punished and lose face for telling the truth, they learn quickly about the wisdom of "the white lie."

. . .

11   So, what to do? Deceive or not deceive? Since we are only humans, perhaps it is not such a cut-and-dried decision. But the problem should not be ignored, since it is responsible for such a large majority of unsuccessful relationships. Certainly, one can choose to deceive, but there may be alternatives to deception which might merit our consideration. In order to do this we must put aside the idea that deception may be good, that too often the truth hurts. We must be willing to face the fact that these beliefs may be no more than a comfortable "cop-out," that although truth may hurt, lying to one you love may do more than hurt, it may be almost totally devastating.

12   Truth in a relationship should begin at the start. Wise individuals, dedicated to growing together in mutual love and trust, whether lovers or possible business partners, should discuss their attitude and expectations regarding honesty early on in the relationship. Among other things, they must consider whether they tolerate lying. There will be some who would rather be lied to than have to face the truth. "To speak the truth among people who do not want to hear it," Nicholas Humphrey said once, "is considered almost an aggressive act—an invasion of privacy, a trespass into someone else's space. Not nice, not done." They may feel it is better not to know than to have to face the anxiety and pain that truth might bring. There are others who will want nothing but the truth, but will want the truth to be offered lovingly. Too often we equate truth with the "brutal reality." Not so. Truth can be communicated gently. "I'm not as fond of this outfit as I am of your blue one. But remember, it's only *my* opinion, and I'm not Yves St. Laurent." This is easier to take than "It's awful! I hate it!" If we decide to accept only the whole truth, then perhaps it can be communicated

less harshly in statements like, "Remember, we decided to always be truthful with each other. So this is how *I* see it, or feel, *now*."

13   It is realistic to believe that we shall have to deal with the conflict of honesty and deception for our entire relating lifetime. How can we expect total honesty with others when many of us engage in lying to ourselves? We must be willing to accept the fact that we may fall from truth from time to time. We must learn to accept these lapses as human and use them as learning experiences to reinforce more truthful behavior at a future time. But it seems to me that if we want our relationships to last and to grow, honesty and truth must be our inevitable goal.

REACT . . .
to the reading selection.

◇ WRITING JOURNAL ENTRY

Write about a time in your life when you were or almost were dishonest. What were the circumstances? What did you learn from the incident?

◇ TEXTBOOK ENTRY

A. Understanding the Content

In the spaces provided, answer the following questions. Refer to the reading selection for answers if needed.

1. What is the main idea of the essay? _____

    _____

    _____

2. What are some reasons people are dishonest, according to the author?

    _____

    _____

    _____

3. What does the author mean when he says we engage in "semantic gymnastics" when we are asked if we know an honest person? _____

    _____

    _____

4. What examples of dishonesty being "rampant in almost every sector of society" does the author provide? _____

    _____

    _____

    _____

5. What are some "alternatives to deception" the author mentions?

    _____

    _____

6. How important is truth and honesty in relationships? _____

    _____

    _____

B. Noticing Writing Techniques and Styles

7. In what paragraph is the thesis best stated? _____

8. Explain how well the opening paragraph relates to the author's thesis? _____

    _____

    _____

9. What is the basic function of paragraph 11? _____

    _____

    _____

10. To what audience do you think the author wrote? _____

    _____

    Why? _____

    _____

PLAN . . .

an essay on some aspect of honesty or ethics.

THE FAMILY CIRCUS   **by Bill Keane**

"Is he the guy who's lookin' for
an honest man?"

In previous units, you have been shown how to select and explore a topic through brainstorming, freewriting, clustering, and PMIs. Here is one more method you might find useful.

STEP 1: Selecting and Exploring a Topic: Reacting to What You Read

By answering the **React** questions that follow the readings in this book, you are, of course, reacting to what you read. Don't overlook your answers to these or some of the **Think** questions as possible sources for essays. However, these questions are supplied for you. They may not require answers that deal with your own questions and concerns. Don't let answering the book's questions keep you from reacting on your own to what you read.

Using the book's questions is a good place to start looking for possible essay topics. For instance, earlier in this unit you were asked to respond to the statement "Honesty is the best policy." How do you really feel about that policy? Is it true? When might it not apply? Is there ever a time when friends, teachers, parents, doctors, lawyers, and governments should lie? Is there such a thing as a "white lie"? Such questions reveal a critical examination and reaction to what is read. Reacting to what you read, then, requires a conscious effort.

Here's a short passage. Read it and then in the space that follows it write down at least four questions or reactions that might serve as possible leads to essay topics if explored further.

> Of course, dishonesty in government—at local, state and national levels—does not always have such noble reasons. A prime example is the so-called Watergate affair. During President Nixon's first term (1969–73), a Committee to Reelect the President was formed. The committee is said to have authorized a group of men to break into the Democratic national headquarters in the Watergate hotel. The idea was to take a peek at the files of the Democratic party. When the burglars were caught, many politicians began scrambling to cover up the story. And President Nixon may have been involved. Most Americans were surprised and outraged by news of the break-in and cover-up. But many Europeans were surprised at our surprise. Some European observers explained that they tend to think of lying, cheating, deception, and corruption as part of politics and government. (Stacia Robbins, "Honesty: Is It Going Out of Style?" *Senior Scholastic* 31 Oct. 1980)

The right or wrong of what you wrote isn't an issue. But just as an example, here are some questions or reactions you might have had as you read the passage:

1. Are we really so different from Europeans in our perception of politicians?
2. What other examples of political corruption could I find in history textbooks?
3. What happened to the people involved in the Watergate break-in? Who were they?
4. Have lying, cheating, deception, and corruption become a part of politics? Have they always been?
5. Was President Nixon involved? Did he resign because he was involved?

There are no doubt many other questions and reactions to the passage, but this gives you an idea of what is meant by reacting to what you read. It means going beyond merely understanding the content and critically thinking about what is said.

◆ TEXTBOOK ENTRY

Following are two more passages related to honesty and ethics. Read them and write some questions or reactions that might lead to a possible topic for an essay on honesty.

A.   Throughout society, all would benefit if the incentive structure associated with deceit were changed: if the gains from deception were lowered, and honesty made more worthwhile even in the short run. Sometimes it is easy to make such a change. Universities, for instance, have found in recent years that parents of incoming students all too often misrepresent their family incomes in order to gain scholarships for their children at the expense of those in greater need of assistance. If, on the other hand, parents are told in advance that they may have to produce their income tax statements on request, such misrepresentation is much less likely to take place. (Sissela Bok, *Lying*. New York: Pantheon, 1978. 246)

_____

_____

_____

_____

_____

B.   Blowing the whistle on corruption, fraud or mismanagement in government or business doesn't have to be as lonely as it once was. Congress, the courts and some federal agencies are taking whistle blowers more seriously. . . . As the number of whistle blowers has grown, so has a network of professionals who specialize in giving them legal, financial and emotional support. The Project on Military Procurement, a nonprofit, nonpartisan group, helps Defense Department workers and contractors who expose wasteful spending. Lawyers at the Government Accountability Project (GAP) help whistle blowers sue for reinstatement or back pay. . . .

Organizations like GAP advise clients to seek anonymity, gather supporting evidence and prepare for financial and emotional stress. And for good reason: nearly all whistle blowers can count on some form of retaliation. Their battles may not be so lonely anymore, but they can be as nasty as ever. (Bob Cohn, "New Help for Whistle Blowers." *Newsweek* 27 June 1988: 43)

_____

_____

_____

_____

_____

◆ WRITING JOURNAL ENTRY

If you don't already have an idea for a topic on some aspect of honesty or ethics, look over the following list for a possible topic. In your journal, explore your idea either through brainstorming, freewriting, clustering, or PMIs.

1. Cheating on exams.
2. Lying about one's age.
3. Should adopted children be told the truth?
4. Distortion of the truth in election campaigns.
5. How colleges should cope with cheating.
6. Should schools have courses on ethics?
7. When is lying beneficial?
8. Should doctors ever lie to their patients?
9. Deception in government.
10. How the public responds to government deceit.
11. Is it worse to plan to lie or to lie on the spur of the moment?
12. "The great masses of the people . . . will more easily fall victims to a big lie than to a small one." (Adolf Hitler, *Mein Kampf*).

STEP 2: Writing a Working Thesis

Sometimes a possible thesis comes before any exploration of the topic. (Remember, we said writing doesn't always follow a step-by-step procedure.) For example, it's possible that after reading item 3 above you react by saying, "Yes, adopted children should be told." There is your working thesis. It's at that point that you would begin listing the reasons that would support your position.

On the other hand, there may be times when you don't feel moved by any of the ideas presented. You may need to go back and reread all or parts of the reading selection or even research some of the sources of paragraphs used in the unit that sound interesting. For instance, you may look over Leo Buscaglia's essay, "Deceive or Not to Deceive?" and some thoughts may occur: Can you make money and be honest these days? Should colleges offer courses in ethics? Is it possible to teach honesty? How does one develop ethics? As you think about your own questions, you may decide that ethics should be taught—a working thesis.

Perhaps paragraph A in the **Textbook Entry** interested you to the point of checking out from the library the book from which it came. Reading more, you come upon this passage:

> The very stress on individualism, on competition, on achieving material success which so marks our society also generates intense pressures to cut corners. To win an election, to increase one's income, to outsell competitors—such motives impel many to participate in forms of duplicity they might otherwise resist. The more widespread they judge these practices to be, the stronger will be the pressures to join, even compete, in deviousness.

This reminds you of what you've heard and read lately about athletes using illegal drugs and steroids to beat the competition, deliberate deceit in a recent election campaign, people lying to receive welfare payments, or your own temptation to cheat on a test in a class in which you weren't doing well. The key word for you here may be *pressure*, and suddenly you have a working thesis: "The pressure to achieve in the system can often cause people to become deceptive."

Topics for essays, as well as working theses, can often come from your reactions to what you read. Don't overlook the possibilities.

◆ TEXTBOOK ENTRY

When you have arrived at a possible working thesis after exploring ideas for an essay on honesty or ethics, write it in the following space for later use.

Working thesis: _____

_____

_____

_____

STEP 3: Analyzing and Organizing Your Ideas

Look carefully at the key words in your working thesis. Make certain you have enough information to support your key points. Organize your ideas into some type of outline you can follow for a first draft. When you are satisfied you are ready, go to the next section.

WRITE . . .

a first draft for an essay on some aspect of honesty or ethics.

The Nutshell Statement

In the space given, write a nutshell statement for the thesis and outline you developed for your essay on honesty or ethics.

The purpose of my essay is _____

_____

_____

My audience is _____

_____

I will support my thesis by _____

_____

_____

Developing Paragraphs by Using Classification and Division

Classification is a way to arrange or divide ideas and information into groups, sections, or categories. Simply put, if you were asked to arrange apples, green beans, pears, potatoes, melons, and broccoli, you would probably arrange the fruit (apples, pears, melons) into one group and the vegetables (green beans, potatoes, broccoli) into another. The two classifications for the food are fruit and vegetable. Of course, you could classify the food by color, nutrition, taste preference, or growing season, depending on the reason or need to classify.

Look carefully at the following list of statements. What do they have in common and how might they be classified?

1. Say "Thank you" when you are given a gift.
2. Place your napkin on your lap.
3. Brush your teeth after every meal.
4. Look before you cross the street.
5. Murder is wrong.
6. We should respond when someone cries for help.
7. The right to live is a fundamental one.

There are several ways these statements can be classified. One way is to break the statements into two groups according to their content: The first four deal with etiquette and safety at a personal level of behavior; the last three deal with a broader social level of behavior. Another way to classify the statements is by their structure. The first four are commands, implying "you" as the subject; the last three are declarative sentences containing the subjects. Another way to classify them is according to those statements you believe in and those you don't.

Usually in a classification paragraph the first sentence introduces the reader to the subject to be divided, and then each division is presented in some logical order. Following is an example:

There are three distinct attributes that promote the growth of language in a child. One, all human infants have a tendency to babble, to play with their vocalizing equipment. Two, humans live in very stable groups so that children hear a consistent language pattern. And three, infants are talked at, very quickly gaining the skill of language because they are accepted into and become a part of the group in which they live.

Notice that the first sentence states that there are three attributes. The rest of the sentences present each of the three in a logical sequence that ranges from the child to the group that influences it.

Here is another example:

> I needed to reduce all that I knew about good writing to a handful of concepts, few enough that I could see them all at once. So I made a list. I came up with . . . or perhaps down to . . . seven. I call them my seven beacons of good writing. They are Brevity, Clarity, Precision, Harmony, Humanity, Honesty, and Poetry, and are posted over my desk. . . . (Gary Provost, "The 7 Beacons of Good Writing." *Writer's Digest* Mar. 1984: 35)

In this example, the author divided what he knew about good writing into seven categories. The rest of his essay, of course, takes each of the seven categories and discusses them in more detail.

One more example should help. As you read it, notice that whereas the author is classifying, some definition is also being used.

> Burnout is progressive, occurring over a period of time. Authors Robert Veninga and James Spradley define five stages that lead from a stressful job to a burnt-out case: 1) The Honeymoon—intense enthusiasm and job satisfaction that, for all but a few dynamos, eventually give way to a time when valuable energy reserves begin to drain off. 2) Fuel Shortage—fatigue, sleep disturbances, possibly some escapist drinking or shopping binges and other early-warning signals. 3) Chronic Symptoms—exhaustion, physical illness, acute anger and depression. 4) Crisis—illness that may become incapacitating, deep pessimism, self-doubt, obsession with one's own problems. 5) Hitting the Wall—career and even life threatened. (Lance Morrow, "The Burnout of Almost Everyone." *Time* 21 Sept. 1981)

The author shows that burnout occurs in five stages: The Honeymoon, Fuel Shortage, Chronic Symptoms, Crisis, and Hitting the Wall (classification). He also defines each one of these stages so that we understand what is meant by the names given to each stage.

◆ TEXTBOOK ENTRY

Read the following passages and answer the questions that follow them.

A.   There are basically two different types of purchasers who respond to advertising. One type rushes out to buy 50 percent of all the products they see advertised. Such buyers help make advertising a highly successful, multibillion-dollar-a-year industry. People of the second type think they are immune to ads; they think most ads are silly, stupid, and "beneath their dignity." This type of purchaser believes ads are aimed at the "suckers" of the first type. Yet 90 percent of the nation's adults who believe themselves immune are responsible for about 90 percent of all purchases of advertised products.

1.   What is being classified? _____

2.   How many divisions are made? _____

3.   Explain each one. _____

_____

_____

B.   We have used several strategies to investigate the phenomenon of worrying. We have compared self-labeled worriers and nonworriers on a variety of psychological measures and tasks and have also studied worry in a laboratory setting in order to identify characteristics of the worry process. Finally, we have looked at methods of intervening therapeutically to reduce this irritating problem among chronic worriers. (Thomas D. Borkovec, "What's the Use of Worrying?" *Psychology Today* Dec. 1985: 60)

1.   What is being classified? _____

2.   How many divisions are made? _____

3.   Explain each one. _____

_____

_____

C.   To begin, you should be aware that there are at least three levels of reading. The first, which might be termed basic reading, you learned in elementary school, where you became acquainted with the alphabet, mastered some system of word or phonetic perception, and gradually acquired a basic vocabulary.

   Another level of reading, which might be termed analytical, involves understanding the full meaning and implications of a written sentence or passage. This level requires not merely a passive act of word recognition but also an active attempt to determine the total message and experience being conveyed. Analytical reading consists of perceiving the central idea, relating subordinate ideas to it, understanding the key words, realizing the logical assumptions, and discerning the reasons supporting the ideas.

   The third level, evaluative reading, consists of formulating a critical judgment about the written work. Evaluative reading requires a questioning attitude, one that constantly challenges the logic of the written statement, searches for the writer's prejudices, weighs the significance of the points, attacks the evidence, considers the stylistic effectiveness of the writing, and then relates the ideas and feelings to other views about the subject.

1.   What is being classified? _____

2.   How many classifications are given? _____

3.   Name each one. _____

Practice in Classification

If you or your instructor feel you need more practice in using the classification pattern, go to page 275.

◆ WRITING JOURNAL ENTRY

1.   Pick at least two of the following, or use your own topics, and practice various ways to classify the ideas or information you have.
     a.   members of your family
     b.   types of cars
     c.   movies
     d.   styles of dress on campus
     e.   farm machinery
     f.   plants around your house
     g.   types of students you know
     When you are finished, you may wish to form groups according to the practices you picked and share your classification patterns with others.
2.   Using the nutshell statement on pages 154–155 and your outline of ideas, write a first draft for your essay. Use the classification pattern where it fits.

REWRITE . . .

your first drafts.

Revise

At this point you should have the first draft of an essay dealing with some aspect of honesty or ethics. Before learning about other revision strategies, check your first draft for the following:

_____ 1.   Does the introductory paragraph use a method that draws the interest of the reader?

_____ 2.   Are you writing about something you know and feel?

_____ 3.   Did you avoid the obvious and take a fresh approach?

_____ 4.   Are the paragraphs organized so that one idea leads smoothly to another? Did you use the appropriate transitional devices?

_____ 5.   Are your paragraphs fully developed and coherent?

_____ 6.   Did you try using description, examples, comparison and contrast, and classification where appropriate? (Don't try to force your ideas into these patterns; only use them when they are the best way to support your ideas.)

_____ 7.   Did you share your essay with someone to obtain another perspective on your writing?

If you are satisfied that you have done the best you can, go on to the next revision strategy.

Overcoming Misplaced and Dangling Modifiers

A modifier is a word or phrase that describes or qualifies some other word or phrase. Adjectives and adverbs are examples of modifiers. It is important to place your modifiers in the correct position in a sentence.

A **misplaced modifier** is one that appears to modify the wrong word or phrase in the sentence. Misplacement can be corrected by repositioning the modifier.

A **dangling modifier** is just that: It dangles in the sentence because it modifies nothing. Correcting dangling modifiers usually requires rewriting the sentence.

Following are examples of both of these common problems in writing.

Misplaced Modifiers [mm]

Obviously, a modifier must have a word to modify. But frequently a modifier is misplaced and modifies the wrong word. Following are three examples:

1. *Example:* All the students passed the test *in this room.*

    Did the students pass the test *in this room,* or did all of the students in the room pass the test? Chances are the sentence should read,

    All the students *in this room* passed the test.

    The prepositional phrase *in this room* is now placed to modify *the students,* not *the test.*

2. *Example:* Lester *almost* understood everything the man said in Spanish.

    Did Lester almost understand, or did he understand almost everything said? The sentence should read,

    Lester understood *almost* everything the man said in Spanish.

3. *Example:* Lester took a Spanish class from adult education *that he liked.*

    Did Lester like the Spanish class or adult education? The sentence should read,

    Lester took a Spanish class *that he liked* from adult education.

    Now the phrase *that he liked* modifies *a Spanish class,* which is what he liked.

Dangling Modifiers [dm or dang]

When a phrase in a sentence does not clearly or logically relate to another word or modify another word in the sentence, it is called a *dangling modifier.* Notice in the examples that follow how the introductory clause does not modify or relate to any word in the sentence.

1.   *Example:* While eating my breakfast, a gunshot attracted my attention.

Who was eating the breakfast, a gunshot? It's not likely. The sentence should read,

> While eating my breakfast, I heard a gunshot that attracted my attention.

The introductory clause now modifies the "I" rather than dangling there modifying nothing.

2.   *Example:* Being intelligent and handsome, I hoped he would ask me for a date.

Is the "I" intelligent and handsome or the person who might ask for a date? The sentence should read,

> I hoped he would ask me for a date, because he's intelligent and handsome.

3.   *Example:* To pass tests, studying should be done on a regular basis.

Who wants to pass tests? It's not clear. The sentence should read,

> To pass tests, students should study regularly.

◆ TEXTBOOK ENTRY

Correct the following sentences for misplaced or dangling modifiers.

1.   Looking out the door, an unusual bird caught my attention.

_____

_____

2.   Being bad grammar, the writer will not use dangling modifiers.

_____

_____

3.   When sitting, my shoulders tend to slump.

_____

_____

4.   Going home, it started to snow.

_____

_____

5.   A dog was found in the city center that belonged to my neighbors.

_____

_____

6.   The instructor explained why misplaced modifiers are incorrect on Thursday.

_____

_____

Practice in Misplaced and Dangling Modifiers

If you or your instructor feel you need more practice on misplaced and dangling modifiers, go to page 308.

Edit for Correct Punctuation: Part I

Looking over your revised essays for correct punctuation is often considered more of an editorial than a revision function. However, as you may have noticed in the discussion of fragments, run-ons, and comma splices, such errors are usually caused by faulty punctuation. In addition, correct punctuation will help your readers know what you really want to say. Notice the difference punctuation makes in the following sentences:

>   During the battle, General Willard ran away.
>   During the battle, General, Willard ran away.

>   My friends say the counselors will get me in trouble.
>   My friends, say the counselors, will get me in trouble.

Just a comma or two can change the entire meaning of a sentence.

Much of the following information may be familiar to you. Use it to review or to learn what you don't know.

The Period [.]

The period is used in the following ways:

1.   After a complete sentence

>   Here is the book I want.

>   She rejected my plea to marry me.

>   Please be more quiet.

>   I asked how I could improve my grade.

2.   After abbreviations

>   Dr. Waldon performed the operation.

>   Ms. Smith was my fifth-grade teacher.

>   He's a member of the U.S. Senate.

3.   After act, scene, and line in drama quotations or chapter and verse in Bible references

> *Macbeth* III. 1. 3–7. (act, scene, lines)

> Revelations 2. 3 (chapter 2, verse 3)

The Exclamation Mark [!]

The exclamation mark is used in the following ways:

1.   After a sentence that carries a strong emotion of excitement

> We won the game! (excitement or disbelief)

> I don't believe it! (incredulity)

2.   After a word or expression of strong emotion

> Fantastic!

> Far out!

> Damn!

The Question Mark [?]

The question mark is used in the following ways:

1.   After a *direct* question, that is, a question that requires an answer

> May I go with you?

> Did you see it happen?

> What time shall we meet tomorrow?

> *Note: Do not use a question mark for indirect questions, such as*

> I asked if I might go with you.

> I asked how I could improve my grade.

2.   After something in doubt, such as the exact date of an event

> The war occurred in A.D. 350 (?).

◇ TEXTBOOK ENTRY

Place the correct punctuation in the following sentences.

1.   What did the teacher want

2.   I asked what the teacher wanted

3.   Oh no I bet I'm late for class again

4.   I can't believe I won

5.   She is late for class again

6.   They asked what her age was

The Comma [,]

The comma, the most used form of punctuation, is used in the following ways:

1. With coordinating conjunctions, such as *and, but, nor,* and *or,* when they link two independent clauses:

> He won the game, but he hurt himself in the process.

> They went to church in the morning, and later that afternoon they went to the park.

> They have not hired any one, nor did they intend to do so in the near future.

Note: Without the coordinating conjunctions in the examples, the sentences would be comma splices, that is, two sentences linked with a comma:

> He won the game, he hurt himself in the process.

> They went to church in the morning, later that afternoon they went to the park.

Note: Replacing the commas in the preceding examples with periods would make the sentences correct, but the use of coordinating conjunctions makes them read better.

2. With items in a series
    a. Use commas with three or more items in a series:

> The VW Rabbit is economical, small, and easy to drive.

> *Incorrect:* The VW Rabbit is small, and easy to drive.

> *Correct:* The novel has well-developed characters, an unusual plot, and an entertaining story.

> He talked about his travels in Ireland, particularly the Irish pubs, Howth Castle, and the Blarney Stone.

   b. Use commas to separate two or more coordinate adjectives (words that describe nouns) used before a noun.

> His short, plump brother hurt his knee.

> The trophy was a tall, thin, silver cup with his name engraved on it.

Note: To test whether or not two or more adjectives can be used together and separated by a comma, read the sentence by inserting only one adjective at a time. For instance,

> His *short* brother hurt his knee.

> His *plump* brother hurt his knee.

or,

> The trophy was a *tall* cup.

> The trophy was a *thin* cup.

> The trophy was a *silver* cup.

3.   With a word or group of words that could be removed from a sentence without changing the meaning

My cousin, I believe, will arrive tomorrow.

In this sentence the phrase "I believe" can be removed from the sentence without changing the meaning. The subject of the sentence is "My cousin," and it is the cousin who "will arrive" (verb). It would be incorrect to write,

I believe, my cousin will arrive tomorrow.

In the preceding sentence the subject is now "I," and it is the "I" who "believes" (verb). The comma's position makes it a comma splice. Following is another example:

Dr. Fast, who loves auto racing, will be a judge at tomorrow's race.

The clause "who loves auto racing" can be removed from the sentence without changing the meaning. Some more examples:

John, *who is my youngest brother*, works for a contractor.

My brother, *taller and stronger than I*, would make a good basketball player.

My brother lives in Alton, *a small town in Illinois.*

In each of these sentences, the information in italics can be deleted because it is not essential to the meaning. These clauses and phrases are called **nonrestrictive modifiers**. In the following sentences, the information in italics is essential to their meaning. Such phrases and clauses are called **restrictive modifiers** and do not have commas separating them:

The man *who loves building model airplanes* lives down the block.

It was my father *who finally convinced me to attend college.*

The exercise *that Mr. Magus gets* is laughable.

4.   To set off introductory words or phrases, such as

Although we arrived late, we still found good seats.

In addition, I want to clarify my previous remarks.

For example, last night we lost five runs in a row.

Because she felt ill, she went home early.

Note: Commas are usually used after the following words or phrases when they begin a sentence:

for example	however	in the first place
in fact	therefore	on the other hand
after	nonetheless	furthermore
although	in general	in addition

5. To set off material with numbers, dates, addresses, and salutory comments, such as

    3,452,611 or 4,500

    9 feet, 6 inches long

    December 12, 1930

    Note: When a date appears in the middle of a sentence, a comma follows the date, as in

    I was born on December 12, 1930, in Missouri.

    711 Sunset Boulevard, Hollywood, California 90012

    Dr. Harold R. Wright, M.D.

    Kurt Vonnegut, Jr.

    Dear Dad,

    Yours truly, *or* Sincerely,

6. To separate direct quotations from the phrase that identifies the speaker

    "Oh, no!" Helen blurted out, "I broke another nail!"

    As my dad always says, "Too old too soon, too wise too late."

    "I thought you were coming with us," Pete said.

◆ TEXTBOOK ENTRY

Place the correct punctuation in the following sentences.

1. He saw the doctor last week but he did not go back as he should have.
2. The history course was interesting informative and unlike any class I've had before.
3. What am I going to do he asked.
4. The car was painted red had white sidewall tires and cost less than the blue one.
5. The long thin velvet dress had been sold when she returned.
6. His teacher however has other things to say about him.
7. However his teacher has other things to say about him.
8. Whatever his teacher says you can be sure he will be noncommital.
9. Sally who never misses class was absent today.
10. The girl who looks like Shirley MacLaine sat near me.

11. In fact, we should take care of that now,

12. He lives at 6431 Oakdale Avenue, San Francisco, California .

13. The man at the lumber yard, cut the board 2 feet 1 inch short .

14. What ever will become of her Aunt Tillie asked ?

15. Shall I go look for the dog John wanted to know ?

Practice in Periods, Question and Exclamation Marks, and Commas

If you or your instructor feel you need more practice in these punctuation marks, go to page 314.

◆ WRITING JOURNAL ENTRY

Return to the last draft on your "honesty" essay. Rewrite and edit by using the following checklist:

_____ 1. Have I fully developed and supported my thesis?
_____ 2. Have I fully developed and supported each paragraph?
_____ 3. Have I used transitional devices to help my reader move from one point to the next?
_____ 4. Have I eliminated sentence fragments, run-ons, comma splices, misplaced and dangling modifiers?
_____ 5. Have I checked for subject-verb agreement?
_____ 6. Have I checked for fallacious thinking or reasoning?
_____ 7. Have I checked for proper punctuation?

A college English professor wrote the words "woman without her man is a savage" on the board, directing the students to punctuate it correctly. He found that men looked at it one way, the women another. The men wrote: "Woman, without her man, is a savage." The women wrote: "Woman! Without her, man is a savage."

Source unknown

Proofread

Read the following student essay, applying the preceding checklist and marking everything that is incorrect. Try to use the symbols *frag* for sentence fragment, *dm* for dangling modifier, and so on. See the inside cover for other editing and proofreading marks. Compare your markings with those of others in the class.

LYING TO MYSELF

Talking with a friend the other day I suddenly realized I have been lying to myself about who I am and what my academic goals should be. As a result. I sat down and listed all the positive and negative things I could think about myself and then listed all the possible goals I might achieve considering whom I am. Three important points emerged first I have been blaming teachers most of my life for not doing well in school. No doubt I did have some poor instructiuon, but as my friend made me realize I am really in charge of my education. And if I want to learn, I can, I could discuss my problems more with my teachers, get tutorial help, use the library and learning centers on campus. But most importantly, I could take school more seriously and learn how to study better. I don't really know how to study.

A second thing I learned was I don't really have any self-confidence. The hardest thing is first convincing myself that I have potential for certain goals if I'm willing to put out the effort. For example I have gone on diets to lose weight but if I don't see a radical change immediately I stop dieting and end up not losing weight and gaining a loss of confidence instead. I'm impatient and want results immediately. Its the same way with my grades. If I spend a few hours studying hard and still don't see a grade improvement. I blame the teacher or the test. I begin to feel I'm not smart enough for college. Down deep I know I am, but my lack of confidence and study skills has kept me from more success in college. The third and final point is that I haven't been realistic about becoming a lawyer. When people have asked me what mygoals are I've always answered a lawyer. I said it so many times I began to believe it myself. But Now I honestly admit to myself that I just said that because it sounded good and that I knew my parents wanted to hear. I don't know what career I want to prepare for and that's alright. I will try to use college as a way to discover more about myself and what I do have the talent for doing.

No more lying to myself.

Return now to your own essay, and when you have done the best rewrite you can, turn it in.

U N I T 6

"You're not here Wilson, I like that in an employee."

CARTOON BY JOHN CALLAHAN

No labor can be beneath one's dignity. On the contrary, all work, no matter how menial, is enobling.

Roshi Philip Kapleau, *The Three Pillars of Zen*

THINK . . .

about the world of work.

◆ WRITING JOURNAL ENTRY

In your journal, discuss what career you would like to pursue and why. How will attending college help you achieve that career?

◆ TEXTBOOK ENTRY

In the spaces provided, answer the following questions.

1. Circle any of the words that define work:

career	employment	job
profession	task	duty
effort	occupation	labor
toil	accomplish	wages

2. Name one job you would definitely *not* want and explain why. _____

    _____

    _____

    _____

3. Do you believe there is a single "right" career for everyone? Explain.

    _____

    _____

    _____

4. Define *work* as you think of it. _____

    _____

    _____

    _____

Read the following statements, answering the questions that follow them.

A.   No one should ever work. Work is the source of nearly all the misery in the world. Almost all evil you'd care to name comes from working or from living in a world designed for work. In order to stop suffering, we have to stop working. (Bob Black, *Semiotext[e]*. New York: Columbia UP, 1987)

1. Do you agree? _____

2.   Explain your position. _____

_____

_____

_____

B.   Work now pervades our non-working lives in unprecedented, widely accepted ways: cellular phones, answering machines, personal and portable computers. The career, for many people, has taken precedence over such time-honored human endeavors as building a strong family or seeking spiritual and philosophical truths. The person who works right up to the point of self-destruction is often accorded far more esteem than the person who seeks a balanced life. Overworking is an American trait, much commented upon by European observers; and it has become the hallmark of strenuous yuppies, whose chief complaint about life is "I don't have enough time." (Fred Moody, *Baltimore City Paper* 23 Oct. 1987)

1.   Explain why you agree or disagree with the statement.

_____

_____

_____

2.   What is more important to you than succeeding in your career?

_____

Why? _____

_____

C.   Choosing a major is a serious step. It's also one that should not be taken just because others tell you a certain field is highly marketable—or something that you otherwise "should" go into. A major field of study should be something you pick because you're comfortable with it. I think we all know inside what we'd most enjoy doing. And remember that a major isn't everything. More and more employers are looking beyond the words printed on a diploma in their search for creative, hard-working graduates. (Karl W. Hardy, "Picking a Career." *Newsweek* 22 Sept. 1986)

1.   What does the author mean by "a major isn't everything"?

_____

_____

_____

2.   What do you think employers are looking for in a worker?

_____

_____

_____

From *Work is Hell* by Matt Groening. Pantheon Books, a division of Random House, Inc., New York.

READ . . .

about a viewpoint on work.

If asked, some people will say they go to work each day to pay for rent, food, car payments, clothes, and a two-week vacation. But is work more than that? Could we do without it? Can we love our work? Can we love our work too much for our own good, becoming workaholics? The following essay offers one person's views on the meaning of work.

Before reading closely, take a moment to read the title and the opening paragraph. Then answer the following questions.

1. What attitude toward the "university intellectuals" who are predicting the future does the author have?

   _____

   _____

2. What do you think is the point of the essay? Why?

   _____

   _____

   _____

3. The meaning an author intends may be lost if the reader does not understand the author's use of certain words and phrases. Make sure that you understand the following words before you read. The number after the word is the number of the paragraph where the word appears.

   a. *preoccupied* (1) = engrossed; completely occupied in the mind
   b. *pipe-dreamed* (2) = wishful; fantastical
   c. *dismal* (2) = gloomy; depressing
   d. *eccentrics* (3) = those who act out of the norm
   e. *composed* (5) = wrote
   f. *array* (6) = an impressive selection
   g. *homesteaders* (12) = those who claim and settle farmland
   h. *drudgery* (18) = tedious, unpleasant work
   i. *chaff* (18) = grain husks

Now carefully read the essay. Practice your marking and note-taking skills.

THE JOY OF WORK

Wendell Berry

1 The university intellectuals are increasingly preoccupied with the future. They are not especially interested in *preparing* for the future—which is something that people do by behaving considerately, moderately, conservingly, and decently in the present—but in *predicting* the future, saying now what will happen then.

2 The most recent vision of the future I have seen is the work of 11 engineering professors at Purdue University. This one proposes what American life will be like at the beginning of the 21st century, and I venture to say that nobody has ever pipe-dreamed a more dismal "logical projection," as the academic futurists call their work. The account offers a glimpse of the daily life in 2001 of "the fictitious Niray family, living in the imaginary Midland City, U.S.A." A few samples of the text will be enough to show what a perfect "world of the future" this is—for machines.

3 The hero of this fiction, Dave Niray, breakfasted on a "cylinder of Nutri-Juice"; in 2001 nobody cooks at home but a few eccentrics: gourmets and old-fashioned people.

4   After drinking his breakfast, Dave began work. "Dave was an editor and feature writer for Trans Com News Service, one of the world's largest electronic news organizations. Although he routinely worked on stories of national and international events, he seldom left the apartment. His video screen gave him access to all of Trans Com's files. He could interview almost anyone in the world—from prime minister to Eskimo trader—via Vision-Phone."

5   By Vision-Phone, Dave interviewed "the minister of agriculture in Buenos Aires," composed his article, and then "activated the house monitor computer system" which reminded him "that Rent-A-Robot would be coming in to clean."

6   Ava, Dave's wife, worked in a factory. She did her work in a "control room" before "an enormous array of keyboards, video screens, and ranks and files of tiny lights." Her work was "kept track of" by a "central computer" known as "the front office." The members of "Ava's crew . . . were, of course, machines." "Although she was called a supervisor, she really did no supervision."

7   In the evening, the Nirays and their son, Billy, played electronic games on their video screens.

8   This is a remarkable world in several respects. These people are apparently able to live an entire day without fulfilling directly any necessity of their lives. They do not take pleasure in physical contact with anything or anybody. It is not recorded that they ever touch or speak to each other. Nor apparently, do they ever think a thought. Their entire mental life is devoted to acquiring things, getting promoted, and being electronically amused.

9   This society is built exclusively on the twin principles of "convenience" and "control"—built, that is, on the dread of any kind of physical activity remotely classifiable as work.

10   This future is so dismal, I think, because it is so nearly lifeless. The only living creatures, or the only ones on view, are humans, and humans are rigidly isolated from one another. They make no direct connections. They deal with each other, as they deal with the material world, only through technology. They live by remote control.

11   And so the first question raised by the work of these fanciful engineers is: Where does satisfaction come from? They apparently think it comes from living in a state of absolute control and perfect convenience, in which one would never touch anything except push buttons.

12   The fact is, however, that a great many people have gladly turned off the road that leads to Midland City, U.S.A. They are the home gardeners, the homesteaders, the city people who have returned to farming, the people of all kinds who have learned to do pleasing and necessary work with their hands, the people who have undertaken to raise their own children. They have willingly given up considerable amounts of convenience—and considerable amounts of control, too—and have made their lives more risky and difficult than before.

13   Why? For satisfaction, I think. And where does satisfaction come from? I think it comes from contact with the materials and lives of this world, from the mutual dependence of creatures upon one another, from fellow feeling. But you cannot talk about satisfaction in abstract terms. There is no abstract satisfaction. Let me give an example.

14   Last summer we put up our second cutting of alfalfa on an extremely hot, humid afternoon. Our neighbors came in to help, and together we settled into what could pretty fairly be described as suffering. The hay field lies in a narrow river bottom, a hill on one side and tall trees along the river on the other. There was no breeze at all. The hot, bright, moist air seemed to wrap around us and stick to us while we loaded the wagons.

15   It was worse in the barn, where the tin roof raised the temperature and held the air even closer. We worked more quietly than we usually do, not having the breath for talk. It was miserable, no doubt about it. And there was not a push button anywhere in reach.

16   But we stayed there and did the work, were even glad to do it, and experienced no futurological fits. When we were done, we told stories and laughed and talked a long time, sitting on a post pile in the shade of a big elm. It was a pleasing day.

17   Why was it pleasing? Nobody will ever figure that out by "logical projection." The matter is too complex and too profound for logic. It was pleasing, for one thing, because we got done. That does not make logic, but it makes sense. For another thing, it was good hay, and we got it up in good shape. For another, we like each other and we work together because we want to.

18   And yet you cannot fully explain satisfaction in terms of just one day. Satisfaction rises out of the flow of time. When I was a boy I used to dread the hay harvest. It seemed an awful drudgery: the lifting was heavy and continuous; the weather was hot; the work was dusty; the chaff stuck to your skin and itched. And then one winter I stayed home and I fed out the hay we had put up the summer before. I learned the other half of the story then, and after that I never minded. The hay that goes up in the heat comes down into the mangers in the cold. That is when its meaning is clearest, and when the satisfaction is completed.

19   And so, six months after we shed all that sweat, there comes a bitter January evening when I go up to the horse barn to feed. It is nearly nightfall, and snowing hard. The north wind is driving the snow through the cracks in the barn wall. I bed the stalls, put corn in the troughs, climb into the loft and drop the rations of fragrant hay into the mangers. I go to the back door and open it; the horses come in and file along the driveway to their stalls, the snow piled white on their backs. The barn fills with the sounds of their eating. It is time to go home. I have my comfort ahead of me: talk, supper, fire in the stove, something to read. But I know too that all my animals are well fed and comfortable, and my comfort is enlarged in theirs. On such a night you do not feed out of necessity or duty. You never think of the money value of the animals. You feed and care for them out of fellow feeling, because you want to. And when I go out and shut the door, I am satisfied.

"The Joy of Work" excerpted from *The Gift of Good Land*, copyright © 1981 by Wendell Berry. Published by North Point Press and reprinted by permission.

REACT . . .

to the reading selection.

◈ WRITING JOURNAL ENTRY

Write about the first time you were paid for doing a job. How old were you? What was the work? Did you enjoy the work? Were you working for the money or the satisfaction of doing a good job?

◇ TEXTBOOK ENTRY

A. Understanding the Content

In the spaces provided, answer the following questions. Refer to the reading selection for answers if needed.

1. What is the main idea of this selection? _____

2. How does Berry react to what he calls the university intellectuals' interest in predicting the future? _____

3. What does Berry find wrong about the futurists' views of life in 2001? _____

4. Where does Berry think satisfaction from work comes from and how does it differ from the futurists' forecasts? _____

5. What two examples of satisfaction from working does Berry provide? _____

B. Noticing Writing Techniques and Styles

6. What is the purpose of paragraph 2? How does it establish both tone and attitude? _____

7. Paragraphs 2 through 6 contain many quotation marks. Why? _____

_____

8. How do paragraphs 11 and 12 work together? What is their function?

    _____

    _____

    _____

9. Why does Berry quote the term "logical projection" in paragraph 17? Where
    and in what context was the phrase used before? _____

    _____

    _____

10. What one word does Berry use repeatedly from paragraph 11 on? How does
    it help him define what his title implies? _____

    _____

    _____

    _____

SALLY FORTH by Greg Howard

PLAN . . .

◇ an essay on some aspect of work.

STEP 1: Selecting and Exploring a Topic: Your Choice

In previous units you have been shown how to use brainstorming, freewriting,
clustering, PMIs, and reacting to what you read by asking questions. Use any

one of these methods to help you select and explore a topic for an essay on some aspect of the world of work.

◆ WRITING JOURNAL ENTRY

If you don't already have an idea for an essay, look over the following list. In your journal, explore one of these or an idea of your own.

Try brainstorming, freewriting, or clustering on

1. working	6. jobless	11. unions
2. careers	7. welfare	12. income
3. future jobs	8. job preparation	13. part-time work
4. tipping	9. welfare	14. coffee breaks
5. co-workers	10. Labor Day	15. work ethics

Or do a PMI on

1. All students should be required to work for two years before enrolling in college.
2. The normal work week should be reduced to four days rather than five.
3. No one should be allowed to work on the same job or in the same career for more than ten years.
4. Women with children should not be permitted to work.
5. People should be paid for not working from the years 18 to 25, then required to work the rest of their lives (reverse retirement).

Or react to and question the following statements

1. Work makes a mockery of freedom. . . . A worker is a part-time slave. The boss says when to show up, when to leave, and what to do in the meantime. He tells you how much work to do and how fast. He is free to carry his control to humiliating extremes, regulating if he so desires, the clothes you wear or how often you can go to the bathroom. With a few exceptions he can fire you for any reason, or no reason. (Bob Black, *Semiotext[e]*. New York: Columbia UP, 1987)
2. Whatever the major, a thorough knowledge of the English language should be included. No matter what you decide to do in life, one day you are going to have to prove to someone, somewhere that you can write and communicate effectively. (Karl H. Hardy, "Picking a Career." *Newsweek* 22 Sept. 1986: 91)
3. . . . The increasing number of jobs requiring a postsecondary education promotes the rumors of a labor shortage. In the American labor pool, 20 percent of adults aged 21 to 25 cannot read at the eighth grade level. These people are not qualified for the skilled jobs the economy is now creating. . . . In the short-sighted race to keep profits at acceptable levels during the 1970s and '80s, business leaders typically lobbied for govern-

ment taxing and spending policies that undermined the desirable job training and educational opportunities. (Jeremy Schlosberg, "Are We Facing a Labor Shortage?" *Utne Reader* Sept./Oct. 1988)

4. If none of these help, look over some of your answers in the **Think** section.

STEP 2: Writing a Working Thesis

After you have selected and explored a possible topic for an essay on work, you should have a list of ideas and some thoughts for a working thesis. Remember that a working thesis is just that, not your final statement. But even a working thesis statement should have one or more key words in it that helps you see what kind of support you are going to need to develop your essay.

There may be times when you can't write a working thesis until you have done Step 3, analyzing and organizing your ideas. Don't worry about it. The three planning steps in this section are not rigid. As mentioned before, the writing process does not usually follow a smooth progression. You may think you are moving along on a topic only to discover that as you do Step 3, a better thesis comes to mind. You may need to do Step 1 over again, which would change the working thesis written in Step 2. That's all part of the writing process and not something you are doing wrong. However, the three planning steps will help you prepare better for a first draft.

◆ TEXTBOOK ENTRY

When you have arrived at a possible working thesis after exploring ideas for an essay on work, write it in the following space for future use.

Working thesis: _____

_____

_____

_____

STEP 3: Analyzing and Organizing Your Ideas

Look carefully at the key words in your working thesis. Make certain you have enough information to support your key points. Organize your ideas into some type of outline you can follow for a first draft. When you are satisfied you are ready, go to the next section.

WRITE . . .

a first draft for an essay on some aspect of work.

The Nutshell Statement

In the space given, write a nutshell statement for the thesis and outline you developed for an essay on work.

The purpose of my essay is _____

_____

_____

My audience is _____

_____

_____

I will support my thesis by _____

_____

_____

_____

_____

Developing Paragraphs by Using Definition

Sometimes when writing you need to define terms, theories, or even ideas for the reader. Using definition means more than supplying a dictionary-type definition. It calls for extended discussion or explanation so that your reader will know exactly how you are using a word or term in a circumstance that may be different from the norm.

The following paragraph uses the extended definition technique to define the word *discipline* as the author means it:

> Actually, the root meaning of *discipline* is "to learn," "to be capable of being taught," "to discover." True discipline is a creative activity. It is inner authority. The aim of discipline, whether in college, in a home, in a career, or anywhere else, is the creation of self-direction and of realistic motives. A truly disciplined person has a self-starting ability to face problems without the compulsions of fear or the

need to lean on others for support. The disciplined adult has learned to accept himself and his capacities as they are, thus freeing him to put all of his faculties to the good use of self-improvement and self-fulfillment.

More than just *discipline* is being defined. The first sentence explains the meaning of the root word. The second and third sentences define the *aim of discipline*. Then a truly *disciplined person* is defined; and finally a *disciplined adult* is defined.

The following example is from an essay in which the author is calling for the abolishment of work. Because the idea seems impractical, the author has to be careful that his use of terms is clear. Notice how differently he defines the word *discipline* in the world of work:

> The degradation that most workers experience on the job is the sum of assorted indignities that can be called "discipline." Discipline consists of totalitarian controls at the work place—surveillance, rote work, imposed tempos, production quotas, punching in and out, etc. Discipline is what the factory and the office and the store share with the prison and the school and the mental hospital. It is something historically original and horrible. . . . Discipline is the distinctively diabolical modern mode of control. (Bob Black, "Abolish Work: Workers of the World, Relax." *Unte Reader* July/Aug. 1988: 48)

Here, the author opens by defining *discipline* as the "sum of indignities" that most workers experience on the job. In the second sentence he offers some examples of these indignities. In the third sentence he compares working situations with prisons, schools, and mental hospitals. In the next sentence he tags on the label "horrible," then concludes by saying discipline is a devilish form of modern control. He not only defines by using examples and comparisons but also, through the use of such words as *degradation, indignities, imposed, horrible,* and *diabolical*, establishes an attitude and tone.

Here is another example of a paragraph that uses definition to support its point. The author is writing about America's economic future, claiming that because of the federal debt, there is a sudden widespread concern with "competitiveness."

> What does *competitiveness* mean? In many American households today it means worry about the future living standards and about whether one's children, ten to fifteen years into their careers, will be able to out-earn their parents. In corporate boardrooms *competitiveness* means the executive nightmare of seeing Americans gorge themselves on goods from foreign firms. For many blue-collar workers, *competitiveness* has an even crueler meaning: layoffs and the understandable desire to get even with the anonymous forces behind them. . . . In Washington *competitiveness* seems to mean nothing and everything. (Peter G. Peterson, "The Morning After." *The Atlantic Monthly* Oct. 1987: 43)

In this case, the author is not trying to define literally the word *competitiveness*, assuming we know the literal definition. Instead, he attempts to show that competitiveness has acquired a negative meaning in different levels of our society.

THE FASTEST-GROWING JOB MARKETS

METRO AREA	ANNUAL JOB GROWTH 1985–2010
1. NAPLES, FLA.	2.81%
2. FORT MYERS, FLA.	2.75
3. FORT PIERCE, FLA.	2.61
4. ORLANDO, FLA.	2.42
5. ATLANTIC CITY, N.J.	2.40
6. ANAHEIM–SANTA ANA, CAL.	2.37
7. LAS VEGAS	2.36
8. WEST PALM BEACH–BOCA RATON–DELRAY BEACH, FLA.	2.33
9. FORT LAUDERDALE–HOLLYWOOD–POMPANO BEACH, FLA.	2.31
10. BRADENTON, FLA.	2.25
11. RENO, NEV.	2.22
12. OCALA, FLA.	2.13
13. PHOENIX	2.11
14. SARASOTA, FLA.	2.09
15. GAINESVILLE, FLA.	2.08
16. BRYAN–COLLEGE STATION, TEX.	2.07
17. TUCSON	2.07
18. BOULDER–LONGMONT, COLO.	2.06
19. PORTSMOUTH–DOVER–ROCHESTER, N.H.	2.04
20. SANTA ROSA–PETALUMA, CAL.	2.02
21. SANTA FE, N.M.	2.01
22. MONMOUTH–OCEAN, N.J.	2.01
23. OXNARD–VENTURA, CAL.	2.01
24. TALLAHASSEE, FLA.	2.00
25. BOISE CITY, IDA.	1.99
U.S. AVERAGE	1.22%

Source: National Planning Assn.

THE BIGGEST NEW-JOB MARKETS

METRO AREA	INCREASE IN JOBS 1985–2010 (thousands)
1. LOS ANGELES–LONG BEACH	1,399.4
2. WASHINGTON, D.C.	1,145.9
3. ANAHEIM–SANTA ANA, CAL.	978.4
4. HOUSTON	957.2
5. ATLANTA	862.5
6. PHILADELPHIA	857.2
7. DALLAS	849.8
8. BOSTON–LAWRENCE–SALEM–LOWELL–BROCKTON, MASS.	814.0
9. CHICAGO	787.2
10. NEW YORK CITY	719.5
11. PHOENIX	880.8
12. SAN DIEGO	850.2
13. MINNEAPOLIS–ST. PAUL	575.8
14. DENVER	565.9
15. NASSAU–SUFFOLK, N.Y.	552.8
16. TAMPA–ST. PETERSBURG–CLEARWATER, FLA.	522.0
17. SAN JOSE, CAL.	502.5
18. SAN FRANCISCO	466.0
19. BALTIMORE	465.2
20. SEATTLE	464.1
21. OAKLAND, CAL.	434.6
22. DETROIT	433.7
23. MIAMI–HIALEAH, FLA.	412.8
24. FORT LAUDERDALE–HOLLYWOOD–POMPANO BEACH, FLA.	412.3
25. ORLANDO, FLA.	408.3
TOTAL, 25 METRO AREAS	17,318.1
U.S. TOTAL	42,977.2

Source: National Planning Assn.

THE FASTEST-GROWING JOBS

OCCUPATION	GROWTH 1985–1995
1. LEGAL ASSISTANTS	98%
2. COMPUTER PROGRAMMERS	72
3. COMPUTER SYSTEMS ANALYSTS	69
4. MEDICAL ASSISTANTS	62
5. COMPUTER SERVICE TECHNICIANS	56
6. ELECTRICAL AND ELECTRONICS ENGINEERS	53
7. ACTUARIES	51
8. ELECTRICAL AND ELECTRONICS TECHNICIANS	50
9. COMPUTER OPERATORS	46
10. HEALTH SERVICES MANAGERS	44
11. TRAVEL AGENTS	44
12. PHYSICAL THERAPISTS	42
13. PHYSICIANS' ASSISTANTS	40
14. PODIATRISTS	39
15. FINANCIAL SERVICES SALES	39
16. ENGINEERS	36
17. LAWYERS	36
18. ACCOUNTANTS AND AUDITORS	35
19. CORRECTIONS OFFICERS	35
20. MECHANICAL ENGINEERS	34
21. REGISTERED NURSES	33
22. PUBLIC RELATIONS	32
23. COMPUTERIZED-TOOL PROGRAMMERS	32
24. OCCUPATIONAL THERAPISTS	31
25. MEDICAL RECORD TECHNICIANS	31

Source: Bureau of Labor Statistics.

TEXTBOOK ENTRY

Read the following short passage and answer the questions that follow it.

MANAGEMENT STYLES

1   There are four basic management styles: *directive, analytical, conceptual,* and *behavioral.* Each style is more effective in some situations than others, and each style has its strengths and weaknesses. Combinations of these styles are used on the job by those in managerial positions.

2   The directive style refers to executives who look for speed, efficiency, and fast results. They are decisive, act on their decisions, and expect others to do the same. Examples of this type of manager are Lee Iacocca of Chrysler Corporation and Frank Lorenzo of Texas Air.

3   Those comfortable with numbers, details, and problem solving are analytical managers. They tend to be thought of as intellectuals, concentrating on technical challenges through the use of logic and careful analysis. Roy Ash and Tex Thornton, builders of Litton Industries, are good examples.

4   The most creative and forward looking are the conceptual managers. The conceptual executive fits organizations that require a concern for others and a broad vision of the present and the future. Steven Jobs, cofounder of Apple Computers, serves as a good example. His vision changed the entire computer industry.

5   Behavioral managers are people oriented. This is a style that rarely shows up by itself but, rather, appears in combination with other styles. Peter Ueberroth describes himself as both friendly and ruthless, a combination of directive and behavioral styles.

1.   What introductory paragraph approach is used in the passage?

2.   What method of paragraph development is used in the introductory paragraph?

3.   What is the point of the passage?

4.   What methods are used to develop the main idea in paragraph 2?

5.   What do the rest of the paragraphs in the passage have in common with paragraph 2?

Practice in Using Definition

If you or your instructor feel you need more practice with paragraphs that use definition, go to page 276.

◆ **WRITING JOURNAL ENTRY**

1.   In your journal, pick two of the following words and write a paragraph or an extended definition for each.

   nice   student   computer
   run   friend   anxiety

2.   Use the nutshell statement, your working thesis, and outline from your essay on work to write the first draft of an essay. Try to incorporate the use of examples and definition if you can, but don't force it.

REWRITE . . .
your first draft.

You should now have a working draft of an essay on some aspect of work. Make sure you have reviewed your draft for the following:

_____ 1. Does your draft have a thesis that reveals to the reader your point of view on the subject?
_____ 2. Does your opening paragraph use a method that draws the interest of your readers?
_____ 3. Are you writing about something you know and feel?
_____ 4. Are your paragraphs organized so that one idea leads smoothly to another?
_____ 5. Have you tried using the paragraph development methods you have learned so far?
_____ 6. Did you share your essay with someone to obtain another perspective on your writing?

If you are satisfied that you have done the best you can so far, go to the next revision strategy.

Revise: Developing Stronger Sentences

At some point during the writing and revision process, look closely at each sentence for the following:

1.   Overused patterns that begin with *It is . . . That . . .* or *There is. . . :*

   Example: There are two questions that need to be considered.

   Better: Two questions need to be considered.

   Example: It is the medicine that makes me ill.

   Better: The medicine makes me ill.

Example: There were four applicants who were waiting to be interviewed.

Better: Four applicants were waiting to be interviewed.

2.   Unnecessary wording:

Example: It is thought in some quarters that the government is not contributing to the lessening of the needs of the poor.

Better: Some people think the government isn't doing enough to help the poor.

Example: The average teacher who works in high school must work all day long and then go home and get ready for the next day's class.

Better: Most high school teachers work long hours.

3.   Sentences that can be combined into one:

Example: The company made a good profit last year. It might not do that well this year because of its loss of tax credits.

Better: Because of tax credit loss, the company may not make the profits it did last year.

Example: It was the fourth time I was late for work. My boss fired me before I had time to sit down at my desk.

Better: Because I was late for the fourth time, I was fired before I had time to sit down at my desk.

◆ TEXTBOOK ENTRY

A. Change the following sentences to read better.

1.   There is one point that you don't want to forget.

_____

_____

2.   It was the seed that I choked on.

_____

_____

3.   It is the medicine that makes me ill.

_____

_____

4.   There were two Dobermans that were standing by the gate.

_____

_____

5.   It was the fourth time that I missed class.

_____

_____

B. Using the words indicated in italics, combine the following sets of sentences, eliminating unneeded words. The first one has been done for you. Remember to punctuate correctly.

1.   a.   The scuba diver nearly drowned.
    b.   He didn't check his tank valve before entering the water.

Use *who:* _The scuba diver who didn't check his tank before entering the water nearly drowned._

2.   a.   The tests did not place us very well.
    b.   They gave tests at the beginning of the course.

Use *which:* _____

_____

3.   a.   John Ambrose is our state senator.
    b.   He is being charged with taking a bribe.

Use *who:* _____

_____

4.   a.   Harry's business netted a huge profit last year.
    b.   Harry's business may be in for financial trouble this year.

Use *which:* _____

_____

5.   a.   The money was returned.
    b.   The money belonged to the lady down the street.
    c.   The thief was caught.

Use *that* and *when:* _____

_____

6.   a.   My dad wanted nothing to do with the military.
    b.   My dad wanted nothing to do with politics.
    c.   His grandfather was a general.

Use *whose:* _____

_____

C. Combine these simple sentences into one as directed. Use correct punctuation. The first one has been done for you.

1. a. The old man clutched his chest.
   b. He was wheezing.
   c. He was frightened.

   Omit needless words: *Wheezing and frightened, the old man clutched his chest. Or: The old man clutched his chest, wheezing and frightened.*

2. a. Tom was unable to stop.
   b. He drove too fast.
   c. He hit the truck head on.
   Change *drove* to *driving* and *hit* to *hitting:*

   _____

   _____

3. a. Tom just sat in his car.
   b. He was stunned by the accident.
   c. He was unable to move.

   Omit needless words: _____

   _____

   _____

4. a. The truck driver felt that death was near.
   b. He yelled in pain.
   c. He panicked for fear the truck would burst into flames.
   Change *yelled* and *panicked* to *yelling* and *panicking:*

   _____

   _____

5. a. Finally, Tom came to his senses.
   b. He rushed to the aid of the truck driver.
   c. The truck driver was now out of his head.
   Change *rushed* to *rushing* and use *who:*

   _____

   _____

6. a. Tom acted none too soon.
   b. He yanked on the truck door.
   c. He pulled the driver out.
   Change *yanked* and *pulled* to *yanking* and *pulling:*

   _____

   _____

7.   a. The truck exploded.
     b. It lit up the dark night.
     c. It sent shock waves that stunned Tom.
     Change *lit* and *sent* to *lighting* and *sending:*

_____

_____

8.   a. Tom carried the truck driver to safety.
     b. He did not know where he got the strength.
     c. The truck driver had passed out.
     Change *know* to *knowing* and use *who:*

_____

_____

Practice in Writing Stronger Sentences

If you or your instructor feel you need more practice in writing stronger sentences, go to page 310.

◆ WRITING JOURNAL ENTRY

1.   Using the revised sentences from Textbook Entry C, organize them in the proper sequential order. Then put them together in paragraph form so that the incidents in each sentence appear in proper order.
2.   Using everything you have learned so far, revise your essay on work. When finished, go to the "Edit" section below.

Edit for Correct Punctuation: Part II

In the last unit you learned about the correct use of end punctuation (periods, exclamation points, and question marks) and commas. In this unit you will learn how to use the other forms of punctuation.

The Semicolon [;]

The semicolon is used for two major purposes:

1.   The semicolon (;), rather than a period, is used between two sentences that are related in thought and equal in importance.

     The car is severely damaged; it may never run again.

     John rode his bike; Jane pushed hers.

2.   The semicolon is used to separate a series of phrases that contain commas.

     The three important speakers were Harry Berry, an actor; Oliver Diddle, the director; and Metro Mayer, the producer.

The Colon [:]

1. The colon is used to direct attention to particular items or statements in a sentence.

   There is only one thing on my mind: food.

   (A dash could be used in place of the colon.)

   The following novels must be read by the end of the month: <u>Deliverance</u>, <u>Slaughterhouse-Five</u>, and <u>The White Dawn</u>.

2. The colon is also used to distinguish the following odds and ends:

   It's exactly 4:15 A.M.

   John 3:16 (Sometimes periods are used instead.)

   <u>New World Beginnings: Indian Cultures in America</u>

   Dear Sir:

The Dash [—]

A dash is generally used in informal writing more than formal writing. It is used in two ways:

1. A dash, like a colon, can be used to direct attention to something in particular, such as

   There's only one thing left to say—forget it!

   (A colon could be used in place of the dash.)

2. A dash is also used to set off information or comments for dramatic effect:

   The BIA (Bureau of Indian Affairs) refused—as it so often has in the past—to listen to the Indians' requests.

   James Dickey's novel <u>Deliverance</u>—his first novel, by the way—was made into a movie.

   Note: When you type, you form a dash with two unspaced hyphens and with no space before or after the dash. When you write, you make the dash longer than a hyphen. In typesetting this dash is designated "em dash" because it is the width of a capital letter M.

Quotation Marks [" "]

1. Double quotation marks are used to show the exact words that someone has said. This is called a direct quote. Do not use quotation marks with an indirect quotation.

   Direct: George said, "I need to borrow five dollars."

   Indirect: George said that he needs to borrow five dollars.

   Direct: "I thought," she said, "that you weren't going."

   Indirect: She said that she thought you weren't going.

"Would you stop putting quotes around everything I say?!"

2. Use double quotation marks to show words being used in a special sense or to indicate slang:

He looked up the word "doppelganger."

That's just a "cop out" on your part.

He's what I term a real "pro" when it comes to sports.

(In formal writing, avoid the use of slang.)

3. Use double quotation marks to indicate the title of short stories, poems, song titles, magazine articles, and chapter titles in books:

"A Day in the Life" is my favorite song in the Beatles' Sgt. Pepper album.

"Witches and Warlocks" is an interesting article in this week's Time magazine.

Important: Titles of complete works such as books, magazines, and record albums are underlined, as the preceding examples show. Titles of chapters, essays, or songs within a complete volume take quotation marks.

4. Single quotation marks are used only to show a quotation or title within another quotation.

"I thought," the student said, "that the statement 'To err is human, to forgive is divine' was from the Bible."

5. Do not use quotation marks when quoting long passages. Instead, indent what you are quoting five spaces to the right, and single-space if you are typing.

Notice the following example:

---

source of quoted material

> On the other hand, in one of the most definitive works on lying, <u>The Right to Lie</u>, the authors, Robert Wolk and Arthur Henley, remark,

long quoted material indented" and single spaced

> A successful marriage is the product of lies as well as love. Although the partners' emotions and attitudes may complement each other well, they are two separate people and their feelings cannot possibly coincide all the time. A policy of total honesty would make them blurt out truths that could be needlessly hurtful or perhaps just untimely. This could wreck the delicate balance of give-and-take so necessary between husband and wife. Constructive, competent and considerate lies can have a mutually protective effect and prevent the partners from stepping on each other's toes. That is why good lying makes good marriage.

shorter quote, not displayed with indent.

> In another place these authors state, "The family that lies together stays together." They are, of course, not speaking of life-destructive untruths, but the day-to-day dishonesty that may protect the relationship from constant trauma.

A *block quote*, as it is called, is usually used when you quote over two lines of print.

The Hyphen [-]

The hyphen should not be confused with the dash. It is not as long as the dash, nor is it used for the same purposes. The hyphen is used for four basic purposes.

1. A hyphen is used to break a word when the word is too long to be continued on the same line, such as

    The hyphen should not be confus-
    ed with the dash.

    The hyphen is used for four basic pur-
    poses.

    Note: Hyphenated words should be divided only at syllables, not anywhere at random.

    Wrong: It is wrong to hyphenate a word an-
                 ywhere you want.

    Correct: It is wrong to hyphenate a word any-
                   where you want.

2. A hyphen is used after the prefixes *all, ex, half, quasi, quarter,* and *self,* and between any prefix and a proper name, as in

    all-American   self-image
    ex-wife   anti-American
    half-dead   quarter-pound

3. A hyphen is used when two or more modifiers are joined before the noun or object it is modifying, as in

    We got the off-season rates.

    Mom bought an all-purpose cleanser.

    There were some not-so-pure Puritans.

    but

    Some Puritans were not so pure.

4. A hyphen is used to express inclusive pages, dates, and ranges, such as

    pages 167-176   1860-1865   3-5 years

    Note: For this purpose, that is, to mean "to" or sometimes "and," the en dash (–) is often used in printed material.

Parentheses [( )]

Parentheses are used to set off comments or information that has no direct point in the sentence's thought and to set off numbers or letters used to list items in a sentence. For example,

   According to Bill (and he is no authority), there will be an eclipse of the moon tomorrow night.

   This unit deals with punctuation, such as the use of (1) the colon, (2) the semi-colon, (3) the question mark, (4) quotation marks, and (5) parentheses.

◆ TEXTBOOK ENTRY

Punctuate the following sentences correctly.

1. Fred said Let's go bowling Friday.

2. *Newsweek's* article Down and Out for the Last Time is interesting reading if you like sports

3. I have only one thing to ask why me

4. What does the word stereotype mean

5. Jackie asked Do we still need to leave at 12 15 PM

6. In a book I read and one of the best I might add I learned about self control

7. Herb runs a fly by night operation it's too risky to buy from him.

The Apostrophe [']

Apostrophes are used for these basic purposes: to form contractions, possessives, and plurals of letters and numbers.

1. Apostrophes are used to form contractions, that is, to show that a letter or letters of a word have been left out.

    they're = they are

    it's = it is

    you're = you are

    we're = we are

2. Apostrophes are used to form singular and plural possessives, such as

    my mother's car
    the man's hat   } *Singular possessive*
    the camera's shutter

    the instructors' workroom
    the girls' locker room   } *Plural possessive*
    the cameras' cases

    Important: If a word ends in *s*, just add the apostrophe: Adams' book.

3. Apostrophes are used to form the plural of letters and numbers, such as

    7's and 11's

    fifteen *d*'s

    Important: Numbers under 10 should generally be written out: seven and eight.

◇ TEXTBOOK ENTRY

1. Punctuate the following sentences correctly.

    a. Its time to go now

    b. We havent eaten yet

    c. She wore her sisters shoes today

    d. Are three 10s and two 8s a good poker hand

    e. We have to read at least three of James Jones novels

2. Form contractions for the following words.

    a. let us _____

    b. I will _____

    c. there is _____

    d. we will _____

    e. she had _____

    f. John is _____

    g. are not _____

    h. would not _____

    i. would have _____

    j. who would _____

    k. does not _____

    l. do not _____

Practice in Punctuation, Part II

If you or your instructor feel you need more practice in punctuation, go to page 316.

◇ WRITING JOURNAL ENTRY

Return to the last draft of your work essay. Rewrite and edit by using the following checklist:

_____ 1. Have I fully developed and supported my thesis?

_____ 2. Have I fully developed and supported each paragraph?

_____ 3. Have I used transitional devices to help my reader move from one point to the next?

_____ 4. Have I eliminated sentence fragments, run-ons, comma splices, misplaced modifiers, and dangling modifiers?
_____ 5. Have I checked for subject-verb agreement?
_____ 6. Have I checked for fallacious thinking or reasoning?
_____ 7. Have I checked for proper punctuation?
_____ 8. Have I written strong sentences?

Proofread

Apply the preceding checklist and mark every incorrect item in the following student essay. Try to use the symbols *frag* for sentence fragment, *dm* for dangling modifier, and so on. See the inside covers for other editing and proofreading marks. Compare your markings with those of others in the class.

WELFARE OR WORK?

According to Teresa Amott and John Miller in the MArch 1988 issue of Dollars & Sense there are some 13 million people who don't have full-time jobs but would like them. Still, they claim there is a labor shortage. How can this be?

The authors feel that the American economy has apparently created a lot of two sorts of jobs. Jobs most people don't want and jobs most people can't get:

"There is a mismatch between what employers are looking for and what job-hunters are seeking. The current shortage is not a shortage of available bodies but a shortage of "employables"--workers who are both able to do the work and willing to acept lousy wages and working conditions."

When recently faced with the dilemma of either working at my present job, earning minimum wage, and having very little interest in my work, or quitting the job and going on welfare. I chose to stay employed.

One reason why I'd rather work, even unhappily, instead of going on welfare is that I have pride in myself. I believe welfare is an easy way out, working is a part of life. It provides valuable experiences. As well as rewarding ones. And if I can't cope with working then how well can I cope with life.

Sure, there are some people who truly need and deserve welfare, and unemployment. Such as a person with a disabling injury, or a person who has been given "the short end of the stick" and left homeless with three kids to feed. However there are also many people that can work but don't. These are the people that give the welfare and unemployment programs both bad names and the budget bigger.

Welfare and unemployment programs are supposed to serve people out of work as intermittent aids. But in too many cases they serve as a lack of incentive for work. Once a person has been given a weekly income without lifting a finger, naturally they're going to become lazy. Theyre going to milk the programs for as much money as they can, and give half hearted attempts at finding a job.

It is for these reasons that I would not go on welfare. I am no different from any other person in that given situation. To get a free ride, I am just as likely to fall into the trap of laziness as the thousands of people who already have.

Return now to your own essay, and when you have done the best rewrite you can, turn it in.

Drawing by Richter; © The New Yorker Magazine, Inc.

*The long-range effect of technology will be to liberate us,
allow us to be freer, more fully human.*

Ben Bova, "In Defense of Technology"

THINK . . .

about technology, its effects, and the future.

◇ WRITING JOURNAL ENTRY

In your journal, discuss what you think is the most important technological achievement or invention ever discovered and explain why.

◇ TEXTBOOK ENTRY

Answer the following questions in the spaces provided.

1. What are some of the everyday advantages you have and take for granted because of technology? _____

    _____

    _____

2. What are some disadvantages that technology has brought?

    _____

    _____

    _____

3. What do you predict would happen if technological advancements were suddenly stopped or outlawed? _____

    _____

    _____

4. Some people seem to fear some of the rapid advancements being made in technology, especially those occurring in computer and robot development. Explain why you feel such fear is or is not warranted.

    _____

    _____

    _____

Respond in the space provided with your views on the following statements:

A.   Anti-technologists have pointed out that the powerful men of society have always used technology as a tool for keeping their power and dominating the poor and weak. Yes, just as they have used superstition and sheer physical force. Over the long run, however, technology has led to a broadening of human freedom, a sharing of wealth and power among the common people, a leavening of power of the elite. (Ben Bova, "In Defense of Technology." *Analog* Sept. 1974)

_____

_____

_____

IS TECHNOLOGY OUT OF CONTROL?

Ask not for whom the reactor tolls; it tolls for thee.

Paul Conrad. © 1986, *Los Angeles Times*. Reprinted with permission Los Angeles Times Syndicate.

B.   To proponents, it's a great new application of technology to improve productivity. To critics, it represents the ultimate intrusion of Big Brother in the workplace. For several million workers today, being monitored on the job by a computer is a fact of life. By installing computer software in a central computer, employers can measure everything from the number of keystrokes entered by a secretary each second to the amount of time a transaction takes, and how many errors are made . . . [which] has provoked questions about the boundaries of worker privacy. . . . (Beth Brophy, "New Technology, High Anxiety." *U.S. News & World Report* 29 Sept. 1988)

_____

_____

_____

READ . . .

about an encounter with a familiar machine.

Have you ever had a machine get the best of you? Most of us have experienced computer foul-ups with bills that took hours of grief to straighten out, telephones that went dead in the middle of a conversation, a dead car battery on the day we're in a hurry, or a vending machine that took all our change and gave nothing in return. The following essay provides a first-person account of an incident so descriptive that we have no trouble understanding the author's plight or his desire to get revenge.

    Before reading closely, take a moment to read the title and the opening paragraph. Then answer the following questions.

1.   What problem is established in the opening paragraph? _____

_____

_____

2.   To whom or what do you think the title refers? _____

_____

3.   What do you think is going to happen? _____

_____

_____

4.   The meaning an author intends may be lost if the reader does not understand the author's use of certain words and phrases. Make sure that you understand

the following words before you read. The number after the word is the paragraph number where the word appears.

a. *appropriate* (1) = correct; right one
b. *customary* (2) = usual
c. *dispensed* (2) = gave out
d. *consistent* (5) = in agreement
e. *livid* (8) = pale from anger
f. *berserk* (8) = crazy; loss of control
g. *frantic* (10) = exasperated; frenzied
h. *taunts* (13) = challenges jeeringly

Now carefully read the essay. Practice your marking and note-taking skills.

BIG WHITE

Skip Rozin

1   A strange calm settled over me as I stood before the large white vending machine and dropped a quarter into the appropriate slot. I listened as the coin clunked into register. Then I pressed the button marked "Hot Chocolate." From deep inside a paper cup slid down a chute, crackling into place on a small metal rack. Through an unseen tube poured coffee, black as night and smoking hot.

2   I even smiled as I moved to my customary place at the last table, sat down, and gazed across to the white machine, large and clean and defiant. Not since it had been moved in between the candy machine and the sandwich machine had I known peace. Every morning for two weeks I had selected a beverage, and each time the machine dispensed something different. When I pushed the button for hot chocolate, black coffee came out. When I pushed the button for tea with sugar, coffee with half and half came out. So the cup of coffee before me was no surprise. It was but one final test; my plan had already been laid.

3   Later in the day, after everyone else had left the building, I returned to the snack bar, a yellow legal pad in my hand and a fistful of change in my pocket. I approached the machine and, taking each button in order, began feeding in quarters. After the first quarter I pressed the button labeled "Black Coffee." Tea with sugar came out, and I recorded that on the first line of my pad. I dropped in a second quarter and pressed the button for coffee with sugar. Plain tea came out, and I wrote that down.

4   I pressed all nine of the buttons, noting what came out. Then I placed each cup on the table behind me. When I had gone through them all, I repeated the process, and was delighted to find the machine dispensing the same drinks as before.

5   None was what I had ordered, but each error was consistent with my list.

6   I was thrilled. To celebrate, I decided to purchase a fresh cup of chocolate.

7   Dropping in two dimes and a nickel and consulting my pad, I pressed the "Coffee with Sugar and Half and Half" button. The machine clicked in response, and a little cup slid down the chute, bouncing as it hit bottom. But that was all. Nothing else happened. No hot chocolate poured into my cup. No black coffee came down. Nothing.

8   I was livid. I forced five nickels into the slot and punched the button for black coffee. A cup dropped into place, but nothing more. I put five more nickels in and pushed another button, and another cup dropped down—empty. I dug into my pocket for more change, but found only three dimes. I forced them in, and got back a stream of hot water and a nickel change. I went berserk.

9   "White devil!" I screamed as I slammed my fists against the machine's clean enamel finish. "You white devil!"

10   I beat on the buttons and rammed the coin-return rod down. I wanted the machine to know what pain was. I slapped at its metal sides and kicked its base with such force that I could almost hear the bone in my foot crack, then wheeled in agony on my good foot, and with one frantic swing, sent the entire table of coffee-, tea-, and chocolate-filled cups sailing.

11   That was last night. They have cleaned up the snack bar since then, and I have had my foot X-rayed and wrapped in that brown elastic they use for sprains. I am now sitting with my back to the row of vending machines. I know by the steadiness of my hand as I pour homemade hot chocolate from my thermos that no one can sense what I have been through—except, of course, the great white machine over against the wall.

12   Even now, behind me, in the space just below the coin slot, a tiny sign blinks off and on:

13   "Make Another Selection," it taunts. "Make Another Selection."

"Big White" published in *Harper's Magazine*. Copyright © 1975 by Skip Rozin. Reprinted by permission of Curtis Brown, Ltd.

REACT . . .

to the reading selection.

◆ WRITING JOURNAL ENTRY

Write a paragraph discussing your reaction to the essay. How did you feel as you read it? What did the selection cause you to think about? Did you enjoy it? Why?

◆ TEXTBOOK ENTRY

A. Understanding the Content

In the spaces provided, answer the following questions. Refer to the reading selection when necessary.

1. What is the thesis of the essay? _____

    _____

    _____

2. Why, in paragraphs 1 and 2, is the author smiling and calm even though the

    machine gave him the wrong beverage? _____

    _____

    _____

3. In paragraph 6, the author is "thrilled," but by paragraph 8 he is "livid." What happens that suddenly puts him in a different mood?

    _____

    _____

    _____

B. Noticing Writing Techniques and Styles

4. The introductory paragraph establishes the fact that "Big White" does not dispense what is selected. What is the function of paragraph 2?

    _____

    _____

5. Why do you think paragraphs 5 and 6 are so short? _____

    _____

    _____

6. Reread paragraphs 12 and 13. With what image of the human being and the machine are we left, especially with the use of the phrase, "Even now, *behind me* . . ."? _____

    _____

    _____

7. What particular descriptions and wording help the author give Big White the personality of an enemy? _____

    _____

    _____

© 1985 Los Angeles Times Syndicate. Reprinted with permission.

PLAN . . .

an essay on some aspect of technology and the future.

STEP 1: Selecting and Exploring a Topic: Your Choice

In previous units you have been shown how to use brainstorming, freewriting, clustering, PMIs, and reacting to what you read by asking questions. Use any one of the methods to help you select and explore a topic for an essay on some aspect of technology and the future.

◆ WRITING JOURNAL ENTRY

If you don't already have an idea for an essay, look over the following list. In your journal, use one of these or an idea of your own.
  Try brainstorming, freewriting, or clustering on

1. technology
2. test-tube babies
3. nuclear power
4. robots
5. automation
6. shopping by computer
7. the year 2090
8. genetic research
9. space colonization
10. future life-styles

Or do a PMI on

1. All shopping should be done by computer and mail order.
2. Every home should have a housekeeping robot that will do everything necessary to keep a house clean.
3. The government should provide special funds to scientists working on the re-creation of life in laboratories.
4. All scientists and technologists who invent, discover, develop, or create substances harmful to humanity should be imprisoned.
5. Every family should be restricted to owning one car and allowed only 25 gallons of gasoline per month in order to reduce air pollution.
6. Television stations should not be allowed to broadcast for more than four hours a day.
7. Animals should be used in scientific research.

Or react to and question the following statements:

1. We are beginning to treat the earth as a sort of domesticated household pet, living in an environment invented by us, part park, part zoo. It is an idea we must rid ourselves of soon, for it is not so. It is the other way around. We are not separate beings. We are a living part of the earth's life, owned and operated by the earth, probably specialized for functions on its behalf that we have not yet glimpsed. (Lewis Thomas, "Man's Role on Earth. *New York Times Magazine* 7 Dec. 1984: 12)
2. The invention of culture depended on another human invention, the greatest one of all history: speech. (Ben Bova, "In Defense of Technology." *Analog* Sept. 1974)
3. I do not admire the computer manufacturers a great deal more than I admire the energy industries. I have seen their advertisements, attempting to seduce struggling farmers into the belief that they can solve their problems by buying yet another piece of expensive equipment. I am familiar with their propaganda campaigns that have put computers into public schools that are in need of books. That computers are expected to become as common as TV sets in "the future" does not impress me or matter to me. I do not own a TV set. I do not see that computers are bringing us one step nearer to anything that does matter to me: peace, economic justice, ecological health, political honesty, family and community stability, good work. (Wendell Berry, "Why I Am Not Going to Buy a Computer." *NER/BLQ* Autumn 1987)

STEP 2: Writing a Working Thesis

Good questions based on your reaction to what you read can sometimes be turned into good working theses by making them direct statements. For instance, what if you were freewriting on an invention, such as the telephone, and you came up with the question "What if all the world's telephones suddenly disappeared?" Turn the question into a statement and complete it: "If all the world's telephones suddenly disappeared . . . life as we know it would come to a standstill" or "chaos would begin" or whatever ideas occur to you.

Maybe after reading statement 2 above, you ask yourself, "Is speech really man's greatest invention?" If after exploring the question you decide yes, turn your question into the statement "Man's greatest invention of all time is speech." Then show why. Or if you don't think so, write, "Man's greatest invention is not speech, it is [name it]" and then support your views.

◆ TEXTBOOK ENTRY

When you have arrived at a working thesis after exploring ideas for an essay on technology, write it in the following space for future use.

Working thesis: _____

_____

_____

_____

STEP 3: Analyzing and Organizing Your Ideas

Look carefully at the key words in your working thesis. Make certain that you have enough information to support your key points. Organize your ideas into some type of outline that you can follow for a first draft. When you are satisfied you are ready, go to the next section.

WRITE . . .

a first draft for an essay on some aspect of technology or the future.

The Nutshell Statement

In the space provided, write a nutshell statement for the thesis and outline you developed for an essay on gender roles.

The purpose of my essay is _____

_____

_____

My audience is _____

_____

_____

I will support my thesis by _____

_____

_____

_____

_____

_____

Developing Paragraphs by Using Analysis: Process and Causal

There are basically two types of analysis in paragraph development. One type is called **process analysis**, which means a close look at how a process works, such as how to read faster, how to milk a cow, how to . . . well, almost "how to" anything. "How to" generally results in an analysis of a process. The other type is called **causal analysis**. Showing the cause of something and the effects it has is causal analysis, which is an attempt to explain why something happens or happened in the past.

The following is a paragraph that deals with process analysis. As you read it, look for the process being described and how that process works.

> A modem, that's short for MOdulator-DEModulator, is a device that connects a computer with a telephone. It converts (modulates) computer signals to sounds that can be sent over the phone line. Here's how it works. Information runs through the computer in groups of eight bits, like cars roaring down a freeway eight abreast. But a telephone line is a one-lane road that can only handle one bit at a time. The modem acts like a funnel. It squeezes a row of eight parallel bits into a serial line of eight bits, one behind the other. (Fred Gebhart, "Plugging In." *Enter* Oct. 1984: 33)

The process being described is how a modem works. First, a modem is defined, then an explanation of how it works is made analogous with a funnel that takes eight cars (eight computer bits) alongside each other on a freeway (the computer line) and squeezes them so that they come out one at a time on a one-lane road (the telephone line).

The following is another example of a paragraph that deals with process analysis.

> Try to make your writing more precise without making it more wordy. Don't make a sentence more precise by hooking up a freight train of details to it. Make it more precise by whittling all the possible word combinations to those few that say exactly what you want to say. Go through your manuscript and change the general word or phrase to the precise word or phrase. Change "They won by a large margin" to "They won by 42 points." If you've written "Various ethnic groups have settled in Newark," change it to "Greeks, Italians and Puerto Ricans have settled in Newark." (Gary Provost, "The 7 Beacons of Good Writing." *Writer's Digest* Mar. 1984)

The topic sentence says you should try to make your writing more precise without making it wordy. Then the rest of the paragraph explains *how:*

♦ Don't make a sentence more precise by hooking up a freight train of details to it.
♦ Make it more precise by whittling all the possible word combinations to a few.
♦ Go through your manuscript and change the general word or phrase to the precise word.

Then examples are provided to make the "how to" more explicit. The process explained, then, is how to make your writing more precise without making it wordy.

Following is another example of process analysis. Don't worry if it sounds too technical at first. Taken out of context from a word processing manual, the paragraph has some symbols in it that may make no sense. Just read it and look for the "how to" explained in it.

> You can store your writing on the disk. To do that, press the ESC key to return to the Main Menu, then type 4 to select the GET/SAVE/REMOVE function. Press CTRL C to continue, and when WRITE displays the Get/Save/Remove Menu, type 2 to select the Save option.

This is rather typical of the way many manuals are written. At first, they seem incomprehensible. But if you take the directions one step at a time, it's not all that bad. Notice the "how to" process from the outline of the paragraph:

Topic sentence: You can store your writing on disk.

How?

1. Press ESC key to get Main Menu.
2. Type 4 to get GET/SAVE/REMOVE function.
3. Press CTRL C.
4. Type 2 when WRITE displays Get/Save/Remove Menu.
5. Type 2 to select Save option.

In this example the process of storing information on a computer disk is explained.

Causal analysis is used to explain *why* something happens or happened rather than *how.* In the paragraph that follows, see if you can recognize a cause and its effect.

Several studies have been done on the effects of hashish smoking. At least one group, a team of army doctors, has found that heavy use of hashish leads to severe lung damage. Also, if the smoker is predisposed to schizophrenia, it can cause long-lasting episodes of that disorder.

This example is easy enough to follow. Basically, the cause in this case is "heavy use of hashish," and two effects are presented: severe lung damage and long-lasting episodes of schizophrenia in those persons who are predisposed.

Following is another example of causal analysis:

Researchers say that sex-typing of school courses can begin as early as second grade. That means the odds are that your daughter will be steered away from math, science, and computer classes. And girls who ignore computer-science classes in grade school and high school often regret that lack of study when they reach the college level and want to consider pursuing a computer-related field. (Charlotte Beyers, "Bridging the Gender Gap." *Family Computing* Aug. 1984)

An outline of the paragraph might look like this:

The cause: Sex-typing of school courses.

The effects: 1.   Females will be steered away from math, science, and computer classes
          2.   Girls may regret it later in life.

When you are writing and you want either to tell your reader how to do something or to show the cause and effect of something, you will need to use analysis.

◈ TEXTBOOK ENTRY

Read the following paragraph and answer the questions that follow.

What has the telephone done to us, or for us, in the hundred or so years of its existence? It has saved lives by getting rapid word of illness and injury from isolated areas. It has crippled the art of letter writing. It has made living alone possible for persons with normal social impulses, and by so doing, broken up the traditional multigeneration household. It has made the waging of war chillingly more efficient than before, yet prevented wars that might have arisen out of international misunderstanding caused by written comunication. (Adapted from John Brooks, *The Telephone: The First Hundred Years.* New York: Harper & Row, 1976)

1.   What type of analysis is taking place, process or causal? Explain. _____

_____

_____

2.   What is being analyzed? _____

3.   Outline the paragraph based on the type of analysis. _____

_____

_____

_____

_____

        What's taking place, of course, is causal analysis. The point of the paragraph is to show the effects the telephone has had in our lives during its 100 years of existence. If the paragraph were discussing how the telephone works or how to do something with the telephone, the analysis would be process analysis. But the paragraph is showing effects. Your outline, then, should list the various effects the telephone has had: saving lives of people in remote areas, crippling the art of letter writing, making living alone possible, and preventing wars.

Practice in Analysis

If you or your instructor feel you need more practice in paragraphs using analysis, go to page 278.

◆ WRITING JOURNAL ENTRY

1. Use analysis to write in your journal about one of the following topics:
    a. How to sleep in class and get away with it
    b. The effects of not studying
    c. How to get a date with someone you don't know but want to
    d. How to make or do something
    e. The effects (pick an invention or discovery) has had on our lives
2. Use your nutshell statement, your working thesis, and outline to write the first draft of an essay. Try to incorporate the paragraph patterns you have learned, but don't force them.

REWRITE . . .
your first draft.

You should now have a working draft of an essay on some aspect of technology. Make sure that you have looked over your paper for the following:

_____ 1. Does your draft have a thesis that reveals to the reader your point of view on the subject?

_____ 2. Does your opening paragraph use a method that draws the interest of your readers?

_____ 3. Are you writing about something you know and feel?
_____ 4. Are your paragraphs organized so that one idea moves smoothly to another?
_____ 5. Have you tried to use the paragraph methods presented so far?
_____ 6. Have you shared your essay with someone to obtain another perspective on your writing.

If you are satisfied that you have done the best you can so far, go to the next revision strategy.

Revise by Using Parallel Sentence Structure [‖]

As you revise your essay, look for _parallelism_ in your sentences. Parallelism in writing means that a pair or series of words or ideas in a sentence should be similar, such as nouns with nouns, adjectives with adjectives, and so on. _Faulty parallelism_ occurs when a series of words or ideas starts out with one element and ends up with another.

To understand parallelism better, read what Gary Provost, a professional writer, has to say:

> If you're still not sure of what parallel construction means, I will give you some familiar but altered examples. Listen to the sound the sentences make when they are put into parallel construction.

Not parallel: Fish gotta swim, and flying is something birds have to do.
Parallel: Fish gotta swim, birds gotta fly.

Not parallel: First I came. Then I saw. Conquering came next.
Parallel: I came, I saw, I conquered.

> In this next example, listen to the way the information gains impact and credibility when the paragraph is rewritten using parallel construction.

Not parallel: I drove to the construction site to see what I could find out from the workers. I talked to the foreman. The electricians and I had a discussion. Also, the carpenters. And the plumbers told me what they thought. The same view was held by everybody. The project would have to be started over.
Parallel: I drove to the construction site to see what I could find out from the workers. I talked to the foreman. I talked to the electricians. I talked to the carpenters, and I talked to the plumbers. They all said the same thing. The project would have to be started over.

(Gary Provost, "Sound Advice," _Writer's Digest_ December 1985: 33)

However, don't get the impression that your sentences should always follow this construction. If you did, you'd be writing sentences that always began with a subject ("I," in the preceding case) followed by a verb ("drove" and "talk"), which can sound boring. In the preceding example, the parallel construction provides emphasis and tone.

Following are some examples of *faulty parallelism*. When you revise, check your sentences for these problems.

1.   *Example:* Sharon *files, types,* and sometimes *will run* errands.

     Notice that the verbs are not parallel in tense. The sentence should read,

     Sharon *files, types,* and sometimes *runs* errands.

     The verbs *files, types,* and *runs* are now all the same tense.

2.   *Example:* Sharon learned how *to type* reports, *to file* correspondence, and *smiles* pleasantly.

     Notice that the pattern *to type* and *to file* is broken with *smile.* The sentence should read,

     Sharon learned how to type reports, to file correspondence, and *to smile* pleasantly.

3.   *Example:* Sharon is *pretty, single,* and *an athlete.*

     The first two adjectives, *pretty* and *single,* describe Sharon, but the noun *athlete* breaks the pattern. The sentence should read,

     Sharon is *pretty, single,* and *athletic.*

     Parallelism is achieved by turning the noun *athlete* into an adjective, *athletic.*

4.   *Example:* Sharon praised the business school she attended *for its instructors* and *because it has up-to-date office equipment.*

     The sentence should be made parallel by using either *for* or *because,* but not both. Notice the change:

     Sharon praised the business school she attended *for its instructors* and *for its up-to-date office equipment.*

     For parallelism, each series of verbs, adjectives, or phrases must be equal or matched in tense and word phrase elements.

◆ TEXTBOOK ENTRY

Rewrite the following sentences, correcting any faulty parallelism.

1.   The judges for the talent show watched her sing, dance, and her acting.

     _____

     _____

2. It is better to run down this street than walking slowly down it.

   _____

   _____

3. We couldn't decide whether to go study in the library or try going home to do it.

   _____

   _____

4. The author of the essay writes so descriptively that we have no trouble understanding both his plight and the revenge he needs to get.

   _____

   _____

5. My German Shepherd enjoys running along the beach, listening to music, and dog food.

   _____

   _____

Practice in Parallelism

If you or your instructor feel you need more practice on parallel construction, go to page 308.

◆ WRITING JOURNAL ENTRY

Using everything you have learned so far, revise your essay on technology and the future.

Edit for Correct Abbreviations and Capital Letters

When you edit your final draft, make certain you have used abbreviations and capital letters correctly. Rules about their use depend on the context in which they are used. Never abbreviate a word if your audience will not understand it. In technical and informal writing, abbreviations are common; in more formal writing they are not. Authorities can disagree on capitalization, but the question of capitalization usage can be answered by looking in a current dictionary. The following guidelines are generally considered standard usage.

Using Abbreviations

1. To refer to someone's title, marital status, or position: Ms., Mrs., Mr., Dr., Jr., Sr., Rev. (Reverend), Gen. (General), Cpl. (Corporal)

   Ms. Linda James

   Dr. Martin Luther King, Jr.

   Gen. Omar Bradley

2. To refer to someone's educational degree: A.A., B.A., Ed.D., M.D., M.S., Ph.D.

   Paul G. Smith, Ph.D. (Never write Dr. Paul G. Smith, Ph.D.)

3. To refer to businesses: Bros., Co., Corp., Inc., Ltd.

   Loman Bros. & Co.

   Apple Computer, Inc.

   General Motors Corp.

4. To refer to time designations: A.M., P.M., A.D., B.C., EST, PST

   We arrived about 10 P.M.

   The shroud dated back to A.D. 1400.

   At 6 A.M., EST, the news story broke on television.

5. To refer to familiar initials: ZIP (Zone Improvement Program code), ESP (extrasensory perception), etc. (and so on), FBI (Federal Bureau of Investigation), ID (identification), TV

   Jane Pauley works for NBC.

   Activities of the CIA have lately come under scrutiny.

   Many of Hemingway's stories are set in Africa (i.e., "The Snows of Kilamanjaro," "The Short Happy Life of Francis Macomber," and "Hills Like White Elephants").

   Note: Geographical locations are seldom abbreviated except for *U.S.S.R.* and *Washington, D.C.* Only use *U.S.* when used as an adjective, such as "U.S. team members."

Using Capital Letters

1. To begin a sentence:

   Have you read any good books lately?

   The election campaign manager was fired for unethical actions.

2. To begin a sentence that is being quoted:

   Art Riddle claims, "Today's cars run smoother, last longer, and are superbly more dependable."

Note: Don't capitalize when the quotation does not begin a new sentence.

"Today's cars," Art Riddle claims, "run smoother, last longer, and are superbly more dependable."

Art Riddle believes that the automobiles of today "run smoother, last longer, and are superbly more dependable."

3.   To refer to specific names, places, or things:

Holden Caulfield

Ireland, Irish culture

Shakespearean theatre

Pulitzer Prize

Oldsmobile Cutlass Supreme

Japanese language

Department of Agriculture

Statue of Liberty

English Composition 1A

Quaker Oats cereal

4.   To refer to titles of honor or esteem:

President Truman

Truman, the only president to use the atomic bomb

Princess Diana

Senator Slim Pickens

5.   To refer to titles of written works:

the *Boston Globe* and the *Los Angeles Times* (The article *the* is not capitalized.)

The Catcher in the Rye (Articles and prepositions, unless the first word, are not capitalized.)

Sylvia Plath's poem "Metaphors"

6.   To refer to geographical regions but not directions:

He traveled widely in the Northwest.

He traveled north.

The North and the South were divided by the Mason-Dixon line.

7.   To begin or end letter introductions and closings:

Dear Sir:	Yours truly,
My dear Mrs. Kottle:	Sincerely,
To whom it may concern:	Sincerely yours,

◆ TEXTBOOK ENTRY

Using the information on abbreviations and capitalization, correct the following sentences.

1. Have you read mark twain's novel tom sawyer?

2. a tv version of his novel will be broadcast at 8 pm.

3. The 1988 summer olympics were held in south Korea.

4. Who was it who said, "we have nothing to Fear but Fear itself?"

5. My sister pam is taking english 302 and plans to major in english.

Practice in Capitalization and Abbreviation

If you or your instructor feel you need more practice in capitalization and abbreviation, go to page 319.

◆ WRITING JOURNAL ENTRY

Return to the last draft of your essay on technology and the future. Rewrite and edit by using the following checklist:

_____ 1. Have I fully developed and supported my thesis?
_____ 2. Have I fully developed and supported each paragraph?
_____ 3. Have I used transitional devices to help my reader move from one point to the next?
_____ 4. Have I eliminated sentence fragments, run-ons, comma splices, misplaced modifiers, dangling modifiers, and faulty parallelism?
_____ 5. Have I checked for subject-verb agreement?
_____ 6. Have I checked for fallacious thinking or reasoning?
_____ 7. Have I checked for proper punctuation?
_____ 8. Have I written strong sentences?
_____ 9. Have I checked for proper abbreviations and capitalization?

Proofread

Apply the preceding checklist and mark every incorrect item in the following student essay. Try to use the symbols *frag* for sentence fragment, ‖ for faulty parallelism, *dm* for dangling modifier, and so on. See the inside covers for other editing and proofreading marks. Compare your markings with those of others in the class.

LIVING WITHOUT A CAR

People are always asking me how I can live without a car. The truth is I wonder how they can stand driving them. In my mind cars cause more trouble and damage than theyre worth. The most harmful effect is the immediate one: death and injury. They have long term bad effects as well, such as the pollution of our atmosphere and the ebbing of natural resources. In addition they take a great deal of money to operate and maintain. Finally, instead of adding ease of life they seem to cause more stress and worry than they relieve.

People don't take into considertion the destructive power one aquires in the drivers seat. The lives of many people are in a single drivers hands. Automobiles are the cause of a great many deaths in the United States. Not ony is this tragic for those thousands of people who die each year. But for those who accidentally kill as well. Their guilt must constantly torture them. The thought of having the power to kill or cripple someone or myself with a mere flick of the wrist makes me shudder, I don't trust myself that much.

Another thing I couldn't bear would to consciously poison the air I breathe. Itonly takes a glance toward the southern horizon where a hazy brown stripe hovers like a dirty blanket to remind me how much pollution cars can cause. People driving cars is like fish dumping poison chemicals into their own aquariums.

Not only do cars destroy our most important natural resource: air, they greedily drink up another resource faster than we can produce it: oil. Because people have an insatiable thirst for getting places in a hurry. New oil rigs are popping up everywhere, and soon there will be no place left, until then, beautiful cities will become dirtied and industrialized in order to support the "car habit."

Supporting that habit takes more than gas, it takes money. Most people would agree that money is scarce. So why spend the thousands of dollars on gas, maintenance, major repairs and insurance, when the money could be spent on travel, home improvment, or a new hot tub?

Despite all of the drawbacks, cars do offer one great advantage: saving time. Ah, but do they? I don't own a car, yet I seem to have more time than my friends who do. This is because I am forced to leave enough time for transportation, since I can't hop in the car and go. While my friends rush to school at the last minute, battling traffic, frayed nerves, I ride the bus, get my homework done in transit, and arrive ten minutes early as well.

How can I live without a car? Easily!

Return now to your own essay, and when you have done the best proofreading you can, turn it in.

A single 30-minute exposure to TV can significantly alter basic beliefs, related attitudes and behavior of large numbers of people for at least several months.

Sandra J. Ball-Rokeach, Milton Rokeach, and Joel W. Grube,
Psychology Today, November 1984.

THINK . . .

about the media.

◆ WRITING JOURNAL ENTRY

Where do you get most of your information about current events? Books? News-papers? Magazines? Television? Radio? Billboards? Fortune cookies? In your journal, write about your favorite media source of information and discuss how well you think you are informed.

◆ TEXTBOOK ENTRY

Answer the following questions in the spaces provided.

1. We are often told that we live in the Information Age because we have access

    to so much media. Do you think most Americans are well informed? _____

    Explain. _____

    _____

    _____

2. From which media do you think most Americans get their information on world

    events? _____

3. Do you see any negative effects in having so much media from which to choose?

    Explain. _____

    _____

4. How much of a part does advertising play in the Information Age? _____

    _____

    _____

    Read the following statements and write what you think about them in the spaces provided.

A. The rapidly increasing concentration of media ownership in the U.S. raises criti-cal questions about whether the public has access to diverse opinion. In 1982, when media expert Ben Bagdikian completed research for his book *The Media Monopoly*, he found that 50 corporations controlled half or more of the media business. By December 1986, when he finished a revision for a second edition, that figure had shrunk to 29 corporations. Six months later . . . the number was down to 26. Some

Wall Street media analysts predict that by the 1990s six giant firms will control most of our media. (Carl Jensen, "Project Censored." *Utne Reader* Sept./Oct. 1988: 84)

B. The media are omnipresent [everywhere] in American society. From morning radio disc jockeys to television's David Letterman at midnight, the media provide non-stop programs of entertainment and information for their audiences. Some critics argue that the media emphasize sex and violence and undermine America's moral values. Others, however, believe that Americans are expert media consumers who can decipher myth from reality in their entertainment and news. . . . The issue of mass media's influence will remain crucial to American society. (David L. Bender, "Chapter Preface," *What Influence Do the Media Have on Society?* St. Paul: Greenhaven Press, 1988. 110)

THINK ABOUT IT . . .

Top 10 U.S. Advertisers

'87 rank	'86 rank	Advertiser	Headquarters	TOTAL U.S. AD SPENDING 1987	1986	% chg.
1	2	**Philip Morris**	New York	$1.56 billion	$1.45 billion	7.4
2	1	**Procter & Gamble**	Cincinnati	1.39 billion	1.50 billion	−7.6
3	5	**General Motors**	Detroit	1.02 billion	838.9 million	22.2
4	3	**Sears**	Chicago	886.5 million	1.11 billion	−19.8
5	4	**RJR Nabisco**	Atlanta	839.6 million	894.2 million	−6.1
6	10	**PepsiCo**	Somers, N.Y.	704.0 million	641.5 million	9.7
7	34	**Eastman Kodak**	Rochester, N.Y.	658.2 million	610.2 million	7.9
8	8	**McDonald's**	Oak Brook, Ill.	649.5 million	591.8 million	9.7
9	6	**Ford**	Dearborn, Mich.	639.5 million	650.9 million	−1.7
10	7	**Anheuser-Busch**	St. Louis	635.1 million	643.9 million	−1.4

Source: Advertising Age

C.   Children spend more time watching television than they spend in the classroom. Because the television medium is familiar to children and because of the advances being made in the electronic media, many educators support television as a teaching tool. Others feel that using television in the classroom places education in the entertainment business and is not the function of the schools.

_____

_____

_____

READ . . .

about some effects of television viewing.

Except for sleeping, no activity occupies more of America's time than television viewing. The consequences of this action are under debate, with some researchers claiming that not enough time is being devoted to reading, thinking, and communication skills. "Pull the plug!" some critics plea. Others feel that television, properly used, can be an effective learning tool. The following reading selection reports some findings on the growing influence television is having on our lives.

Before reading closely, take a moment to read the title, the first paragraph, and the three subheadings. Then answer the following questions.

1.   What position on the effects of television does the author take? _____

_____

_____

2.   Based on the opening paragraph, what support for her position will the author use? _____

_____

_____

3.   Do you think you will agree or disagree with the author? _____

Why? _____

_____

_____

4.   The meaning an author intends may be lost if the reader does not understand the author's use of certain words and phrases. Make sure that you understand

the following words before you read. The number after the word is the paragraph
number where the word appears.

a. *rebuttal* (1) = reply; answer
b. *adverse* (1) = negative; bad
c. *correlated* (2) = shown to be parallel
d. *fosters* (2) = encourages; cultivates
e. *aspirations* (6) = hopes; future goals
f. *electorate* (7) = those qualified to vote
g. *discourse* (7) = verbal exchange, either spoken or written
h. *incoherence* (8) = unclear; lacking order
i. *affability* (9) = friendliness
j. *drivel* (9) = childish talk; foolishness

WHAT RESEARCH IS SAYING ABOUT TELEVISION

Kate Brody

1   Arguments go back and forth. Critics claim that television is to blame for declin-
ing Scholastic Aptitude Tests, a growth of nation-wide violence, and a lowering of
moral and ethical standards. The broadcasters' rebuttal is that they are being unfairly
blamed for simply giving the public what it wants, arguing that their influence is exaggerated. But there is some growing evidence, based on research, that television *is*
having some adverse effects on our lives, negative enough information that we should
consider more seriously than we are.

2   For a long time, defenders of television argued that there was no clear evidence
that viewing violence on TV was linked to aggressive behavior. Now, a report by the
federally sponsored National Institute of Health says that "violence on television does
lead to aggressive behavior by children and teenagers who watch the programs" (Mann
27). After studying 732 children over a five-year period, NIH reports that "several
kinds of aggression—conflicts with parents, fighting, delinquency—were all positively
correlated with the total amount of television viewing" (27). In addition, the findings
of the report found that

> more than half the parents thought their children learned more about sex from
> TV than from any other source except the parents themselves [and that it] fos-
> ters bad habits by glamorizing highly advertised junk foods and frequent use of
> alcohol. (27)

The study made note that among the most avid TV watchers are the very young and
the very old, women, and minorities. Heavy viewers tend to be less educated.

3   For some time, educators suspected that television had a negative influence on
the attention span of students. A research project by a Purdue University psychologist,
Jacob Jacoby, indicates that viewers retain less from television than from reading.
Jacoby found that

> more than 90 percent of the 2,700 people he tested misunderstood even such
> simple fare as commercials or questions on the detective series "Barnaby Jones."
> Only minutes after watching the typical viewer missed 23 to 36 percent of the
> questions about what he or she had seen (28).

A partial explanation for this has to do with the brain's structure. The left half of the brain is where our ability to think and analyze occurs. The right half of the brain specializes in emotional responses. By connecting viewers to instruments that measure brain waves it was found that television's pictures stimulate the right side of the brain by a ratio of 2 to 1 (29).

4   The quick images projected through television gives viewers little chance to pause and reflect on what they have seen. One image follows another with no chance to review or digest what has been said or seen. By electronically measuring the high proportion of alpha waves received while viewing, scientists have shown that there is a numbing effect on the brain (28). Alpha waves are normally associated with a day-dreaming or dream state.

5   Researchers at the Edith Nourse Rogers Memorial Veterans Hospital in Bedford, Mass., tested subjects for attention spans. They

> attached 40 young viewers to an instrument that shut off the TV set whenever the children's brains produced mainly alpha waves. Although the children were told to concentrate, only a few could keep the set on for more than 30 seconds (29).

Since the average child aged 2–11 watches over 25 hours of television a week, it would seem there is some validity to heavy viewing of fast-paced images and sound to the inability of youngsters to concentrate for very long.

6   A federal report, "Television and Behavior," has found other negative aspects of television viewing—unrealistic career expectations among young people:

> Heavy viewers want high-status jobs but do not intend to spend many years in school. For girls, there is even more potential for conflict between aspirations and plans; the girls who are heavy viewers usually want to get married, have children, and stay at home to take care of them, but at the same time they plan to remain in school and have exciting careers (82).

Television seems to say that problems can be solved as quickly as they are in a 30-minute situation comedy or a 30-second commercial. When problems are not resolved quickly, people become frustrated. According to social scientists, the frustrations caused by these expectations can lead to destructive outbursts from misbehavior in school to ghetto riots.

7   Neil Postman, professor of communications arts and sciences at New York University, believes that television "has culture by the throat." In his book, *Amusing Ourselves to Death: Public Discourse in the Age of Show Business*, Postman calls television "the command center of the culture," believing that:

> We possibly have the most ill-informed electorate in the West because people rely so much on television for their understanding of the world. Television makes Americans know of a lot of things, but about very little. Knowing about implies a historical dimension, an inkling of the implications.
>
> It's different from other media in that people don't go to movies to get the weather or find out political information or get the ball scores. We go to television to get everything. And the problem that results is that television, because of its entertainment format—its visual nature—turns all forms of discourse into entertainment packages (59).

Many educators agree with Postman, arguing that students spend too many hours in front of television seeing entertaining irrelevance and incoherence. The result is a majority of students who lack substance of thought and expect their teachers to entertain them.

8   Even some journalists seem to be aware of the negative power of television. Among them, Bill Moyers, public television journalist, believes that America's social behavior is changing. Americans have "ceased talking to one another" and instead now "entertain one another, and they do so in all sorts of places where entertainment is beside the point and corrupting. Under the tyranny of affability and simplicity, public discourse, politics, religion, and education have collapsed into smiling drivel" (Moyers 46).

9   In a country where television has become such a strong force in most people's lives, the consequences of its negative effects are worth considering. Since more and more research seems to indicate that television influences us on everything from what we eat to who we elect for president, we have cause to be concerned for our future. As Benjamin Barber, political science professor at Rutgers University says, "We stand—prepared or not—on the threshold of a new age that promises to revolutionize our habits as viewers, as consumers and ultimately as citizens" (Mann 30).

Mann, James. "What Is TV Doing to America?" *U.S. News & World Report* 2 Aug. 1982, 27–30.

Moyers, Bill. "The Power of Television," *KCET Magazine* Sept. 1988, 45–47.

Postman, Neil. *Amusing Ourselves to Death: Public Discourse in the Age of Show Business.* New York: Viking, 1985.

Stein, Ben. *The View from Sunset Boulevard: America as Brought to You by the People Who Make Television.* New York: Basic Books, 1979.

U.S. Government Pamphlet. "Television and Behavior" 1985.

REACT . . .

to the reading selection.

◆ WRITING JOURNAL ENTRY

Write a paragraph in your journal that discusses why you do or do not agree with Kate Brody's thesis in the essay you just read.

◆ TEXTBOOK ENTRY

A. Understanding the Content

In the spaces provided, answer the following questions. Refer to the reading selection when necessary.

1.   What is Brody's thesis? _____

_____

_____

_____

2. What evidence does she provide to support her contention? Are there any reported negative effects that are not backed up by research? _____

_____

_____

_____

_____

3. What specific negative effects of television are presented? _____

_____

_____

_____

4. What side of the brain is primarily used for watching television and what effect does this have on the viewer? _____

_____

_____

_____

B. Noticing Writing Techniques and Styles

5. What introductory paragraph method is used? _____

_____

6. What is the point of paragraphs 2 and 3? What method of development is used? _____

_____

_____

7. Why are there no quotation marks around the quoted material in paragraphs 2, 3, 5, and 7? _____

_____

_____

8. How appropriate is the quoted material? Is it necessary? _____

_____

_____

_____

PLAN . . .

an essay on some aspect of the media.

STEP 1: Selecting and Exploring a Topic

In previous units you have been shown how to use brainstorming, freewriting, clustering, PMIs, and reacting to what you read by asking questions. Use any one of these methods to help you select and explore a topic for an essay on some aspect of the media.

◆ WRITING JOURNAL ENTRY

If you don't already have an idea for an essay, look over the following list below. In your journal, explore one of these items or an idea of your own.
  Try brainstorming, freewriting, or clustering on

1.	radio	6.	junk mail
2.	newspapers	7.	TV network news
3.	advertising	8.	MTV
4.	magazines	9.	rock music lyrics
5.	TV commercials	10.	publishing

Or do a PMI on

1. No person or corporation should be allowed to own more than two major newspaper publications, radio stations, or television stations.
2. All television commercials should be played at the beginning and end of a program so that there are no interruptions.
3. There should be government regulations to keep the media from showing sex, violence, and crime on television and in movies.
4. People running for government office should not be allowed to advertise or debate on television but instead restricted to newspapers and radio.

5. Advertisements for tobacco products and alcoholic beverages should be banned.

Or react to and question the following statements:

1. Please remember that in television the product is not the program; the product is the audience and the consumer of that product is the advertiser. The advertiser does not "buy" a news program. He buys an audience. The manufacturer (network) that gets the highest price for its product is the one that produces the most product (audience). (Linda Ellerbee, *And So It Goes.* New York: Putnam, 1986. 95)

2. One reason that propaganda often works better on the educated than on the uneducated is that educated people read more, so they receive more propaganda. Another is that they have jobs in management, media, and academia and therefore work in some capacity as agents of the propaganda system—and they believe what the system expects them to believe. By and large, they're part of the privileged elite, and share the interests and perceptions of those in power. (Noam Chomsky, "Propaganda, American-style." *Utne Review* Sept./Oct. 1988: 81)

3. Controversy—the heart of politics—has gotten a bad name in the textbook business, and publishers have advised their writers to avoid it. This fear of controversy is distorting our children's education, leaving us with biology texts that neglect evolution and history texts that omit the important influence of religion. . . . Controversy and compromise are the engines of democracy, and they provide the forum for citizen involvement, but if students are led to believe that the system is smoothly self-perpetuating and that no problems need solving, they will see no need for their participation. (Arthur J. Kropp, "Let's Put an End to Mediocre Textbooks." *Houston Post* 2 May 1987)

STEP 2: Writing a Working Thesis

A working thesis, remember, is just a starting point, a statement about your subject that you think you'd like to prove or develop. It may not be your final thesis statement, but it serves as a guide to help you take the information you have gained from exploring the topic through freewriting, brainstorming, clustering, or whatever method you've used.

Your working thesis should contain at least one key word that indicates the thrust of your viewpoint, as in the following thesis statements:

Rock music lyrics can have a *negative effect* on youth.

The media's influence on America's morals is *limited.*

The present forms of media advertising are *detrimental on a worldwide scale.*

There should be *no government regulations imposed* on the media.

The italicized words in each of the thesis statements require support and development. Look for the key words in your working thesis.

Steve Kelley. San Diego Union.

◆ TEXTBOOK ENTRY

When you have arrived at a working thesis for an essay on the media, write it in the following space for future use.

Working thesis: _____

_____

_____

_____

STEP 3: Analyzing and Organizing Your Ideas

Look carefully at the key words in your working thesis. Make certain that you have enough information to support and develop them. Organize your ideas into some type of outline that you can follow for a first draft. When you have finished, go to the next section.

WRITE . . .

a first draft for an essay on some aspect of the media.

The Nutshell Statement

The probable thesis of my essay is _____

_____

_____

My purpose is _____

_____

_____

The audience is _____

_____

_____

I will support my thesis by _____

_____

_____

_____

Developing Paragraphs by Using Description

In previous units you have learned that there are several paragraph patterns that writers use frequently: illustration or example, comparison and contrast, classification, definition, and analysis. This unit will focus on the use of **description**.

The trick to using description is to have enough but not too much. Look at the following sentence:

The cat sat on the table.

There's no problem from the standpoint of correct English. But with added description, such as

The black cat sat hunched on the kitchen table ready to spring to the floor.

We now have the cat's color, a vision of the way the cat sat, and on what table. The reader has been provided with sensory and specific description.

Description can be overdone, however, to the point of losing the reader because there is so much going on. For instance,

> The dirty, black cat with bald spots caused by a recent illness due from lack of diet, sat hunched like a striped tiger sitting on a tree branch in the jungle ready to spring on its prey on the kitchen table that still had dirty dishes from this morning's breakfast.

Descriptive? Yes, but what happened to the cat sitting on the table? What is important in the sentence has become lost in all the description. Look at a few examples of various types of descriptions that work well.

> Printout receptacles provide convenient security when and where you need it. A large mouth provides an ample opening to receive thick quantities of material, yet unique interior baffling insures security—even if the can is turned completely upside down. Hinged top is only removable when unlocked by key. Fire-resistant construction of heavy gauge steel features nylon feet to protect floors, and a vinyl bumper that surrounds the receptacle at its widest area to protect the furniture and walls. It comes 37 inches high, is 14 × 14 inches wide, and holds 27 gallons.

Obviously, this is a catalogue-style description. If you were in the market for a printout receptacle, the description provides enough information to let you know if it's what you want. A visual description of size is provided as well as a working description. Following is a different type of description:

> Traffic now surges in the street, and mid-morning sunshine, though hot, grows fuzzy with smog. A man carrying a large sack of merchandise musically chants his business: "Buying—shoes, curtains, rugs." This one-man conglomerate will sell his rummage on poorer streets. He is followed by our roving plumber, who announces his presence by blowing three notes on a pipe. (Bart McDowell, "Mexico City: An Alarming Giant." *National Geographic* Aug. 1984)

Notice the key words that bring the scene alive: *traffic surges, mid-morning sunshine, fuzzy smog, musically chants,* and *one-man conglomerate.* If we read closely, we hear the traffic, we feel the heat, we see the smog and the man with the sack, and we hear his words and the plumber's pipe sounds. Yet the description is not overdone. Following is still another description. Notice the words that help give sensory feelings.

> One prisoner had been brought out of his cell. He was a Hindu, a puny wisp of a man, with a shaven head and vague liquid eyes. He had a thick, sprouting moustache, absurdly too big for his body, rather like the moustache of a comic man on the films. Six tall Indian warders were guarding him and getting him ready for the gallows. Two of them stood by with rifles and fixed bayonets, while the others handcuffed him, passed a chain through his handcuffs and fixed it to their belts, and lashed his arms tight to his sides. They crowded very close about him, with their hands always on him in a careful, caressing grip, as though all the while feeling him to make sure he was there. It was like men handling a fish which is still alive and may jump back into the water. But he stood quite unresisting, yielding his arms limply to the ropes, as though he hardly noticed what was happening. (*Shooting an Elephant and Other Essays* by George Orwell; copyright 1950 by Sonia Brownell Orwell)

This passage, in addition to using description in a manner already discussed, uses similes and metaphors. A **simile** is a comparison of two unlike things. For example here are two similes from the passage:

> He had a thick, sprouting moustache, absurdly too big for his body, rather *like the moustache of a comic man on the films.*

> It was *like men handling a fish which is still alive and may jump back in the water.*

Similes use the words *like* or *as* to introduce the comparison. **Metaphors**, like similes, make a comparison but don't use the words *like* or *as*. Instead, they make implicit comparisons, such as *liquid eyes* (eyes aren't liquid, yet the use of the word as a descriptive adjective helps us visualize the look in his eyes at that moment). Following is an example of a simile and metaphor appearing together:

> You see men of eighty still vital and straight as oaks; you see men of fifty reduced to gray shadows in the human landscape. The cellular clock differs for each one of us. . . . (Sharon Curtin, "Aging in the Land of the Young. *The Atlantic,* July 1972)

The phrase *straight as oaks* is a simile, comparing the stature of 80-year-old men to oak trees; *gray shadows in the human landscape* is a metaphor for 50-year-old men who are old before their time. *The cellular clock* is also a metaphor for the aging process.

As you know, a topic sentence, as well as a thesis, requires support, and the type of support needed is often determined by the way the topic sentence is phrased. In a topic sentence that reads

> I recall my first evening in La Gritta.

it's reasonable for a reader to assume that a description of that visit will follow. Of course, that's exactly what the author provides:

> I recall my first evening in La Gritta. It was evening and I was sipping Campari and soda while candles flickered and a mandolin whispered the melody of a love song whose lyrics spelled out desire, along with life's search for fulfillment. As the sun slipped low, clouds filled with fire bathing the horizon. Starry-eyed visitors, young and old, were in the mood for the language of love. (Jerry Hulse, "Traveling in Style." *Los Angeles Times Magazine* 18 Oct. 1987: 27)

Notice the details the author uses to describe the scene for his readers: "sipping Campari and soda" (not just having a drink), "candles flickered" (not just burned), "a mandolin whispered" (not played), "lyrics spelled out" (not lyrics said), and "clouds filled with fire bathing the horizon" (not the setting sun). A descriptive paragraph provides readers with language that touches the senses, creating sights, sounds, smells, taste, and touch.

Look closely at the use of description in this paragraph:

> We were walking out on a sweep north of Yay Ninh City, toward the Cambodian border, and a mortar round came in about thirty yards away. I had no sense of those distances then; even after six or seven weeks in Vietnam I still thought of that kind of information as a journalist's detail that could be picked up later, not some-

thing a survivor might have to know. When we fell down on the ground, the kid in front of me put his boot in my face. I didn't feel the boot; it got lost in the tremendous concussion I made hitting the ground, but I felt a sharp pain in a line over my eyes. . . . Some hot, stinking metal had been put in my mouth; I thought I tasted brains there sizzling on the end of my tongue, and the kid was fumbling for his canteen and looking really scared, pale, near tears, his voice shaking. (Michael Herr, *Dispatches*, New York: Avon, 1978)

It would be difficult to find a topic sentence in the paragraph, but in this case, the author is attempting to describe the horrors of war and to create a topic sentence that would say "war is hell," or "war is scary" or "I had a horrible experience in Vietnam." A topic sentence would not be effective in this paragraph, where the author is describing the event as it was occurring.

Here is one more example of the use of description to make a point:

They might yet be reeling from manic Monday. At the Silverdome, where they had beaten the Celtics nine straight times, the only basket the Pistons could throw anything into was the wastebasket, which is exactly what they did with copies of the final box score. During one stretch of the first half, they missed *20 straight shots*. They went from off-target to awful to aw-come-on-this-is-ridiculous. And, the Celtics weren't much better. It was basketball without baskets. It was a game that belonged in a YMCA. (Mike Downey, "How Low Can It Get?" *Los Angeles Times* 31 May 1988: III, 1)

It is not difficult to detect the author's tone and opinion about the basketball game he witnessed. Phrases, such as "manic Monday," the only basket the Pistons could throw anything into was the wastebasket," and "off-target to awful to aw-come-on-this-is-ridiculous," describe enough for us to envision a very bad game.

◆ TEXTBOOK ENTRY

Read the following paragraphs and then in the blanks provided fill in the correct responses.

A. We assume that you have seen enough Lucky Strike ads so that you will be able to follow our description without too much trouble. The ad is very simple. It presents a photo of a young woman (perhaps 23 or 24 years old) in a sweater, in a field or meadow, wearing a scarf, with one hand in her pocket and the other resting lightly on her windblown hair, holding an unlighted cigarette. She gazes straight out of the frame. The words "Light My Lucky" appear in quotation marks, very prominently displayed, starting just below her chin and extending across the right margin of the page. At the bottom of the frame, on the left, is the well known warning from the Surgeon General, which says: "Smoking By Pregnant Women May Result in Fetal Injury, Premature Birth, and Low Birth Weight." The Surgeon General's warning refers to pregnant women. But the woman in the ad is anything but pregnant. . . . she is positively healthy. The idea that smoking is unhealthy is obliterated by these contradictory messages, leaving only pregnancy connected to ill health. This is an extremely clever and well-made ad. (R. Scholes et al., *Textbook*. New York: St. Martin's Press, 1988. 122)

1.   What is being described? _____

2.   What is the topic sentence of the paragraph? _____

    _____

3.   How does the description help support the topic sentence? _____

    _____

    _____

    _____

B.   On Sunday morning, as winds reached gale force, two boats that had anchored in the harbor began drifting toward the rocks. One of the boats, a 36-footer from Newport Beach, already had engine problems. The other, a 30-foot sloop, could not use its engine because its propeller apparently had become entangled in an anchor line. The larger boat was the first to go. It went into the rocks and disintegrated in about 10 minutes. Three of the people on board managed to get into a life raft. The fourth person managed to swim ashore. Ten minutes later, the sloop slammed into the rocks. The people on board were swept between the jagged rocks and the boat's splintered hull. Then they were no longer in sight.

1.   What is being described? _____

2.   What is the topic sentence? _____

    _____

3.   What words help describe what is taking place? _____

    _____

    _____

C.   When our class was assigned to Mr. Fleagle for third-year English I anticipated another grim year in that dreariest of subjects. Mr. Fleagle was notorious among City students for dullness and inability to inspire. He was said to be stuffy, dull, and hopelessly out of date. To me he looked to be sixty or seventy and prim to a fault. He wore primly severe eyeglasses, his wavy hair was primly cut and primly combed. He wore prim vested suits with neckties blocked primly against the collar buttons of his primly starched white shirts. He had a primly pointed jaw, a primly straight nose, and a prim manner of speaking that was so correct, so gentlemanly, that he seemed a comic antique. (Russell Baker, *Growing Up*. New York: Congdon and Weed, 1982)

1.   What is being described? _____

2.   What is the topic sentence? _____

    _____

3.   Why does the author repeat the words *prim* and *primly?* How does it help or

    hinder the description? _____

_____

_____

D.   Behind the coalbox, a kitten sits watching her brother who is seated in the middle of the kitchen floor unaware of this scrutiny. Like a bloodthirsty tiger the watcher quivers with anticipation, whips its tail to and fro, and describes the movements of head and tail which are performed also by adult cats. . . . Instead of leaping on its brother as on a prey . . . it assumes a threatening position while still galloping, arching its back and advancing broadside on. (Konrad Lorenz, "On Feline Play," _Man Meets Dog._ Boston: Houghton-Mifflin, 1953)

In the space provided, write the words and phrases that you feel help describe the events in this passage. There's a simile in the passage; see if you can find it.

_____

_____

_____

_____

E.   I sat waiting for the teacher to hand out the test. I was very nervous. I spent a lot of time studying, but I was still nervous anyway. Tests always make me uneasy. I failed the last test and if I fail this one, I will fail the class.

Without overdoing it, rewrite the above passage, making it more descriptive. Make the reader sense the situation better than it is stated.

_____

_____

_____

_____

_____

Practice in Writing Descriptive Paragraphs

If you or your instructor feel you need more practice with descriptive paragraphs, go to page 281.

◇ WRITING JOURNAL ENTRY

1.   As practice, pick any one of the following topic sentences and write a descriptive paragraph for each. Try to use words that deal with the senses, avoiding com-

monly used descriptive phrases or words. Place the topic sentence where it works best.

    a. The day started out well enough, but it didn't last long.

    b. From the moment I first saw him (her), love conquered all.

    c. It's the most insulting advertisement I have ever seen.

    d. It was obvious he didn't know I was watching.

    e. It's not easy to forget a face like that.

2.   Look over your nutshell statement and organizational plan on the media that you wrote in your writing journal. Write a first draft based on your notes. Try to include a paragraph using description if you can. However, don't use the method if it doesn't help you say what you want.

"SHHH, I'M WATCHING TV"

Television is a powerful force in the lives of most American families. Many families report that they spend time together, but further questioning reveals that much of that time is spent silently watching television. Although a television program might foster discussion and debate among family members, this is not often the case. In fact, many families now have multiple television sets so that watching television may be done alone by each family member separately.

    . . . The term *television widow* is no joke to many families. A woman remarked on a talk show, "I can't get worried about whether there's life after death. I'd be satisfied with life after dinner in our home."

    It is interesting to note that many families place the TV in the "family room." R. G. Goldberg suggests that this is a misnomer since talking and communicating among family members is usually discouraged when the TV is being watched. The family room containing a TV set might more aptly be named the "antifamily room."

    Many families simply have the TV on whenever anyone is in the house. It is like background noise. The only problem is that because it activates two senses, hearing and sight, it is far more difficult to avoid attending to it than to noise alone. I'm sure we've all had the experience of visiting someone who leaves the television on during our visit. Communication is next to impossible even though one tries to converse. Eyes keep wandering to the television. In a sense, leaving the television on when someone comes in to converse is the not-so-subtle message, "Television is more important than your communication."

    A. C. Nielsen Company estimates that the average American television set is on approximately forty-four hours per week. With scarcity of time being one of the American family's major problems, it is clear that television often usurps what little togetherness time a family may have.

REWRITE . . .
your first draft.

You should now have a working draft of an essay on some aspect of the media. Make sure that you have looked over your paper for the following:

_____ 1. Does your opening paragraph reveal the subject or topic of your essay?
_____ 2. Does your opening paragraph contain a thesis or hint at your views or feelings toward your topic?
_____ 3. Does your opening paragraph use a method that draws the interest of your readers?
_____ 4. Did you write about a topic you know or have feeling for?
_____ 5. Did you avoid the obvious and take a fresh approach to your topic?
_____ 6. Did you share your essay with others for their opinions?

If you are satisfied that you have done the best you can, go to the next revision strategy.

Revise by Using Descriptive Language

As you revise your essay, try to use descriptive language where appropriate and possible. When you notice that you have written a cliché, or stale metaphor, try to say the same thing in fresh language. Admittedly, it is not easy and requires practice, but a good thesis and argument can lack effectiveness if the language used isn't powerful enough to stir the reader.

When Martin Luther King, Jr., spoke out against racism and segregation, he often used strong metaphors to end his speeches. At his famous speech in 1963 at the Lincoln Memorial, King said that Lincoln's Emancipation Proclamation "came as a great beacon light of hope to millions of Negro slaves who had been seared in the flames of withering injustice." Think about this image. Lincoln's words are made analogous to "a great beacon light of hope" for a group of slaved people being "seared," or burned, in the flames of withering or shrinking injustice. He went on to say that 100 years later "the life of the Negro is still sadly crippled by the manacles of segregation and the chains of discrimination." His use of *manacles* and *chains* makes a strong image of a people still held in a bondage of racial discrimination and hatred. Such description gives power to the meaning behind his words.

Lively description can be found in the daily newspapers and magazines. In his book *Metaphors and Symbols: Forays into Language*, Roland Bartel provides several examples:

Baseball great Babe Ruth was said to resemble "A swollen ballet dancer with those delicate, almost feminine feet and ankles."

Nolan Ryan's fastball was called a "liquid streak of white."

Darrel Porter at the plate "looks like a man trying to swing a bat on the deck of a ship in a storm."

Charles Berlitz said that knowing one language is like living in a large house and never leaving one room.

An economist said that successful taxation is the art of plucking the goose without making it hiss.

A drama critic claimed Katherine Hepburn's voice was implacable, like a dental drill.

Reporters call Nancy Reagan an iron butterfly.

A London reporter said that Nancy Reagan attending the royal wedding looked like John Wayne riding into the sunset.

All of these descriptions provide tone, attitude, and interest to what is being read.

Beware of overused descriptions. We are all too familiar with some of the following. Invent your own sayings when you catch yourself using any of these:

Bury the hatchet. From the American Indian custom of burying hatchets, scalping knives, and war clubs when a war ended so that the war could be forgotten.

Clincher. From the practice of clinching nails so they cannot be easily pulled out.

Raking someone over the coals. Refers to the old practice of extorting money from Jews by hauling them over the coals of a fire until they agreed to pay.

Sold down the river. Selling slaves from worn-out tobacco farms and sending them down the river to more prosperous tobacco farms.

Crocodile tears. From the belief that crocodiles shed tears while they ate their victims.

Cut and dried. From curing hay or timber.

Have one's work cut out. Tailors used to cut out garments and give them to others in the shop to make into clothes.

Earmarked. From the practice of marking the ears of sheep and cattle for identification.

Making both ends meet. A rope must be long enough to go around whatever is being tied up; the ends of the rope must meet.

Laugh up one's sleeve. Goes back to the time when people wore sleeves that were so large that they could hide their faces in their sleeves while they were laughing.

To a T. Refers to the accuracy of the T-square used by carpenters. Variantly, short for "to a tittle," the small sign used as a diacritical marking in printing.

Handwriting on the wall. Warnings and omens, as in the book of Daniel.

Pull up stakes. Refers to boundary stakes.

Old stamping ground. Places where animals and later people gathered.

Put one's shoulder to the wheel. Help a horse pull a cart out of the mud or up a hill.

Over the barrel. Nearly drowned persons used to be laid over a barrel for resuscitation.

Get it in the neck. Refers to the way chickens are killed for eating.

Throw the book at someone. The maximum punishment, all the rules in the book.

Keep your shirt on. Fighters used to remove their shirts before fighting.

Sailing under false colors. Pirates changed flags to avoid attack.

Low man on the totem pole. The figure carved at the bottom of the pole seems to bear the weight of all those carved above.

Feel one's oats. A horse full of oats often displays its energy.

Touch and go. In a near collision, cars or ships may barely touch and keep on going.

Not dry behind the ears. When a colt or calf is born, the last spot to dry is the area behind the ears, hence, someone newly born—naive and credulous.

In the bag. The merchandise is in the bag, ready for delivery. Before the advent of bags, the expression was "all wrapped up."

Come to the end of one's rope. Animals staked for grazing are limited by the length of the rope. Alternately, a reference to the hangman's rope and the end of one's life.

Get the brush-off. To be treated like lint that has to be brushed off. The expression may also refer to the actions of a porter who, suspecting a small tip, gives a person just a few flicks of the brush.

Sucker. A dupe or simpleton as naive as a young animal that still sucks.

Fly off the handle. Losing one's temper as suddenly as an axe head flies off the handle.

Excerpts from *Metaphors and Symbols.* Copyright © 1983 by the National Council of Teachers of English. Reprinted by permission.

◆ TEXTBOOK ENTRY

Write in the blanks what you think is being described in the following statements.

1. in the dog house: _____

   _____

2. That's the way the ball bounces: _____

   _____

3. bent out of shape: _____

    _____

4. Hold your horses: _____

    _____

5. Read between the lines: _____

    _____

6. all fired up: _____

    _____

7. All the world's a stage. (Shakespeare): _____

    _____

8. May those who sow in tears reap with shouts of joy. (Psalm 126:5): _____

    _____

9. Husbands are like fires. They go out when unattended. (Zsa Zsa Gabor):

    _____

10. a limp tail hanging like a shoelace from its mouth (Marianne Moore):

    _____

◇ WRITING JOURNAL ENTRY

Using everything you have learned so far, revise your essay on the media.

Edit: Documenting Sources

Frequently it is useful and often necessary to quote other sources in your essays. When you do, identify your source, even if you are summarizing and not quoting directly. Never just stick in a quotation because you think it fits what you are saying. Always lead in to the quote, such as

In her book *Unplugging the Plug-In Drug*, Marie Winn says . . .

According to Winn . . .

Linda Ellerbee states that . . .

Kropp is correct when he says . . .

Also, make certain that you follow an acceptable documentation form. The following information, based on the Modern Language Association's recommendations, is required of formal essays.

Bibliographies

If you are using information from another source in your paper, attach a bibliographical page at the end that contains an alphabetical list of all the material you borrowed or paraphrased. What follows is an explanation of some common sources. Consult the *MLA Handbook for Writers of Research Papers* if you need information not explained here. Notice the order, the punctuation, and the spacing required. The names of book publishers can be shortened to one or two identifying words, that is, Holt, Rinehart & Winston = Holt.

Listing books:

   Ellerbee, Linda. *And So It Goes.* New York: Putnam's, 1986.

Note: If your typewriter or computer cannot italicize book or magazine titles, underline them:

   Ellerbee, Linda. <u>And So It Goes</u>. New York: Putnam's, 1986.

   Singer, Dorothy and Jerome L., and Diane Zukerman. *Teaching Television—How to Use Your Child's Advantage.* New York: Dial, 1981.

Listing articles in academic journals:

   Joffe, B. H. "Commercial Television Can Be Used for Teaching." *Education Digest* X(1986): 444–449.

   Dietz, W. H., and S. L. Gortmaker. "Do We Fatten Our Children at The Television Set?" *Pediatrics* 75 (1985): 403–445.

Listing articles in popular magazines:

   Greenfield, Meg. "The Media Made Me Do It." *Newsweek* 7 April 1985: 68.

   "The Top 12 Censored Stories of 1987." *Utne Reader* Sept./Oct. 1988: 84–91.

Listing articles in newspapers:

   Kropp, Arthur J. "Let's Put an End to Mediocre Textbooks." *Houston Post* 2 May 1987: A4.

Citing Sources

At the end of the information you are quoting or summarizing, identify the page number of your source material. For instance, notice that in the following example, the author and book title serve as a lead-in to the quotation, with the page number in parentheses at the end.

   In *Unplugging the Plug-In Drug*, Marie Winn argues that "great numbers of parents today see television as a way to make child-rearing less burdensome" (7).

If readers want to know the publisher and date of publication of the book, they can look at the bibliography for full source information.

   If you are citing an author with two sources or more listed in the bibliography, and not using the book title in your lead-in because it has been mentioned before, you add to the page number the first or second word of the book to which you are referring. Marie Winn, for instance, has written *The Plug-In Drug* and *Unplugging the Plug-In Drug*. If both texts appeared on the bibliography, the preceding example would be written like this:

> Winn argues that "great numbers of parents today see television as a way to make child-rearing less burdensome" (*Unplugging* 7).

Notice the punctuation in the example.

Sometimes information is summarized or paraphrased in your own writing. In that case, include the author and page number at the end of the statement:

> The primary danger of the television screen lies not so much in the behavior it produces as in the behavior it prevents (Bronfenbrenner 32).

This citation lets readers know that the information is taken from page 32 of a work by someone named Bronfenbrenner. For full citation, readers can look at the bibliography at the end of the paper.

◆ TEXTBOOK ENTRY

Make correct documentation citings for the following works. Underline book and magazine titles.

1. *What to Do After You Turn Off the TV* by Frances Moore Lappe, published in 1986 by Ballantine Books in New York.

    _____

    _____

2. *The Daily Herald*, July 18, 1985, Tom Valeo's "Television and Kids: Breaking the Habit," E-3.

    _____

    _____

3. Rob Lamp's "The World of 'Dark Rock,' " February 17, 1986, in *The New American*, pages 65–66.

    _____

    _____

4. November 1984, "30 Minute Exposure," *Psychology Today*, Sandra J. Ball-Rokeach, Milton Rokeach, and Joel Grube.

    _____

    _____

◆ WRITING JOURNAL ENTRY

Return to the last draft of your essay on the media. Rewrite and edit by using the following checklist:

_____ 1. Have I fully developed and supported my thesis?
_____ 2. Have I fully developed and supported each paragraph?
_____ 3. Have I used transitional devices to help my reader move from one point to the next?
_____ 4. Have I eliminated sentence fragments, run-ons, comma splices, misplaced modifiers, dangling modifiers, and faulty parallelism?
_____ 5. Have I checked for subject-verb agreement?
_____ 6. Have I checked for fallacious thinking or reasoning?
_____ 7. Have I written strong sentences?
_____ 8. Have I checked for proper abbreviations and capitalization?
_____ 9. Have I used descriptive words to strengthen my sentences?
_____ 10. Have I checked for proper punctuation and documentation?

Proofread

Apply the preceding checklist and mark every incorrect item in the following student essay. Compare your findings with those of others in your class.

TV IS A HIDDEN COMPETITOR FOR ALL OTHER ACTIVITIES

The fact that children are likely to choose watching television over having a story read aloud to them, orplaying with a stamp collection, or going out for a walk in the park does not mean that watching televison is actually more entertaining or gratifying than any of these activities It does mean, however, that watching television is easier.

In most families, television is always there as an easy and safe competitor. With 98 % of American homes containing one or more TV set, it's easy to see why (Singer, page 45). When another activity is proposed, it had better be really special, otherwise it is in danger of being rejected. The parents who have unsuccessfully proposed a game or a story end up feeling rejected as well, they are unaware that television is still affecting their childrens' enjoyment of other activities, even when the set is off.

It is for this reason that one of the most important Don'ts suggested by Jim Trelease in his valuable guide The Read Aloud Handbook is the following

> Don't try to compete with television. If you say, "Which do you want, a story or TV?" they will usually choose the latter. That is like saying to a 9-year-old "Which do you want, vegetables or a donut?" Since *you* are the adult, *you* choose. "The television goes off at eight-thirty in this house. If you want a story before bed, that's fine. If not, that's fine too. But no television after eight-thirty." But don't let books appear to be depriving children of viewing time. (The Read Aloud Handbook 9)

Adapted from Marie Winn, *Unplugging the Plug-In Drug.* (New York: Penguin, 1987), pp. 8–9.

Return now to your own essay, and when you have proofread it the best you can, turn it in.

UNIT 9

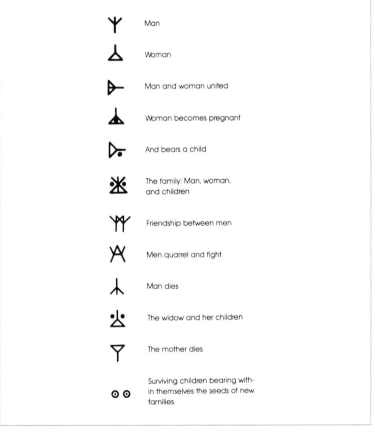

Ψ	Man
⅄	Woman
▷	Man and woman united
⚇	Woman becomes pregnant
▷•	And bears a child
✻	The family: Man, woman, and children
ΨΨ	Friendship between men
Ж	Men quarrel and fight
人	Man dies
•⅄•	The widow and her children
Υ	The mother dies
⊙ ⊙	Surviving children bearing within themselves the seeds of new families

Marriage is a great institution, but I'm not ready for an institution yet.

Mae West

THINK . . .

about relationships, marriage, and family.

◇ WRITING JOURNAL ENTRY

Pretend you are bringing home someone you care about. Prepare that person by describing how each member of your family will behave.

◇ TEXTBOOK ENTRY

Think about the following questions and write your answers in the spaces provided.

1.   Describe your ideal mate and decide whether or not such a person exists.

_____

_____

_____

2.   List at least six words or phrases that you feel are keys to a good marriage or relationship (i.e., love, trust, sex, fidelity, etc.).

_____

_____

_____

3.   Explain why you feel that marriage is or is not an important social institution.

_____

_____

_____

4.   Define what you think is meant by a "family unit." _____

_____

_____

_____

5. For what reasons do you think divorce is justified. _____

_____

_____

_____

Think about each of the following statements. Then write your personal reactions, feelings, or thoughts in the spaces provided.

A. Three out of four people say that their number one reason for choosing their mate is "our ability to laugh and have fun together." Significantly, these people have happier and more sexually satisfying marriages than other couples. Fifty-five percent of those surveyed consider "a sense of humor very important" to marital happiness. They rate it ahead of "sex," which only 32 percent call "very important." (Claire Safran, "Why More People Are Making Better Marriages." *Parade* 28 Apr. 1985: 2)

_____

_____

_____

B. The word *family,* when narrowed down to its nucleus, evokes primal feelings. The college-age students who watch afternoon reruns of "Ozzie and Harriet" don't just tune in for its camp humor. There is also a hunger for an entry into those

---

THINK ABOUT IT . . .

In his classic book *The Art of Loving,* Erich Fromm defines love as an active power that breaks through the walls that separate people from each other. In love we find the paradox of two beings becoming one yet remaining two. Like the Greeks, Fromm discusses several kinds of love, including brotherly and maternal love. Brotherly love is characterized by friendship and companionship with affection. Maternal love is characterized by an unselfish interest in your partner and a placing of yourself second to your partner's needs. For Fromm mature love includes attachment plus sexual response. More importantly it includes the four basic elements necessary to any intimate relationship: care, responsibility, respect, and knowledge. People who share all of the elements of mature love are pair-bonded. The relationship is reciprocal. Fromm goes on to suggest that a person's need to love and be loved in this full sense arises from our feelings of separateness and aloneness. Love helps us escape these feelings and gain a feeling of unitedness.

Frank Cox, *Human Intimacy.* St. Paul: West, 1987. 65.

dated vignettes. To be mom and dad and us kids for a half-hour. (Ellen Goodman, "Something Shared, Something Missing." *Los Angeles Times* 26 Jan. 1988: II, 7)

_____

_____

_____

C.   In addition to the growing number of single people through divorce, we also have other dramatic changes in the family unit. Many heterosexual single adults have been permitted to adopt children and set up single-parent families. Some women have deliberately chosen to bear children out of wedlock and raise them alone. Gay men and women have petitioned the courts for the right to marry each other and to adopt children. Increasing numbers of married couples are choosing to remain childless. Clearly, attitudes have changed a great deal in just three decades. (George Gallup, Jr., "The Faltering Family," *Forecast 2000*. New York: Morrow, 1984)

_____

_____

_____

READ . . .

about the effects of changing social relationships.

It wasn't too long ago that the typical American family was depicted as a man and a woman, married to each other, with two children. The man went off to work while the mother stayed home and took care of the house and children. And, of course, they all lived happily ever after.

It's become increasingly obvious that this is no longer the case, if it ever was. Some social scientists claim that the "traditional" family structure as we often think of it existed only in our minds. Some researchers are predicting that the traditional family as we know it will fade in the future. Others believe that the changes in family life-style represent a decline in America's morals and soon a decline of the country as a world power. The selection you are about to read, by the author of *Alone in America: The Search for Companionship*, shows a different effect that is occurring because of these changes in relationships and family life-style.

Before reading closely, take a moment to read the title, the first paragraph, and the three subheadings. Then answer the following questions.

1. What is the subject of this reading selection?

    _____

2. What questions do the subheadings raise that you want answered?

    _____

    _____

3. What do you think you might learn from reading this essay?

    _____

    _____

4. The meaning an author intends may be lost if the reader does not understand the author's use of certain words and phrases. Make sure that you understand the following words before you read. The number after the word refers to the paragraph number where the word appears.
    a. *sublimate* (2) = hide or ignore in our subconscious
    b. *permeates* (3) = spread throughout; seemingly everywhere
    c. *vulnerable* (3) = exposed or open to being hurt
    d. *privitized* (5) = made private; secluded; alone
    e. *vestige of the past* (8) = a sign or representation of something that exists no more
    f. *paradoxically* (10) = seemingly to be contradictory, yet true

Now carefully read the selection, practicing note-taking and marking skills.

LONELINESS AS AN AMERICAN EPIDEMIC

Louise Bernikow

1   Everyone goes through a period of loneliness, but now too many people are lonely too much of the time. Many of them are among the growing ranks of those who live alone, though living by yourself doesn't necessarily mean you are lonely any more than living with others means that you have a sense of connectedness. Many people who are married have a horrendous time feeling connected to anything.

2   It's the women who talk about this more easily. Lots of men I tried to interview said they were not lonely. Men seem to have better defenses or were able to sublimate the feeling. They seem to deny loneliness much more easily than women. They are more likely to lose themselves in work or get absorbed with possessions. One guy kept buying presents for his motorcycle after his divorce as though it had become his wife.

"Selling Friendship"

3   Loneliness permeates the culture. Look at the ads. New York Telephone says: "Don't be lonely, pick up the phone." AT&T's recent ad campaign urged people to "reach out and touch someone." In beer ads people don't drink by themselves; they're with others. The ads are not selling alcohol; they're selling friendship. Sellers of goods are increasingly aware of how vulnerable we are and how loneliness is a button to be pushed to make people buy.

4   Why is all of this happening? For one thing, there are huge numbers of people who lived through the 1960s and had a feeling of belonging to something larger than themselves, whether the antiwar, women's or civil-rights movements or the youth culture. A lot of the people I interviewed who are now 40 miss that feeling.

5   American life has become privatized. People are wrapped up in selfish, individual pursuits of material goods. We're not often encouraged to value people.

6   We also live in a world where it's not so clear what others are for any more. The television, the computer, the bank-teller machine allow us to do without others what we used to have to do with them. There are great numbers of people who have VCR's, stay home and watch a movie on TV instead of being, in a sense, forced to go to a movie theater where they would be around others. All the advances in our life may not cause isolation, but they have made it more possible to live that way.

Fantasies of Mom, Pop, Dick and Jane

7   In a broader sense, loneliness is the product of unabsorbed changes in society. When it comes to family life, we still have fantasies of Mom, Pop, Dick, Jane, and Spot. Television promotes that image. People still think it's the norm when it isn't. But they long for it, and feel lonely if they don't have it. The relationship between the sexes is another area in which we have not adjusted to change. Relationships used to be so simple. Everybody knew what to expect; they hooked up and settled down. Today, many men don't really know how to deal with women and vice versa. Increasingly, women do not need to be married just for economic reasons. Some people assume that these single women are doomed to lonely and loveless lives. But, in fact, they seem often to have a great deal of intimacy and friendship in their lives without being married.

8   Lifetime employment with one company is also a vestige of the past. All the mergers and takeovers have made what used to be a more secure life much more unstable. You can't make a relationship in the office when you think you're going to be out on your ear the next day. Of all the places I visited, the area south of Pittsburgh was where people seemed most lonely. The steel mills were the connecting point in their lives, and they lost that. Many retreated into horrendous isolation. They stayed home, watched TV, drank beer and beat their wives. Family life fell apart under the stress.

Senior Citizens as Pioneers

9   Social scientists say older men living alone are most at risk of dying from loneliness. But that may be a generational problem. These are men who depended on women for life support. When you talk to them, you realize they don't know how to cook for themselves; their wives made dentist appointments and handled social life. So I'm not sure that they're at risk only because of their age. It may well be that their social habits are the problem. Perhaps younger generations of men will behave differently and be much less at risk when they age.

10   Paradoxically, while there are special problems among older men, the real
pioneering activity in dealing with loneliness is going on among senior citizens. Many
of them recognize that loneliness can kill you, so they try to create companionship
through collective housing or by building their own institutions. In Miami Beach, for
example, there's a senior citizens' orchestra. The members have said to me, "This
orchestra keeps me alive." It provides a community.

11   Maybe that's what is meant to fill the gap, not a boyfriend or a girlfriend or even
making peace with being alone, but creating a community. The least lonely people I
met have done this. They also have strong friendships. They are connected to people
not exactly like themselves. They also have physical and emotional intimacy and a feeling of membership in something bigger than themselves.

cathy®   **by Cathy Guisewite**

REACT . . .

to the reading selection.

◇ WRITING JOURNAL ENTRY

Pick out one thing from the reading selection that struck you as true, struck you
as false, or created a new awareness, and write about it in your journal.

◇ TEXTBOOK ENTRY

In the spaces provided, answer the following questions. Refer to the reading
selection when necessary.

A. Understanding the Content

1. What does Bernikow mean by her title? _____

   _____

   _____

   _____

2. According to the author, are more women lonely than men? Explain.

   _____

   _____

   _____

3. Bernikow states, "Loneliness permeates the culture." What examples does she offer to support this claim? _____

   _____

   _____

   _____

4. What does the author mean when she says we still have fantasies when it comes to family life? _____

   _____

   _____

   _____

5. How do relationships differ today from what they were, according to Bernikow? _____

   _____

   _____

   _____

6. Based on what older people have discovered, what does Bernikow think may "fill the gap" of loneliness? _____

   _____

   _____

   _____

B. Noticing Structure and Style

7. How well does Bernikow support paragraph 5? Explain. _____
_____
_____

8. Based on the way the essay is structured, how helpful are the three headings? _____
_____
_____
_____

9. How well does the author support her title? Explain. _____
_____
_____
_____

FEIFFER®

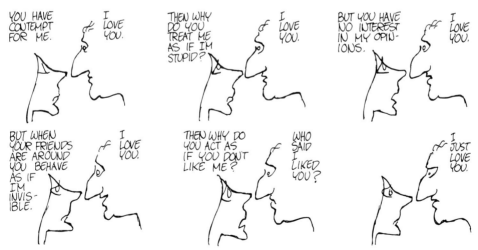

PLAN . . .

an essay on some aspect of relationships, marriage, or family.

STEP 1: Selecting and Exploring a Topic

In previous units you have been shown how to use brainstorming, freewriting, clustering, PMIs, and reacting to what you read by asking questions. Use any of these methods to help you select and explore a topic for an essay on some aspect of relationships, marriage, or family.

◇ WRITING JOURNAL ENTRY

If you don't already have an idea for an essay, look over the following list. In your journal, explore one of these or an idea of your own.

Try brainstorming, freewriting, or clustering on

1. friendship	6. co-workers	11. day care
2. togetherness	7. classmates	12. sex roles
3. dating	8. divorce	13. single
4. relatives	9. parenting	14. intimacy
5. marriage	10. partners	15. cohabitation

Or do a PMI on

1. High schools should require students to take a course on how to raise a family.
2. All prospective parents should be required by law to attend monthly workshops on child development, family dynamics, and communication skills.
3. All employers should provide paid paternal leave for fathers.
4. Marriage and divorce should not be legal matters.
5. For the good of global relations, all governments should participate in an exchange program wherein 18-year-olds are required to live with a family of another country for one year.

Or react to and question the following statements:

1. The family performs four important functions. First, it produces and socializes children. Second, it acts as a unit of economic cooperation. Third, it assigns status and social roles to individuals. Fourth, it provides

a source of intimate relationships. Technology, industrialization, mobility, and other factors are altering the way the family performs its functions. (Bryon Strong and Christine DeVault, *The Marriage and Family Experience*. St. Paul: West, 1986. 5–6)

2. We can't depend on having the same neighbors for any length of time, the same school friends, the same workmates or the same employer. As a result, people are more frequently assessed by others simply on the basis of their appearance. . . . (Ellen Berschied, "Beautiful People: An Unfair Advantage in Life." *U.S. News & World Report* 1 Nov. 1982)

3. Country-loving woman, 32, seeks caring relationships with nurturing men. Am pretty, sensual, creative, funny, independent and romantic. I value honesty, kindness and physical and emotional intimacy. Am content to enjoy several relationships but a special someone who shares my dreams of family life in the country could change all that! (Classified ad in the *Santa Barbara Independent*)

STEP 2: Writing a Working Thesis

A working thesis, remember, is just a starting point, a statement about your subject that you think you'd like to prove or develop. It may not be your final thesis statement, but it serves as a guide to help you organize the information you have gained from exploring the topic through freewriting, brainstorming, clustering, or whatever method you've used.

Your working thesis should contain at least one key word that indicates the thrust of your viewpoint, as in the following thesis statements:

Although we hear that the modern family has lost some of its traditional functions, it has *gained some new ones.*

Research suggests that there are *six major qualities* shared by a strong, healthy family.

Successful communication is the *cornerstone of a good relationship.*

Maintaining a friendship is *not always easy.*

The italicized words in each of the preceding thesis statements require support and development. Look for the key words in your working thesis.

◆ TEXTBOOK ENTRY

When you have arrived at a working thesis for an essay on relationships, marriage, or family, write it in the following space for future use.

Working thesis: _____

_____

_____

_____

STEP 3: Analyzing and Organizing Your Ideas

Look carefully at the key words in your working thesis. Make certain that you have enough information to support and develop them. Organize your ideas into some type of outline that you can follow for a first draft. When you have finished, go to the next section.

"I've called the family together to announce that, because of inflation, I'm going to have to let two of you go."

CARTOON © 1974 THE NEW YORKER AND JOSEPH FARRIS

WRITE . . .
a first draft for an essay on some aspect of relationships, marriage, and family.

The Nutshell Statement

The probable thesis of my essay is _____

_____

_____

My purpose is _____

_____

_____

The audience is _____

_____

I will support my thesis by _____

_____

_____

_____

_____

Writing Concluding Paragraphs

A concluding paragraph should be a strong one that reaffirms what you have been saying by summarizing what has been said, drawing a conclusion, or stirring the reader into thinking about the subject and thesis. As with introductory paragraphs, there is no one way to do this, but here are some methods that work effectively:

1. Leave the reader with a question that calls attention to your point.
2. Use a quotation or anecdote that is relative to and supports your thesis.
3. Summarize your main points without repeating what has already been said.
4. Stress the need for awareness, change, or concern for the topic.
5. Make conclusions based on the information presented.

Which approach to use will depend on what seems a natural way to end what you have been writing. Read the following concluding paragraphs to understand the methods just mentioned.

1. *Leave the reader with a question that calls attention to your point.* This method can be used to jar or stimulate the reader into thoughtful action. Notice how questions are used to conclude an essay on marital partner awareness training:

> Partner awareness involves knowing accurately what your partner is experiencing in terms of his or her own self-awareness. How does this behavior affect my partner? Is my partner happy, sad, or indifferent? How can I best communicate with my partner? What does my partner think or feel about this? Answering such questions accurately is the goal of partner awareness training. (S. Miller et al., "Recent Progress in Marital Awareness Communications." *The Family Coordinator* 24 Apr. 1975: 756)

By leaving the reader with these questions, the author summarizes the goal of partner awareness training.

2. *Use a quotation or anecdote that is relative to and supports your thesis.* If you know an anecdote or a quotation from a source that supports your point of view, it is often a good way to end an essay. It shows that others agree with you. Notice how the following concluding paragraph uses a line from a song and a quotation from the husband of a successful marriage to help conclude the author's point that we must look for positive aspects in our life partners:

> An old song from the 1940s suggests "accentuate the positive, eliminate the negative." Since few of us can be a 100 percent perfect spouse to our mate, expecting perfection can only lead to disappointment. Perhaps an attitude of accentuating the positive is best found in a comment made by one of the persons interviewed in the Lauer study of successful marriages. A husband of twenty-four years said, "She isn't perfect but I don't worry about her weak points, which are very few. Her strong points overcome them too much." (Frank Cox, *Human Intimacy.* 4th ed. St. Paul: West, 1987)

3. *Summarize your main points without repeating what has already been said.* By using this method, you leave your readers with a clear-cut statement of your supporting points. However, be careful when you use this method. If in the body of the essay, the main ideas are clearly stated in a "first, second, third" fashion, this method would not be appropriate. In the following example, notice how the three main points of an essay on good communication in a relationship are summarized:

> Thus, three basic conditions must be met before good communication can be assured. First, there must be a commitment to communicate. Both parties must want to communicate with one another. Second, the partners must be oriented to growth and to improving the relationship. Each must be willing to accept the possibility of change. Third, neither partner must try to coerce the other with communications. Communication should not be so aversive and attacking as to cause a partner to be defensive or to withdraw. (Bryan Strong and Christine DeVault, *The Marriage and Family Experience.* St. Paul: West, 1986)

4. *Stress the need for awareness, change, or concern for the topic.* To get readers to react to your proposal or views, you may want to state how important it is for readers to be aware of or concerned with your topic and viewpoint. Here is the conclusion of an essay that deals with the importance of learning to communicate properly in intimate relationships:

> It seems clear that building a satisfying intimate relationship is a difficult and complex task. Many factors will influence the success of such relationships. Certainly if we prepare ourselves to meet the problems so often found in intimate relationships of all kinds and learn the skills of open communication and problem solving before hostilities and inability to communicate make problem solving more difficult, we stand a better chance of maintaining and fulfilling intimate relationships. (Frank Cox, *Human Intimacy.* 4th ed. St. Paul: West, 1987)

5. *Make conclusions based on the information presented.* Depending on what has already been said, you may want to base a prediction or a conclusion on the information you've presented. In the following example, the author draws a conclusion based on research presented in the essay:

> The final remarriage myth is a watered-down version of the divorce myth. Although the effects of parental remarriage on children are typically not perceived as negative as are the effects of parental divorce on children, there is clearly a widespread belief in our society that all stepchildren have a difficult time. . . . The empirical research on stepchildren, however, does not support the view that parental remarriage has harmful effects on children. (Glen Norval, "The Psychological Well-Being of Children of Divorce." *Journal of Marriage and the Family* 47 (Aug. 1983): 641)

The preceding methods for developing paragraphs should not be considered the only approaches. But they can serve as models until you feel comfortable with appropriate methods of your own.

◇ TEXTBOOK ENTRY

Read the following concluding paragraphs. In the blanks provided, write what methods you feel are being used. You may see more than one method used in some paragraphs.

A.   The key goal of the Friends of Families strategy would be to make it clear that we all share problems in family life, that we need to share our stories about what is happening in our families, and that we need to be aware of the ways that the economic and political order shapes our personal lives. (*Surplus Powerlessness*, Institute for Labor and Mental Health, 1986.)

_____

_____

B.   "Even in a positive office family, people can get stereotyped," concludes Levine-Shneidman. "Those who are on top in a positive family may be happy, but those on the bottom of the heap are not. There is a pressure to conform to roles, and the group does not allow for much individuality. Even those on top have an image to keep up, and that can be stultifying." (Jean Callahan, "Our 9 to 5 Family." *The Boston Globe* 28 Aug. 1987)

_____

_____

C.   Call it a clan, call it a network, call it a tribe, call it a family. Whatever you call it, whoever you are, you need one. You need one because you are human. You didn't come from nowhere. Before you, around you, and presumably after you, too, there are others. Some of these others must matter. They must matter a lot to you and, if you are very lucky, to one another. Their welfare must be nearly as important to you as your own. Even if you live alone, even if your solitude is elected and ebullient, you still cannot do without a clan or a tribe. (Jane Howard, *Families.* New York: Simon, 1978)

_____

_____

D.   The problem is that we have not even begun to admit how much fun bullying is. C.S. Lewis writes of the elaborate brilliance of psychological abuse in his essay "The Inner Ring." He understood that it is exhilarating to exclude someone from a club, to put people down—and best of all, to do it gravely, civilly, and publicly. . . . So let's ask the helping professions to focus their wonderful ingenuity on the bullying instinct in us all, and the bullying traditions of our groupings. And let's ask them: When shall we start teaching children about bullying? (Carol Bly, "Of Bullies and Mascots: Playing Family Roles." *Utne Reader* May/June 1988: 72)

_____

_____

E.   Self-actualizing people essentially are people who feel comfortable about themselves and others. They are able to meet most of the demands of life in a realistic fashion. They tend to use their past experiences and ideas about their future to enhance the present rather than to escape from it. They are not prisoners of their past but are free to use it to improve the present. Intimacy includes the commitment to help each other realize to the fullest possible degree all of the human potential inherent in each individual family member. Granted this is a difficult and at times impossible task, yet it is a worthy goal toward which to strive. (Frank Cox, *Human Intimacy.* 4th ed. St. Paul: West, 1987)

_____

_____

Practice in Concluding Paragraphs

If you or your instructor feel you need more practice in writing concluding paragraphs, go to page 284.

◆ WRITING JOURNAL ENTRY

Look over the nutshell statement and organizational plan on relationships, marriage, or family that you wrote earlier. Write a first draft based on your notes. Try to write a strong concluding paragraph that fits the point of your essay.

REWRITE . . .
your first drafts.

You should now have a working draft of an essay on some aspect of relationships, marriage, or family. Make sure that you have looked over your paper for the following:

_____ 1. Does your opening paragraph use a method that draws the interest of your reader?
_____ 2. Did you write about a topic you know and have feeling for?
_____ 3. Did you avoid the obvious and take a fresh approach to your topic?
_____ 4. Did you write a strong concluding paragraph that fits the point of your essay?

If you are satisfied with these points, go to the next revision strategy.

Revise for Proper Tone and Attitude

When you speak, you use a tone of voice that lets others know if you're feeling angry, happy, sad, bored, or whatever. When you write, the words you select and the way you phrase them also create a tone. If you are careless in wording and phrasing, you might convey the wrong tone to the reader. If the tone of an essay is inconsistent, it can confuse the reader about your true attitude toward the topic. The reader may think your attitude is phony, absurd, condescending, or stuffy simply because you failed to provide a proper or consistent tone.

Theodore Cheney, in *Getting the Words Right*, explains the importance of tone and attitude well:

> Beginning writers not yet in command of their diction will sometimes set the wrong tone early in a piece. In the very first sentence they may establish (unintentionally and inappropriately) an informal tone for what is going to be a serious piece: "The nurse came in with a cheerful 'Time for our shot' and stabbed him in the butt." Later in the piece, we find that the patient is a fine young man who dies

in his hospital bed. The initial lighthearted tone was established because the writer didn't stop to think that *butt* is a very informal word and one frequently used in jokes. The misled reader does not discover that the intended tone is one of serious concern until he has read a number of subsequent paragraphs. The reader has a right to be upset with the writer for such lack of sensitivity. (Cincinnati: Writer's Digest Books, 1983. 39)

Cheney's point should serve as a revision strategy reminder. Check your essay's wording, or better yet, have someone else read and detect your tone. If you are being serious, make certain your tone reflects seriousness. If you intend to be sarcastic, make certain your tone reflects that attitude.

A good tone is one that is unaffected, not put on. Don't try to write like someone you are not. The more you write, the more you will develop your own style. Given the same topic, each writer will find his or her way to express his or her views. The best way is your way—provided, of course, you have applied everything you have learned so far.

Edit

The previous units have given you numerous items to look for when editing. This is a good time to review all units for the editing advice offered in each one. When you have finished reviewing, rewrite and edit by using the following checklist:

_____ 1. Have I fully developed and supported my thesis?
_____ 2. Have I fully developed and supported each paragraph?
_____ 3. Have I used transitional devices to help my reader move from one point to the next?
_____ 4. Have I eliminated sentence fragments, run-ons, comma splices, misplaced modifiers, dangling modifiers, and faulty parallelism?
_____ 5. Have I checked for subject-verb agreement?
_____ 6. Have I checked for fallacious thinking or reasoning?
_____ 7. Have I written strong sentences?
_____ 8. Have I checked for proper abbreviations and capitalization?
_____ 9. Have I used descriptive words to strengthen my sentences?
_____ 10. Have I checked for proper punctuation and documentation?
_____ 11. Have I checked for proper and consistent tone?

Proofread

Apply the preceding checklist above and mark every incorrect item in the following student essay. Compare your findings with those of others in your class.

THE INGREDIENTS FOR A HEALTHY FAMILY

Certainly the first, and perhaps the most important, relation-ships we encounter are those within our family. Relationships with parents, siblings, and other close relatives are so strong that they effect us for our entire lives. While the media may often portray co-called "ideal families" with incredibly understanding parents, its doubtful such families exist. Some families are no doubt happier and get along better than others, but it's probably safe to bet that all families have their problems. But what is it that makes a "good family" good? What would all families need in order to reach a real "ideal" family?

I think my family comes close to being "ideal." After examining us as a unit, I think I have discovered the ingredients that makes us so special and that other family's should imitate: (1) friendliness to each other as well as outsiders, (2) holiday rituals, (3) a display of affection, (4) a connection to family history, and (5) a sense of home.

We are very friendly in my family. Sure, we have arguments and sometimes I yell to my sister that I hate her, but that passes. In fact, thats that nice part about it. We can get angry and let off steam, but when we cool down we are aware that we really care about and love each other. But more importantly, its the little things, like saying "Good morning" to each other, or asking each other how things are going. We are also friendly to others when they come into our home, we try to make every one feel comfortable.

We are also very affectionate. We have gotten into the habit of hugging and kissing each other goodbye in the morning. Nothing dramatic, just a nice gesture of our affection. I used to think it was silly, but now that I'm older I can see that it is important to display our affection.

ANother thing that makes our family strong are our holiday rituals. Especially Christmas. Ever since I can remember, we have celebrated Christmas the same way. It's become a tradtion for my dad and I to get the tree two days before Christmas. Then on Christmas eve we all decorate the tree together. Most of the ornaments are ones that we've had since my sister and I were kids. We sing songs and exchange gifts that night. The we have a special wine concoction my mother has always made.

We have moved around alot because of my dads job, but no matter where we go there is always a since of home. My mom always tries to place the living room furniture in the same position. My mom has had two candle sticks from her young girl days which are always placed on the mantle.

These characteristics make our family a pleasant unit. We can count on one another for support and love we feel good about ourselves. While each one of us are individuals, we have a strong sense of "we." I'm thankful for these traits, they are going to help me when I start to raise a family of my own.

Return now to your own essay, and when you have proofread it the best you can, turn it in.

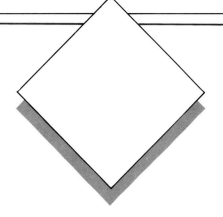

PRACTICES IN . . .

◆ PRACTICES IN WRITING INTRODUCTORY PARAGRAPHS

Practice 1.   Read the introductory paragraphs below, and in the spaces provided after each, write which one of the following six methods for writing opening paragraphs is used and what you would expect the topic and the thesis of the essay to be.

Method 1. The use of question(s)
Method 2. The use of an anecdote
Method 3. The use of quotation
Method 4. The brief overview
Method 5. The stressing of importance
Method 6. The use of various combinations

A.   Is love an art? Then it requires knowledge and effort. Or is love a pleasant sensation, which to experience is a matter of chance, something one "falls into" if one is lucky? Even though the majority of people believe the latter, we believe it is the former.

Paragraph method used: _____

Topic of essay: _____

Probable thesis: _____

B.   Each person has a mental picture of what the "world out there" is like. For centuries, this picture was shaped by personal experiences and education. These two factors are still present in shaping mental pictures, but there is a third force that assumes an ever increasing importance. Today, the mass media play a major role in teaching people what the world is like.

Paragraph method used: _____

Topic of essay: _____

Probable thesis: _____

C.   There is no issue more important than the avoidance of nuclear war. Whatever your interests, passions or goals, they and you are threatened fundamentally by the prospect of nuclear war. We have achieved the capability for the certain destruction of our civilization and perhaps of our species as well. (Carl Sagan, "To Preserve a World Graced by Life.")

Paragraph method used: _____

Topic of essay: _____

Probable thesis: _____

D.   I never learned hate at home, or shame. I had to go to school for that. I was about seven years old when I got my first big lesson. I was in love with a little girl named Helene Tucker, a light-complexioned little girl with pigtails and nice manners. She was always clean and she was smart in school. I think I went to school mostly to look at her. I brushed my hair and even got me a little handkerchief. It was a lady's handkerchief, but I didn't want Helene to see me wipe my nose on my hand. . . . (Dick Gregory, "Shame," *nigger.* New York: Dutton, 1964)

Paragraph method used: _____

Topic of essay: _____

Possible thesis: _____

E.   There are two classes of people in the world, observed Robert Benchley, "those who constantly divide the people of the world into two classes, and those who do not." Half of those who divide quote Benchley and his fellow aphorists. The other half prefer proverbs. And why not? The aphorism is a personal observation inflated into a universal truth. . . . A proverb is anonymous human history compressed to the size of a seed. . . . (Stefan Kanfer, "Proverbs or Aphorisms?" *Time* 11 July 1983)

Paragraph method used: _____

Topic of essay: _____

Probable thesis: _____

F.   It is generally agreed that the American educational system is in deep trouble. Everyone is aware of the horrible facts: school systems are running out of money, teachers can't spell. Most of us know, or think we know, who is to blame: liberal courts, spineless school boards, government regulations. It is easy to select a villain. But possibly the problem lies not so much in our institutions as in our attitudes. It is sad that although most of us profess to believe in education, we place no value on intellectual activity. (Carolyn Kane, "Thinking: A Neglected Art." *Newsweek* 14 Dec. 1981)

Paragraph method used: _____

Topic of essay: _____

Probable thesis: _____

G.   Gail Tietjin was eighteen when the accident happened. Her nineteen-year-old boyfriend was driving her home from a dinner party. He was drunk. About 1:30 A.M. that July morning in 1982, he drove the car around a curve and into a tree. It was two hours before the crash was discovered. Police thought Gail was dead until they heard a gurgle in her throat. (John Lempesis, "Murder in a Bottle." *Reader's Digest* Apr. 1982)

Paragraph method used: _____

Topic of essay: _____

Probable thesis: _____

H.   More and more people think the unthinkable. The possibility that human life will be extinguished by a full-scale nuclear war is no longer seen as imaginary but as *real*. . . . The more nuclear weapons are made, the more difficult it is to prevent their deliberate or accidental use. The more suspicious the governments of superpowers grow of each other, the greater the chances of desperate recourse to a first strike. Given this volatile situation, it is only realistic to fear the worst. (Konstantin Kolenda, "Under the Mushroom Cloud." *The Humanist* Jan./Feb. 1983)

Paragraph method used: _____

Topic of essay: _____

Probable thesis: _____

Practice 2. In the spaces given, explain what is wrong with the following opening or partial paragraphs.

A. Anyone who bases his daily actions on the position and movement of the stars must not be very bright. I'm no expert on the subject, but I read a book on astrology and I think it's a fraud.

_____

_____

B. In my essay, I would like to tell you about my nutrition class. It is very interesting and I like it.

_____

_____

C.   JIM THORPE: ALL-AMERICAN

This was the best book I ever read. It was about sports, and I like sports; so the book was very interesting to me. I've always been active in sports.

_____

_____

D. Jerry is a good friend. He is charming, intelligent, and never seems to get angry. His favorite food is cheese. Tall girls always seem to be attracted to him even though he is short. I met him when we were in the army.

_____

_____

E. The point of my essay will be to discuss the following points in more detail. One, I will. . . .

_____

_____

Practice 3. Rewrite the introductory paragraphs for any two essays in this book. Turn them in to your instructor.

◇ PRACTICES IN USING ILLUSTRATION AND EXAMPLE

Practice 1.   Circle the key words in the topic sentences that follow. Then fill in the blanks, using the topic sentence as your guide. Don't be afraid to use exaggeration or humor. There are no "right" answers.

A.   Our wedding was different from most. For example, _____

_____

Also, we _____

_____

Then, unlike most weddings, _____

_____

_____

B.   College is (not) exactly as I thought it would be. For instance, _____

_____

_____

Plus, _____

_____

In addition, _____

_____

_____

Practice 2.   Circle the key words in the topic sentences that follow. Then place a checkmark in front of the ones that require illustrations or examples to support them.

_____ 1. The audience in the last movie I saw really irritated me.
_____ 2. There were many types of televisions from which to choose.
_____ 3. The image of the male as portrayed on television is quite different from reality.
_____ 4. The most fundamental kind of love, which underlies all types of love, is brotherly love.
_____ 5. His ideas of marriage compared with hers caused the problems.

Practice 3.   Read the following paragraphs. Then outline them in the spaces provided.

A.   Burnout seems to hit everyone sooner or later. Burnout runs through the teaching profession like the Asian flu, possibly because it depresses people to be physically assaulted by those they are trying to civilize. Social workers and nurses burn out from too much association with helplessness. Police officers burn out. Professional athletes burn out. Students burn out. Executives burn out. Housewives burn out. And, as every parent knows, there usually comes a moment in late afternoon when baby burnout occurs—all of its little circuits become overloaded and sleeplessness develops.

Main idea: _____

_____

Supporting points: _____

_____

_____

_____

_____

B.   When she speaks English, the Valley Girl speaks her version of surf talk, including some words, like *barf*, that go back to the 1940s and earlier. *Awesome* means "good"; *bag your face* is an expression of disagreement; *max* means "maximum" or "to score high"; *mondo* is the Valspeak for "very"; *billies* are "dollar bills" or "money"; *for sure* is an expression of either support or scorn; *grody* is "unspeakably awful"; *totally* is "very good"; *tubular*, which originated in surfing to describe a well-curved wave, also means "very good"; *vicious*, which seems to owe something to Black street talk, is "extremely desirable." (Robert McCrum, William Cran, and Robert MacNeil, *The Story of English*. New York: Viking, 1986: 349)

Main idea: _____

_____

Supporting points: _____

_____

_____

_____

_____

C.   In late June, for example, when the sun is supposed to be in the constellation Cancer according to traditional astrology, it is actually one constellation over, in Gemini. Gemini is really Taurus, Taurus is Aries, and so on. Thus most horoscopes that you read in the newspaper or get from astrologers apply to a completely different sign from the one assigned to your birthday. (John Blair, "Astrology's off Target." *Harper's* Apr. 1988)

Main idea: _____

_____

Supporting points: _____

_____

_____

_____

_____

Practice 4.   Read the following paragraph; then rewrite it by changing negatives to positives or vice versa. For instance, the first sentence says, "Television is addictive." You change this to "Television is *not* addictive." It may sound crazy, but try it. See if you can do this and still have the paragraph make sense but now support the opposite view. Rewrite in your journal. (Your instructor may have you do it on another sheet of paper to turn in.)

Television is addictive. For example, when a set breaks, more families rush to have it repaired, often renting one if the repair process takes longer than a day or two. When "nothing's on TV," people experience boredom with their lives, not knowing what to do with themselves. Volunteers who were paid to do without television for a year did well for the first month, spending more time with children, reading, and visiting friends. But then tension, restlessness, and quarreling increased. Once they returned to their TV sets, their lives became normal again.

◇ PRACTICES IN USING COMPARISON AND CONTRAST

Practice 1.   Read the following paragraphs and answer the questions after each.

A.   There is nothing more alone in the universe than man. He is alone because he has the intellectual capacity to know that he is separated by a vast gulf of social memory and experiment from the lives of his animal associates. He has entered into the strange world of history, of social and intellectual change, while his brothers of the field and forest remain subject to the invisible laws of biological evolution. Animals are molded by natural forces they do not comprehend. To their minds there is no past and no future. There is only the everlasting present of a single generation. . . . Man, by contrast, is alone with the knowledge of his history until the day of his death. (Loren Eiseley, "The Long Loneliness: Man and Porpoise," *The Star Thrower.* New York: Quadrangle/Times Books, 1978)

1.   Does this paragraph compare or contrast?

_____

2.   What is being compared or contrasted?

_____

3.   Write your own topic sentence for this paragraph.

_____

_____

_____

B.   But what is the difference between the scientist who observes in his microscope the most minute and unexpected signs of life, and the old farmer who by contrast can barely read or write, who stands in his garden in springtime and contemplates the buds opening on the branches of his trees? Both are confronted with the riddle of life. One may be able to describe life in greater detail, but for both it remains equally inscrutable. . . . (Albert Schweitzer, *Reverence for Life.* New York: Harper & Row, 1969)

1.   What is being compared?

_____

2.   What is being contrasted?

_____

3.   Write your own topic sentence for the paragraph.

_____

_____

_____

C.   We're all wild about the stupid. If you're so dumb that you move your lips when you sign your name, you're probably likeable, pleasant, and always welcome. If you're up to your ass in brains, however, you're probably intimidating, resented, distrusted and your company is about as enjoyable to normals as a plague of toads. . . . Americans may love winners, but we like and identify with the losers, without whose slashing ignorance our own mediocrity would be unbearable. (Robert S. Wieder, "Dumb Is Good." *Penthouse* Feb. 1983)

1.   Write a topic sentence for this paragraph.

_____

_____

2.   What is being compared or contrasted?

_____

_____

D.   In other words, I think kids in the 1920s were very much like kids are in the 1980s—they were getting drunk, and they were flappers, or whatever. Driving fast cars. Many were concerned with death and suicide, just as they are now. The hippies in the '60s were just another variation. MTV gives you a way to see what the kids are thinking and feeling, and I see a certain continuity and sameness. (Joshua Hoffs, "Getting Its Message Across," Calendar Section. *Los Angeles Times* 8 July 1984)

1.   In the space given, outline the paragraph.

_____

_____

_____

_____

2.   What advice would you give the author for rewriting this paragraph?

_____

_____

Practice 2.   Read the following two paragraphs. In the space given, write a paragraph that compares and contrasts these two views of MTV that appeared in the July 8, 1984, *Los Angeles Times*.

View A

   I'm not against MTV in any way. I think it's fascinating, and I don't feel at all moralistic about whether it's good or bad. I'm just impressed with its being a communications medium in today's world that seems to be rivaling and will probably out do print communication. That's not a new concept. MTV is getting its message across to millions of people, and who knows what influence it might have?

View B

   "Burning Down the House" (by Talking Heads) is another tape that disturbs me. They smash doors, they smash windows, they smash heads. That's not scary. That's violent. . . . In "Burning Down the House" the violence is random. I think if someone was inclined to burn down a house, that video makes it look fun and glamorous. After all, you've got it on TV and you keep watching it and watching it. After a while, if you see it enough, you can get to thinking. "It must be an OK thing to do, or why would it be on television?"

_____

_____

_____

_____

_____

Practice 3.   Write a paragraph on a separate piece of paper, deliberately using the following transitional words or phrases.

a. first   c. third   e. finally
b. second   d. in addition   f. thus or finally

Practice 4.   Write two paragraphs contrasting the economy of owning any model VW with owning a Cadillac. Use at least three of the following transitional words or phrases to link the two paragraphs together smoothly.

a. but   c. yet   e. on the other hand
b. however   d. nevertheless   f. in contrast to this

Practice 5. Write at least two paragraphs describing in part what you did yesterday. Use as many of the following words or phrases as possible.

a. then   d. meanwhile   g. later
b. next   e. afterward   h. finally
c. after   f. subsequently

◆ PRACTICES IN USING CLASSIFICATION

Practice 1. Read the paragraphs and answer the questions that follow.

A. There are at least four ways for schools to teach English to students who speak another language at home. One is to immerse students totally in English, not allowing students to speak their native language. Another is to provide short-term bilingual education, directed toward moving students into English-language classes as rapidly as possible. Still another is to provide dual curriculum, which permits students to spend several years making the transition. And last, there is language and cultural maintenance, which seeks to enhance students' mastery of their first language while teaching them English.

1. What is being classified? _____

   _____

2. How many classifications are there? _____

   _____

3. What transitional words or devices are used to help you go from one division

   to the next? _____

4. Rewrite the topic sentence to this paragraph so that it incorporates all four classifications. Obviously, you will have to use only the key words of each classification.

   _____

   _____

   _____

   _____

B. It is important to identify habits of the mind that can interfere with clear thinking. Some of them are uniquely our own, based on background and experience. However, there are a number of habits with which all of us are familiar. In *The Art of Thinking*, Vincent Ryan Ruggiero calls these habits the mine-is-better habit, face-saving, resistance to change, conformity, stereotyping, and self-deception.

1. What is being classified? _____

_____

2. How does the word *however* help narrow down more specifically what is being
classified? _____

_____

_____

3. What would you expect the next paragraph to discuss? Explain. _____

_____

_____

_____

C.   In a certain sense we all listen to music on three separate planes. For lack of a
better terminology, one might name these: (1) the sensuous plane, (2) the expres-
sive plane, (3) the sheerly musical plane. The only advantage to be gained from
mechanically splitting up the listening process into these hypothetical planes is the
clear view to be had of the way we listen. (Aaron Copeland, *What to Listen for in
Music*. New York: McGraw-Hill, 1957)

1. What specifically is being classified? _____

_____

2. Are these real divisions? Explain. _____

_____

_____

3. According to the author, what is the advantage of dividing up the listening

process? _____

_____

_____

D.   All American thinking about nuclear weapons is strongly influenced by two popular myths. One myth says that nuclear weapons were decisive in bringing World
War II to an end. The second myth says that if Hitler had got nuclear weapons first
he could have used them to conquer the world. Both myths were believed by the
scientists and statesmen who built the first nuclear weapons. They are still believed
by most Americans today. Since we cannot explore the might-have-beens of history
we cannot know for sure whether these myths are true. I believe that both myths
are false. (Freeman Dyson, "Cutting Nuclear Myths Down to Size." *Science 84:* 88)

1. What is being classified? _____

_____

2. How many classifications are there? _____

3. What is the point of the paragraph? _____

_____

_____

_____

Practice 2. Put the following scrambled sentences into what you think is the correct order for a classification paragraph. Don't just write down the numbers; write out the entire paragraph in the correct order.

1. Devote the remaining 9 minutes to moving through the paper page by page.
2. Second, turn to the News Summary and Index of the paper and read it through.
3. Let us suppose you can spare only 15 minutes first thing in the morning for reading the newspaper.
4. This condensation covers everything except the relatively minor articles in the news.
5. Begin by reading every headline on page 1; it's the show window of the paper where leading pieces of news are displayed.

Practice 3. In your journal or on a separate sheet, write a paragraph classifying the types of introductory paragraphs discussed in Unit 1.

◆ PRACTICES IN USING DEFINITION

Practice 1. Read the paragraphs and answer the questions that follow.

A. With these important considerations in mind, we can attempt a more formal definition of thinking. *Thinking is any mental activity that helps formulate or solve a problem, make a decision, or fulfill a desire to understand. It is a searching for answers, a reaching for meaning.* Numerous mental activities are included in the thinking process. Careful observation, memorizing, remembering, wondering, imagining, inquiring, interpreting, evaluating, and judging are among the most important ones. (Vincent Ryan Ruggiero, *The Art of Thinking.* New York: Harper, 1984. 2)

1. What specifically is being defined? _____

2. What was probably defined in the previous paragraph or passage? _____

_____

3. In helping to define, the paragraph also uses examples. What are the examples helping to define? _____

_____

4. What are some of the specific examples? _____

_____

B. For the French, friendship is a one-to-one relationship that demands a keen awareness of the other person's intellect, temperament and particular interests. A friend is someone who draws out your own best qualities, with whom you sparkle and become more of whatever the friendship draws upon. Your political philosophy assumes more depth, appreciation of a play becomes sharper, taste in food or wine is accentuated, enjoyment of a sport is intensified. (Margaret Mead and Rhoda Metraux, "A Way of Seeing." *Saturday Review* Mar. 1970)

1. What is being defined? _____

   _____

2. List all the areas given that friendship helps us to develop.

   _____

   _____

   _____

   _____

C. Fables . . . are also folk tales handed down from generation to generation. "A fable seems to be, in its genuine state, a narrative in which beings irrational, and sometimes inanimate, are, for the purpose of moral instruction, feigned to act and speak with human interests and passions" (Samuel Johnson). Often sanctimonious, sometimes amusing, the fable always explicitly states a moral truth; there is no hidden meaning, nothing is left to our imagination.

   The fairy tale, in contrast, leaves all decisions up to us, including whether we wish to make any at all. It is up to us whether we wish to make any application to our life from a fairy tale, or simply enjoy the fantastic events it tells about. Our enjoyment is what induces us to respond in our own good time to the hidden meanings, as they may relate to our life experience and present state of personal development. (Bruno Bettelheim, *The Uses of Enchantment.* New York: Random House, 1976)

1. What methods of paragraph development appear in the two paragraphs?

   _____

   _____

2. According to the passage, what is a fable?

   _____

   _____

   _____

3. How is a fairy tale different from a fable? _____

   _____

   _____

   _____

4.   What is the key transitional phrase used in the passage?

_____

Practice 2.   In the space given, finish the following paragraph, writing an extended definition. Feel free to use any combination of methods to develop your definition.

To me, a good friend is _____

_____

_____

_____

_____

_____

_____

_____

◇ PRACTICES IN USING PROCESS AND CAUSAL ANALYSIS

Practice 1.   Read the paragraphs and answer the questions that follow.

A.   Mothers who shy away from the computer keyboard are setting a poor example for their daughters. If young women are to keep pace with their brothers and boyfriends, mothers must enter the computer age—and then their daughters will follow eagerly.

1.   Is this paragraph using process or causal analysis? Explain. _____

_____

2.   What is being analyzed? _____

_____

_____

3.   If _____ happens

this will happen _____

_____

B.   When you're exposed to a threat, your body responds by releasing powerful stimulating hormones into the bloodstream. Those hormones make the heart beat more strongly and more rapidly and also direct blood flow to where it's most needed. In a time of stress the blood supply is usually diminished to the abdomen and the skin, and is increased to the muscles. Most of the physical symptoms of anxiety—cold feet, butterflies in the stomach, sweating, dilation of the pupils of the eyes and skin pallor—are caused by these hormones. (David Viscott, *The Language of Feeling.* New York: Arbor House, 1976)

1. What is the process being analyzed here? _____

_____

_____

2. The cause is: _____

_____

The effects are: _____

_____

_____

_____

_____

C. The temptation of the educator is to explain and describe, to organize a body of knowledge for the student, leaving the student with nothing to do. I have never been able to understand why educators do this especially where books are concerned. Much of the time they force their students to read the wrong books at the wrong time, and insist that they read them in the wrong way. That is, they lecture to the students about what is in the books, reduce the content to a series of points that can be remembered, and if there are discussions, arrange them to deal with the points. (Harold Taylor, "The Private World of the Man with a Book." *Saturday Review* Aug. 1961)

1. What is being analyzed? _____

_____

2. What is it the author feels most teachers do wrong?

_____

_____

_____

3. What is the result of this mistake? _____

_____

_____

Practice 2. Read the following paragraph, then write a one-sentence statement explaining the cause and effects being discussed.

By pushing aside the limitations of experience and schooling, mass media have created a nation of people who have opinions on just about every subject and mental pictures of places never visited, people never encountered, and events experienced only as tiny images on a television screen. News and entertainment media distribute so much information about the world that many educators claim schools are no longer the main source of learning for most people. Mass media have taken over the role of forming our mental image of the world.

_____

_____

_____

_____

Practice 3.   In the space provided, outline the following paragraph.

For all people under forty years old, driving is the leading cause of death. What can be done to reduce this terrible toll? First, change the laws to reduce the amount a driver may legally drink, to discourage the average person from driving drunk, and to deal more effectively with problem drunken drivers. Second, motivate and train police to spot and arrest intoxicated motorists. And, finally, on the individual level, change attitudes that permit if not encourage drunken driving. (John Lempesis, "Murder in a Bottle." *Reader's Digest* Apr. 1982)

1.   What process is being analyzed? _____

      _____

2.   What transitional words or phrases are used to help the reader understand the

      steps in the process? _____

      _____

3.   Fill in the following outline of the paragraph:

                   How to Reduce the Drunken Driving Death Toll

      Step One:

      a. _____

      b. _____

      c. _____

      Step Two:

      _____

      _____

      Step Three:

      _____

◇ PRACTICES IN WRITING DESCRIPTIVELY

Practice 1.   Read these paragraphs and answer the questions that follow.

A.   When was the last time you remember a street alky stumbler with nothing on top? Black, white, old, young, short, tall, all of them had a full mop. And hair that wouldn't quit. It leaped up as if it were electrified, or shagged down in complete asocial indifference, or zoomed back absurdly neat, gray-black and glued. Inexplicably, it seemed that boozing burned out the guts but grew hair. (George DeLeon, "The Baldness Experiment." *Psychology Today* Oct. 1977)

1.   What is this paragraph about? _____

_____

2.   Explain the following terms in less descriptive words:

    a.   a street alky stumbler _____

    b.   a full mop _____

    c.   leaped . . . as if . . . electrified _____

    d.   zoomed back _____

    e.   boozing burned out the guts _____

3.   Is the sentence fragment used effectively? Explain.

_____

_____

B.   Standing in a subway station, I began to appreciate the place—almost to enjoy it. First of all, I looked at the lighting: a row of meager electric bulbs, unscreened, yellow, and coated with filth, stretched toward the black mouth of the tunnel, as though it were a bolt hole in an abandoned coal mine. Then I lingered, with zest, on the walls and ceiling: lavatory tiles which had been white about fifty years ago, and were now encrusted with soot, coated with the remains of a dirty liquid which might be either atmospheric humidity mingled with smog or the result of a perfunctory attempt to clean them with cold water; and, above them, gloomy vaulting from which dingy paint was peeling off like scabs from an old wound, sick black paint leaving a leprous white undersurface. Beneath my feet, the floor was a nauseating dark brown with black stains upon it which might be stale oil or dry chewing gum or some worse defilement; it looked like the hallway of a condemned slum building. Then my eye traveled to the tracks, where two lines of glittering steel—the only positively clean objects in the whole place—ran out of darkness into darkness above an unspeakable mass of congealed oil, puddles of dubious liquid, and a mishmash of old cigarette packets, mutilated and filthy newspapers, and the débris that filtered down from the street above through a barred grating in the roof. (From Gilbert Highet, *Talents and Geniuses*, 1957)

1.   What is your reaction to this descriptive paragraph?

      _____

2.   Underline all of the similes used.

3.   Why does the author say he "began to appreciate the place"?

      _____

      _____

      _____

C.   I don't think I said anything, but I made a sound that I can remember now, a shrill blubbering pitched to carry more terror than I'd ever known existed, like the sounds they've recorded off of plants being burned, like an old woman going under for the last time. My hands went flying everywhere all over my head, I had to find it and touch it. . . .

    Twenty yards in front of us men were running around totally out of their minds. One man was dead (they told me later it was only because he'd been walking forward with his flak jacket open, another real detail to get down and never . . . [forget] again), one was on his hands and knees vomiting some evil pink substance, and one, quite near us, was propped up against a tree facing away from the direction of the round, making himself look at the incredible thing that had just happened to his leg, screwed around about once at some point below his knee like a goofy scarecrow leg. He looked away and then back again, looking at it for a few seconds longer each time, then he settled in for about a minute, shaking his head and smiling, until his face became serious and he passed out. (Michael Herr, *Dispatches*. New York: Avon Books, 1978)

1.   What is this passage about? _____

      _____

2.   What is meant by "another real detail to get down"? _____

      _____

3.   What can you infer is a "flak jacket"? _____

      _____

4.   Explain any similes used. _____

      _____

      _____

      _____

      _____

5.   How real do the events in this passage seem? Explain. _____

      _____

_____

_____

D. It is 3 A.M. Everything on the university campus seems ghostlike in the quiet, misty darkness—everything except the computer center. Here, twenty students, rumpled and bleary-eyed, sit transfixed at their consoles, tapping away on the terminal keys. With eyes glued to the video screen, they tap on for hours. For the rest of the world, it might be the middle of the night, but here time does not exist. As in the gambling casinos of Las Vegas, there are no windows or clocks. This is a world unto itself. Like gamblers, these young computer "hackers" are pursuing a kind of compulsion, a drive so consuming it overshadows nearly every other part of their lives and forms the focal point of their existence. They are compulsive computer programmers. Some of these students have been at the console for thirty hours or more without a break for meals or sleep. Some have fallen asleep on sofas and lounge chairs in the computer center, trying to catch a few winks but loath to get too far away from their beloved machines. (Dina Ingber, "Computer Addicts." _Science Digest_ May 1981)

1. Circle all the words or phrases that help describe the scene and action.

2. To what are those computer addicts being compared? _____

_____

3. To what is the computer center being compared? _____

_____

4. As written in this passage, what are these comparisons called? _____

_____

5. Which descriptive words or phrases seem familiar? _____

_____

_____

Practice 2.   In the following sentences, identify metaphors or similes and explain each.

1. Emotions hurried over his face as if many colored lights had been switched on and off. _____

_____

_____

2. I hung like a marionette from the threads, my arms dangling, floating at the mercy of the breeze. _____

_____

_____

3. His hair was wiglike and resentful of the comb.

4. He clammed up and wouldn't talk.

5. Her eyes flashed fire at him.

Practice 3. Pick two of the following topics, and in your journal, write a descriptive passage for each. If you don't have any of these, pick your own topic.

1. Your favorite place
2. Your bedroom
3. Your best friend
4. Your typical day
5. Your dream mate
6. Your pet

◆ PRACTICES IN WRITING CONCLUDING PARAGRAPHS

Practice 1. Read these concluding paragraphs from essays and answer the questions that follow.

A. In the last 24 hours, 68 people have been killed by drunken drivers. In the next 24 hours, another 68 will die. Tragedies like these will not be stopped without strict laws, stiff mandatory penalties, better education of both the public and the police, and our own intervention.

1. Does this concluding paragraph
   a. summarize
   b. make conclusions
   c. stress need for change
   d. both b and c

2. Explain your selection:

B. We have a scarcity of heroes and heroines these days for the simple reason that they go unnoticed. We pay close attention to the millionaires, the beauty queens, baseball stars, and television personalities who conform to what self-fulfillment is supposed to be all about; and, though we may take them for our models, they are not heroes in the historic sense of the word. They have not made great sacrifices and taken great risks. They have only pursued the soaring bird and caught a fistful of feathers. (Shari Miller, "Self-Fulfillment Through Service to Others." *The Humanist* Jan./Feb. 1983)

1. Does this paragraph
   a. leave the reader with a question
   b. stress the need to change
   c. draw conclusions about the topic
   d. none of the above

2. Explain your selection. _____

   _____

   _____

   _____

C.   Henry James had something of all of this in mind in some advice he gave to young writers: "Oh, do something from your point of view; an ounce of example is worth a ton of generalities . . . do something with life. Any point of view is interesting that is a direct impression of life. You each have an impression colored by your individual conditions; make that into a picture, a picture framed by your own personal wisdom, your glimpse of the American world. The field is vast for freedom, for study, for observation, for satire, for truth." (James E. Miller, "Discovering the Self," *World, Self, Reality.* New York: Harper, 1972)

1. What can you guess the essay was about?

   _____

2. What method of concluding paragraph is being used? _____

   _____

3. When would this type of ending not be appropriate? _____

   _____

   _____

D.   I have dwelt at some length on the weaknesses of Tsipis and Schell. They share these weaknesses with almost all American experts who write about nuclear weapons. Their strengths are their own. Tsipis' strengths are a lucid style and a firm grasp of technical details. Schell's strengths are a bold vision of the future and a moral conviction that will move mankind to make his vision come true. If we can combine Tsipis' technical competence and Schell's prophetic zeal with a more skeptical attitude toward American strategic dogmas, we shall have the essential ingredients for a hopeful future. (F. Dyson, "Cutting Nuclear Myths Down to Size." *Science 84:* 90)

1. What can you guess the essay was about? _____

   _____

2. What method is being used? _____

    _____

3. Explain your selection: _____

    _____

    _____

    _____

    _____

Practice 2.   Read the concluding paragraphs from two essays in this book and write your own concluding paragraph for each. Turn them in to your instructor.

◆ PRACTICES IN ORDERING AND ORGANIZING

Practice 1.   It is highly unlikely that the following list would really be used for an essay, but for the sake of practice, order by color (red, yellow, blue-black) the following ten items of fruit.

Unordered Support	**Ordered Support**
1. strawberries	_____
2. bananas	_____
3. peaches	_____
4. pomegranates	_____
5. red apples	_____
6. grapefruit	_____
7. blueberries	_____
8. tomatoes	_____
9. blackberries	_____
10. lemons	_____

Practice 2.   In the spaces below, place the ordered support in Practice 1 into an outline that could be used for writing an essay. The first part has been done for you.

Paragraph 1
  I. Introduction, mentioning the three main types of fruit
    A.   *red fruit*
    B.   *yellow fruit*
    C.   *blue-black fruit*

Paragraph 2

II. _____

    A. _____

    B. _____

    C. _____

    D. _____

Paragraph 3

III. _____

    A. _____

    B. _____

    C. _____

    D. _____

Paragraph 4

IV. _____

    A. _____

    B. _____

Paragraph 5

  V. Conclusion, summarizing three main types of fruit

    A. _____

    B. _____

    C. _____

Practice 3. Rearrange the following list of tools into a more logical or orderly form.

Unordered Support	Ordered Support
1. claw hammer	_____ ⎫
2. pliers	_____ ⎬ A. ____
3. jigsaw	_____ ⎭
4. ball peen hammer	_____ ⎫
5. vise grips	_____ ⎬ B. ____
6. handsaw	_____ ⎭
7. sledgehammer	_____ ⎫ C. ____
8. bench vise	_____ ⎭

Practice 4. In the spaces below, place the ordered support in Practice 3 into an outline that could be used for writing an essay.

Paragraph 1

    I. Introduction, mentioning three main types of tools

        A. _____

        B. _____

        C. _____

Paragraph 2

  II. _____

        A. _____

        B. _____

        C. _____

Paragraph 3

  III. __ _____

        A. _____

        B. _____

        C. _____

Paragraph 4

IV. _____

        A. _____

        B. _____

Paragraph 5

  V. Conclusion, summarizing three types of tools

        A. _____

        B. _____

        C. _____

Practice 5. Rearrange the following fish into two categories: freshwater and saltwater.

Unordered Support   **Ordered Support**

1.   trout   _____

2.   shark   _____

3. goldfish   _____

4. saltwater fish   _____

5. sea bass   _____

6. perch   _____

7. freshwater fish   _____

8. stingray   _____

9. bluegill   _____

10. catfish   _____

11. swordfish   _____

12. tuna   _____

Practice 6. Place the ordered list of fish from Practice 5 into an outline that could be used for writing an essay on types of fish. Use the space that follows.

Practice 7. Rearrange the following list into an orderly form. Two items in the list *do not* belong.

Unordered Support   **Ordered Support**

1. ice skating   _____

2. water sports   _____

3. skin diving   _____

4. snow skiing   _____

5. sports   _____

(continued on next page)

6. swimming   _____

7. jogging   _____

8. waterskiing   _____

9. winter sports   _____

10. snow sledding   _____

11. table tennis   _____

12. sailing   _____

Practice 8.   Place the ordered list in Practice 7 into an outline that could be used for writing an essay. Do this on a separate sheet and turn it in to your instructor.

Practice 9.   Place each item on the following brainstorming list under their appropriate heading.

nail biting   medical intern
exercise regularly   frequent illness
police officer   irritability
inner-city high-school teacher   get a massage
insomnia   maintain a sense of humor
hunger for sweets   meditate
eat more sensibly   air-traffic controller
quit   miner
rapid pulse   lack of concentration

Tough Jobs	Signs of Stress	Ways to Cope
_____	_____	_____
_____	_____	_____
_____	_____	_____
_____	_____	_____
_____	_____	_____
_____	_____	_____

Practice 10.   Following are two sets of sentences taken from opening paragraphs and scrambled. See if you can rearrange the sentences in their proper order. Do this ordering in your journal or on a separate sheet of paper.

A.   1. But like most college students, you'd probably like to improve your reading.
     2. You may have already found that college professors expect you to read, understand, remember, and draw inferences from assignments.

(continued on next page)

3. You'd like to be able to concentrate better, to read faster, to remember more of what you've read, and to analyze and evaluate more effectively.

4. How can you cope with this heavy reading load?

5. Obviously, you can read.

B. 1. Others miss too much school because of illness and feel it would be too difficult to catch up on all the work.

2. However, lack of interest, although one reason for dropping out, is not the only reason.

3. Some students find it financially necessary to leave school to go to work.

4. But many students leave because they find college disappointing.

5. When a student drops out of college, many instructors feel that the student is not really interested in the subject or in developing his or her academic potential.

◆ PRACTICES IN TOPIC SENTENCES

Practice 1.   Put brackets [ ] around the topic sentences in the following paragraphs. Then in your own words write the main idea. Make sure you write complete sentences. If there is no topic sentence, write what you think could be a topic sentence for the paragraph.

A.   Here is a four-step method to prevent your mind from wandering while reading. First, before you attempt to read anything, look over the length of the material to see if you have time to read it all; if not, mark the spot where you intend to stop. Second, read the title and the first paragraph, looking for the thesis of the article. Next, read any boldface headings and the first sentence of each paragraph. Finally, read the last paragraph, which probably contains a summary of the material. This four-step method helps you focus on what you are about to read, pushing aside other thoughts that might interfere with your concentration.

Main idea: _____

_____

_____

B.   The patients wandered aimlessly about, mumbling incoherently. Violent ones were wrapped in wet sheets with their arms pinned, or they wore straitjackets. Attendants, in danger of assault, peered at their charges through screens. The floor lay bare, because rugs would have quickly been soiled with excrement. These were the conditions of a large mental institution 30 years ago.

Main idea: _____

_____

_____

C.   To the orthodox Muslim the use of pork by Americans is revolting, and to the orthodox Hindu the thought of eating beef is almost as horrifying as the thought of eating human flesh is to Americans. East Africans find eggs nauseating. The

Chinese students in the United States have sometimes become ill at seeing people drink milk.

Main idea: _____

_____

_____

D.   Dazzled by the magic of television, we tend to forget what we might have been doing without it. We might have read more, thought more, written more. We might have filled the hours with games such as bridge or Scrabble. We might have played more musical instruments, spent more time outdoors, embroidered, knitted, whittled. We might have spent more time relating to others.

Main idea: _____

_____

_____

Practice 2.   Select two of the paragraphs in Practice 1 and in the spaces given, write in your own words the main idea; then list the supporting points. In effect, you are outlining the two paragraphs you select.

A.   Main idea: _____

_____

Supporting points: _____

_____

_____

_____

_____

_____

B.   Main idea: _____

Supporting points: _____

_____

_____

_____

_____

_____

Practice 3.   Rewrite any of the following topic sentences so that the main idea and control are obvious. Some may not need revising.

1. Weddings are an important tradition in our society.

    _____

    _____

2. I love my wife.

    _____

    _____

3. My parents are the greatest people I know.

    _____

    _____

4. Love is a many-splintered thing.

    _____

    _____

5. Some people marry for companionship.

    _____

    _____

6. Marriage is more than enjoying being close to each other.

    _____

    _____

7. *When You Marry* is a good book.

    _____

    _____

Practice 4.   Read the following topic sentences, and circle the key words that control what the rest of the paragraph will develop.

1. There were at least four major reasons for the fight.

2. The counselor gave them many examples of broken homes.

3. Our wedding was different from most.

4. There were many types of wedding gowns from which to choose.

5. The couple had several problems to work out between them.

6. Her idea of marriage and his were quite different.

7.   The food at the wedding reception was unusual and delicious.

8.   The couple had to decide which of these three places to go on their honeymoon.

9.   Honeymoons are not a good idea despite the tradition behind them.

10. Some people marry for all the wrong reasons.

Practice 5.   On a separate sheet, pick *one* of the topic sentences from Practice 4 and write a paragraph that develops the key words in that sentence. Turn it in to your instructor.

◆ PRACTICES IN REVISING SENTENCES

Practice 1.   Rewrite the following sentences so they sound better.

1.   Jogging on city streets can be very dangerous because it endangers the joggers who might get hit by cars when drivers don't see them.

2.   It is a fact that there is a great deal of money in the field, and that is why stockbrokers get into it.

3.   In the area of revision, you should try to use as few words as possible when revising, selecting words that really mean what you want to say.

4.   The new clinic gives poor free legal help.

Practice 2.   Read the following student paragraph, and in the space provided, make comments that you feel would help the student improve on the paragraph. Each sentence has been numbered for reference.

Student's First Draft

> (1) Advertising subconsciously teaches us. (2) And we need to be more aware of it. (3) It teaches us that failures can be avoided if we use the right products Are you having trouble getting a girl? (4) Maybe its your breath. (5) Try Listermint. (6) Maybe your smile. (7) Try Ultrabrite. (8) Maybe you have body odor. (9) Try Ban. (10) Such ads create a problem, it teaches us that there are instant solutions to almost every problem.

Helpful remarks:

◇ PRACTICES IN CORRECT WORD CHOICE

Practice 1.   Correct any error in the following sentences—agreement, verb usage, correct words, punctuation, and so forth.

1. My sister Kate don't care what she say to no one.

2. Moe will except the award at the meeting tonight.

3. It don't matter to me, man!

4. I didn't want to go anyways its a dumb way to spend money.

5. That night in jail was the baddest night I ever spend.

6. I can't hardly believe I got through it.

7. Sammy could of won if he hadn't tripped.

8. Its the best candy in the world.

Practice 2. Select the correct word within parentheses for the blanks in the following sentences. Some of the word choices were not discussed in this chapter. If you are in doubt about any word, look it up in your dictionary.

1. She does not want to _____the fact that she needs psychological help. (accept, except)

2. He _____the older part so that it fit the new one. (adopted, adapted)

3. Let's hope the medicine will not have an _____effect on her. (adverse, averse)

4. My _____is not to _____him on the matter. (advise, advice)

5. The story completely _____him. (alluded, eluded)

6. I'm _____to go. (all ready, already)

7. For years, he has _____the guilt alone. (born, borne)

8. The new _____building cost a fortune. (capital, capitol)

9. Upon this _____, I'll build my home. (cite, sight, site)

10. The material felt very _____to the touch. (course, coarse)

11. Why is _____always served last? (dessert, desert)

12. She was _____a waitress. (formerly, formally)

13. If you want to go, _____fine with me. (it's, its)

14. Use the _____one mentioned in the list above. (latter, later)

15. The tie was _____about his neck. (loose, lose)

16. Wow, I _____my history test! (past, passed)

17. He has been the _____at this school for four years. (principal, principle)

18. He was _____right, you know. (quiet, quit, quite)

19. The sun _____brightly on the water. (shown, shone)

20. I am older _____you are. (than, then)

Practice 3. Underline the correct word within parentheses in the following sentences.

1. (Who's, Whose) idea was it to invite her?

2. The man (who, which, that) lives upstairs teaches creative writing.

3. Marianne didn't want to (loose, lose) her job, so she stayed late to finish her work.

4. While riding the (stationary, stationery) bike for exercise, his father reads the newspaper.

5. Sue's English teacher (implied, inferred) on her last essay that she had creative talent.

6. When they are (all ready, already), call me and I'll pick them up.

7. (Its, It's) difficult to believe (its, it's) mid-term time again.

8. Just (among, between) us three, I'm not sure I can finish my essay on time.

9. My mother felt (bad, badly) yesterday.

10. The music had a strange (affect, effect) on the crowd.

Practice 4. Explain what is wrong with these statements.

1. The doctor testified in a horse suit.

   _____

2. The British arrested 126 protesting missiles.

   _____

3. Today the police begin a campaign to run down jaywalkers.

   _____

4. The court ordered the minister to produce women.

   _____

5. She pulled me over to the window with a smile.

   _____

6. The waitress dropped the bowl on the bar she had been carrying.

   _____

Practice 5. Underline the word that sounds best in the following sentences.

1. Please (transmit, send) my best wishes to your mother.

2. We should (stop, discontinue) using pesticides on food.

3. Let's hope the matter is (terminated, ended).

4. Are you (familiar with, conversant with) the new rules?

5. Frank's boss wants to (initiate, begin) a new program.

◇ PRACTICES IN TRANSITIONAL DEVICES

Practice 1.   Using the transitional devices given, fill in the blanks in the passage following.

but	second	third
finally	first of all	for instance
thus	in the end	of course
as well as	for if it is	

_____, the media teach many things, _____I should like to mention four of their biases which are in special need of opposition by the schools.

The media are, _____, attention-centered. Their main goal is to capture and to hold the attention of their audiences. The content of media is of little importance. _____, its only function is as bait.

_____, the media are vastly entertaining. Nothing will appear on television or the movie screen outside of school unless it has "entertaining value." This means it must not be demanding or disturbing; _____, the audience will turn away.

_____, the media, especially television, are image-centered. Television consists of fast-moving, continuously changing visual images which compress time. The average length of a shot on "The Love Boat," _____, is about three seconds. On commercials, the average length of a shot is two seconds.

_____television, _____movies, work against the development of language.

And _____, most of what children see on television and in the movies takes the form of stories. . . .

Practice 2.   Use the transitional words or phrases given to make the two paragraphs following read more smoothly.

also	today
for example	in those days
in the past	in fact
last	second
as a consequence	as a result

_____the housewife was the guardian of the children. _____ she gave them their early education and initiated them into principles of religion.

_____, she taught them respect for others. She _____taught them to take care of material goods, and _____ she made them understand the work ethic. _____ the housewife was busy cooking, making clothes, and enjoying her family's development.

_____ such a woman is rare. _____ such a woman would be considered old-fashioned, a square. With affluence has come all the electric gadgets for her kitchen which she can't do without. _____, today's women have more leisure time, and too many have gone into the job market or taken to drinking or to other women's husbands. _____, family values have become distorted.

◆ PRACTICES IN WRITING CORRECT SENTENCES (frags, r.o., c.s.)

Practice 1.   In the spaces given, correct any of the following sentences that need correction, and identify what type of error you are correcting. One needs no correction.

1. She does not have the prettiest teeth in the world. As you can see when she smiles.

   (Type of error: _____)

   _____

2. While I was heading for school, hitchhiking as usual.

   (Type of error: _____)

   _____

3. Critically evaluate the books we have read by ranking them in order of your favorite to least liked explain the reasons for your ranking.

   (Type of error: _____)

   _____

4. He would rather watch television than read, as I'm sure many boys his age would.

   (Type of error: _____)

   _____

5. Dr. Causet lectured on many interesting things. For example, black magic, devil worship, and other occult ideas.

   (Type of error: _____)

   _____

   _____

6. A sentence is usually described as a group of words expressing a complete thought, it contains a subject and a predicate and is an independent unit of expression.

   (Type of error: _____)

   _____

   _____

7. Every morning, my grandmother used to go for a walk in the park in the afternoons she watched her favorite television serials.

   (Type of error: _____)

   _____

   _____

8. As we are all going in the same general direction.

   (Type of error: _____)

   _____

   _____

9. We used to walk through the woods in the fall finding a nice spot in the warm sun, we usually stopped and had lunch.

   (Type of error: _____)

   _____

   _____

10. When the irate customer asked for his money back.

   (Type of error: _____)

   _____

   _____

Practice 2. In each of the following paragraphs there is a *sentence fragment.* Find it, and rewrite it correctly in the space provided.

A. If you stand to lose a considerable sum. Don't be reluctant to threaten legal action if your complaint is justified but a merchant refuses to refund your money.

More and more often, courts are backing the customer who has a legitimate grievance.

_____

_____

B.   The judge ruled he should receive a cash refund inasmuch as repairmen had been unable to make the air conditioner work during the warranty period. Dozens of others who bought similar defective air conditioners yanked them out of their cars and took a heavy loss. Rather than engage in legal action.

_____

_____

C.   Few families can afford to waste money if goods or services are not satisfying, especially with inflation a grim reality. Think back on your own purchases in the past year. Did you throw out expensive meat because it was spoiled by the time you got it home from the market? How about the blanket that shrank after a first washing? The $7.00 wash-and-wear shirt whose color faded mysteriously?

_____

_____

D.   We aren't chronic complainers, but if a roast is of poor quality or a child's coat has a defective lining, we speak right up to the butcher or the clothing store manager. We're not bashful about asking for a replacement or a refund. If we believe our request is justified.

_____

_____

Practice 3.   Circle all the cliff-hanger words, and then change all of the following fragments into complete sentences.

1.   Inasmuch as there is no school tomorrow. _____

_____

2.   Before we leave on our cruise. _____

_____

3.   Because of the grades I earned in high school. _____

_____

4.   Unless the money arrives before Tuesday. _____

_____

5.   If I were the president of the United States. _____

_____

6. After you have finished this week's assignment. _____

_____

7. When we all heard that Aunt Sally was coming for a visit. _____

_____

8. Although the students knew of the teacher's feelings. _____

_____

9. As I mentioned to you the last time we met. _____

_____

10. Until the end of the week. _____

_____

Practice 4.   Rewrite the following run-on sentences and comma splices by insert-ing transitional words *and/or* the correct punctuation. Review the section on transitional words in Unit 3 if necessary.

1. The brakes went out on his bike he managed to stop it.

_____

_____

2. His dentist has never hurt him, he still hates the thought of going.

_____

_____

3. He was happy that finals were over, he wasn't certain of his grades.

_____

_____

4. The instructor was friendly enough his assignments were not easy.

_____

_____

5. Everything seemed to go wrong, the projector blew a bulb and the screen fell off the wall.

_____

_____

Practice 5. Following are sets of sentences. Combine each set of sentences into *one* sentence by eliminating words you don't need. The first one has been done for you. Don't end up with fragments or run-on sentences.

1. a. The American flag is red.
    b. The American flag is white.
    c. The American flag is blue.

    The American flag is red, white, and blue.

2. a. Milo's car is a '65 Chevy.
    b. Milo's car is painted maroon.
    c. Milo's car is a convertible.

    _____

    _____

3. a. My history teacher is distinguished.
    b. My history teacher has been invited to speak at the United Nations.
    c. My history teacher was once nominated for the Nobel Prize.

    _____

    _____

4. a. José is proud of his Mexican heritage.
    b. He does not like to be called a Chicano.

    _____

    _____

5. a. Our biology textbook is well illustrated.
    b. It has many study guides.
    c. It is fairly easy to understand.

    _____

    _____

6. a. Larry is more handsome than clever.
    b. He should learn to keep his mouth shut.

    _____

    _____

7. a. Sandy is better at English than the rest of us.
    b. Sandy is always impressing our teacher.
    c. She has a better background in languages.

    _____

    _____

8.   a. Julie is afraid of the instructor.
      b. She seldom speaks in class.
      c. Julie hates our psychology class.

_____

_____

9.   a. Shelly wrote a story.
      b. Shelly wrote a poem.
      c. Shelly wrote an essay.
      d. While she was recovering from her accident, Shelly wrote.

_____

_____

10.   a. Richard Bach is the author of *Jonathan Livingston Seagull*.
      b. He also wrote *Illusions*.
      c. *Illusions* is about the adventures of a reluctant messiah.

_____

_____

◆ PRACTICES IN AGREEMENT

Practice 1.   Change the verbs in the following sentences to agree with the subject. Some sentences may be correct.

1.   Our new car, like many new cars, don't seem to be as well built as older models.

2.   My brothers, who look much like my dad, seems to have taken their physical characteristics from Dad's side of the family.

3.   John, as well as Mary and Ted, were late for class.

4.   The students, bored with the speaker's topic, was getting restless and noisy.

5.   Each of us are in need of the money.

6.   My teacher, mother, and father want me to try for the scholarship.

7.   Some of the pieces of wood is wet.

8.   Anyone who wishes to go with us are welcome.

9.   Each book and its cover have to be returned next week.

10.   "Guadalajara" and "Sin ti" is on my favorite record of Mexican music.

Practice 2.   Rewrite the following sentences, changing the subjects of the following sentences to plural subjects, and changing the verbs to fit the plural subjects. Some pronouns may also need to be changed to plural form.

1.   The principal wants all parents to attend the meeting.

   _____

2.   The letter took a long time to reach us.

   _____

3.   The book is overdue at the library.

   _____

4.   The diamond ring fell through the grate.

   _____

5.   After eating his fill, the pony rubbed his neck on the fence.

   _____

6.   Only one of the boys wants to go with us.

   _____

7.   Their philosophy professor expects them to write good essay exams.

   _____

8.   The astronaut takes proper precautions before turning the dials.

   _____

9.   The *New York Times* is larger on Sundays than weekdays.

   _____

10.   The tree in the backyard is losing its leaves.

   _____

Practice 3.   In the following sentences, change the pronouns that do not agree with the subject.

1.   Each person must tell the story in their own way.

2.   Neither that car nor mine works as they should.

3.   The doctors wanted to be certain he was understood.

4.   Everybody wants to see an A on their paper.

5.   Someone left their keys on the table.

6.   Anyone can get some type of job if they really want to.

7. One of us must give our report on Tuesday.

8. The store has a reputation for not giving refunds for their faulty goods.

9. Every man and woman should vote according to their own conscience and judgment.

10. The group of laborers announced their decisions regarding the proposed labor law.

Practice 4.   Write a sentence by using the following subjects and making certain there is a pronoun reference that agrees with the subject.

1. Each one of the members _____

    _____

2. Neither you nor I _____

    _____

3. The group of doctors _____

    _____

4. Everyone must _____

    _____

5. Either one _____

    _____

6. None of the parents _____

    _____

7. The class _____

    _____

Practice 5.   In the following sentences, underline the subjects with one line and the verbs and auxiliaries with two lines.

1. The reruns of "M.A.S.H." are more enjoyable than some of the newer programs.

2. The cat and the mouse scurried around the cabin.

3. In some colleges, men and women live in the same dormitories.

4. The flower blossoms are bright and colorful.

5. Mr. Petersen, along with his wife, left for England today.

6. Mr. Petersen's children, as well as their friends, did not want them to go.

7. Please go to the store for me before it closes.

8. Each of us is aware of her problems.

9. Some of the cars are a total wreck.

10. None of us want to do it.

Practice 6.   In the following sentences, underline the correct verb form within parentheses.

1. Sales of scuba equipment (has, have) dropped during the winter months.

2. Orchid corsages (is, are) very popular at proms.

3. An orchid, of all the different types of flowers, (are, is) the most popular.

4. Jane, as well as Alice and Paul, (were, was) late.

5. The girls, who don't care much for their brothers, (was, were) about to leave without them.

6. My mother, father, and sisters (wants, want) to come, too.

7. Everybody (was, were) ready to help him.

8. Each book and short story (have, has) to be read by the end of the week.

9. Mathematics (is, are) my favorite subject.

10. Joey (don't, doesn't) want to go with us.

Practice 7.   In the blanks, write in the correct form of the verb within parentheses.

1. Neither my girlfriend nor my best friends _____ to go. (to want)

2. The television and the stereo set always _____ down when I need them. (break)

3. Either the divan or the chair _____ to be moved. (have)

4. Our new dishwasher, like many new appliances, _____ not seem to be built too well. (do)

5. Julia _____ n't want to go with us. (do)

6. The coin _____ through the grate. (fall)

7. The novel *Shogun* _____ with, among other things, the difficulty in learning humility. (deal)

8. The diving teams _____ n't want to compete in the shark tagging tomorrow. (do)

9. After eating, the cat _____ its paws. (to clean)

10. Neither the book nor the movie version _____ the truth. (to show)

◆ PRACTICES IN PARALLEL CONSTRUCTION AND MODIFIER PLACEMENT

Practice 1. Fill the blank with words parallel to the ones already in the sentence.

1. Alice plans to be a typist, _____, or file clerk.

2. My dad likes hunting, _____, and sailing.

3. We will dance, _____, and sing all night.

4. After the movie, we _____,
_____, and _____.

5. The teacher said that we were _____,
_____, and _____.

Practice 2. Explain why each of the following sentences is not correct.

1. The car slid to the left while daydreaming.

_____

_____

2. Because he was late, the boss fired him.

_____

_____

3. Sally helped her sister to put icing on the cake.

_____

_____

4. While watching the movie, my purse was stolen.

_____

_____

5. One should always try to do his best in whatever one undertakes.

_____

_____

Practice 3. Correct each of the sentences in Practice 2.

1. _____

_____

2. _____

_____

3. _____

_____

4. _____

_____

5. _____

_____

Practice 4.   Correct the following sentences.

1.   She put on her bathing cap, walked to the diving board, changing her mind at the last minute.

_____

_____

2.   After standing too long, my head begins to ache.

_____

_____

3.   The actress spent months traveling to locations by jet, train, car, and once even rode a burro.

_____

_____

4.   He always plays the piano with ease, with confidence, and takes pleasure in it.

_____

_____

5.   Stunned by the end of the story, the television program left me very upset.

_____

_____

6.   Humans are really animals and one should not expect so much from us.

_____

_____

7.   Shaking his fist, he yelled and was making faces at the old man.

_____

_____

8.   The instructor pretended to be stupid, but he is really very sharp.

_____

_____

9.   Because it would not run, he sold the car.

_____

_____

10.   She would rather watch television with glasses on.

_____

_____

◊ PRACTICES IN WRITING STRONGER SENTENCES: SENTENCE COMBINING

Practice 1.   Combine each set of sentences into one sentence. Use correct punctuation. The first one has been done for you.

1.   a.   Sammy ran quickly from the room.
     b.   His face was wet with tears.
     Change *was wet:* *His face wet with tears, Sammy ran quickly from the room. Or: Sammy ran quickly from the room, his face wet with tears.*

2.   a.   The car slowed to a stop.
     b.   The headlights were pointing right at us.
     Change *were pointing:*

     The car slowed to a stop, the headlights pointed right at us.

3.   a.   When I saw him, Joe was sitting in front of the TV set.
     b.   The dog was lying at his feet.
     Change *was lying:*

     _____

     _____

4.   a.   The men up and down the hills fought against the fire.
     b.   They were sweating profusely.
     c.   They were worried they might lose the battle against the flames.
     Change *were sweating* and *were worried:*

     _____

     _____

5. a. The coach sat on the bench alone.
    b. His head was hanging low.
    c. His hands were clutched together.
Change *was hanging* and *were clutched:*

_____

_____

6. a. When the teacher returned, she could not believe the mess.
    b. Books were scattered on the floor.
    c. Graffiti were scribbled on the blackboards.
    d. Students were dancing on their desk tops.
Use a dash after the independent clause:

_____

_____

_____

7. a. Janet hung up the phone.
    b. Janet was obviously pleased with the conversation.
    c. She had a huge smile on her face.
Experiment with different possibilities:

_____

_____

_____

Practice 2.   On another sheet of paper, combine each set of the following sentences into one sentence. You are free to use words such as *who, which, that, although, before, because,* and so on, as well as changing verbs to *-ing* endings. There is no one answer but many options. Compare your versions with those of others.

1. a. José was strong and quick.
    b. José was not particularly heavy.
    c. Being strong and quick aided José's running ability.
2. a. Shirley picked up a hitchhiker.
    b. He looked down and out.
    c. The hitchhiker had a little dog.
3. a. My aunt Polly arrived on Sunday.
    b. We were not ready for her arrival.
    c. Her room was not prepared.
4. a. The colonel moved among his troops.
    b. He briefed his staff before he moved among his troops.
    c. The colonel seemed to be looking for someone in particular.
5. a. Mac went home to await the election result.
    b. Mac voted early.
    c. He was a candidate for mayor.

6.   a.   Broward Community College is excellent in most respects.
     b.   It has upgraded its vocational course offerings.
     c.   It also prepares students who want to go on to a four-year college.
7.   a.   *The Reader's Digest* has a large circulation.
     b.   It condenses everything from its original form.
     c.   It rewrites everything to a fourth-to-sixth-grade level.
     d.   I prefer to read things in their original form.
8.   a.   I read James Michener's novel *Centennial*.
     b.   It was made into a television miniseries.
     c.   I preferred the book to the TV program.
     d.   The book seemed more realistic.

Practice 3.   Combine each of the following sets of sentences into one effective sentence. Use any way that works. There is usually more than one way, but some sound or read better than others. Use correct punctuation.

1.   a.   A gift was promised to me.
     b.   It was promised by my father.
     c.   The gift was a Jeep.

     _____

     _____

     _____

2.   a.   When Hank Aaron snapped his wrists, the bat hit the ball, sending it over a 385-foot sign.
     b.   It brought him his 715th home run.
     c.   It broke the Babe's long-standing record.

     _____

     _____

     _____

3.   a.   Some soldiers were across the gulch.
     b.   They began shooting at me.
     c.   But I got back to the others.
     d.   I was not hurt at all.

     _____

     _____

     _____

4.   a.   The horse was made of spirit.
     b.   He himself was made of spirit.
     c.   The trees were made of spirit.
     d.   The grass was made of spirit.

  e. The stones were made of spirit.
  f. Everything was made of spirit in Crazy Horse's dream.

_____

_____

_____

5. a. In just three seconds, a cigarette makes your heart beat faster.
  b. It makes your blood pressure go up.
  c. Smoke takes the place of oxygen in your blood.
  d. It leaves cancer-causing chemicals in your body.

_____

_____

_____

6. a. Next to parents, television has become the most powerful influence on the beliefs of young people.
  b. Television influences young people's attitudes and values.
  c. Television affects the way humans learn to become human beings.

_____

_____

_____

7. a. J. Allen Hynek is director of the Center for UFO Studies.
  b. He is a professor of astronomy at Northwestern University.
  c. He testified before the House Committee on Science and Astronauts.
  d. Hynek stated that the UFO problem may be far more complex than we imagine.

_____

_____

_____

8. a. Even though the government reports have linked smoking with cancer, the U.S. Congress, in 1970, spent $84 million to help the tobacco industry.
  b. Congress spent $2.7 million in research to find a new way to grow tobacco more cheaply.

c. They spent $250,000 in advertising overseas to get foreign nations to buy American tobacco.

d. Congress guarantees a minimum price per acre for tobacco crops.

◆ PRACTICES IN PUNCTUATION: PART I

Practice 1.   Place commas and periods wherever they belong in the following sentences.

1. A Jeep just might make it but our little VW Bug won't

2. Swamps they warned sometimes bury the road

3. The letter was simply addressed, "Dr. Frankenstein"

4. For my next dangerous trick I would like to attempt to cut this lady in half with no harmful effects to her person

5. Mr. Johnson is a US senator from California

Practice 2.   Use whatever end punctuation (period, exclamation, question mark) is necessary for the following sentences.

1. I just can't believe we won

2. His only response was, "You're kidding"

3. May I ask where you bought that dress

4. I asked where she bought her dress

5. Oh, man It's too impossible to believe

Practice 3.   Place commas wherever they belong in the following sentences.

1. He never asked for the book but I knew he wanted it.

2. Here's what I need: four cans of oil two boxes of concrete floor cleaner and a new broom.

3.   She is a long-legged willowy blond and has a great sense of humor.

4.   My father as far as I know wants to go too.

5.   Although she didn't say it I think her feelings were hurt.

6.   In fact we need to do more of this.

7.   Mr. Smythe who is my English professor just published his first novel.

8.   Mr. Smythe my English professor just published his first novel *Sweet Sweet Smythe*.

9.   My doctor however wants to consult another doctor.

10.   It was 4 feet 6 inches.

11.   He was born December 12 1901 near Mobile Alabama.

12.   She has a new address: 722 Nepal Avenue Phoenix Arizona.

13.   "Tell me" Rita said "where did you get those shoes?"

14.   For example there were six cases of beer four bottles of Coke and 12 packages of pretzels.

15.   However long it takes I will wait for her.

Practice 4.   Place correct punctuation marks wherever they belong in the following paragraphs.

A.   Technology is toolmaking the human animal doesn't have the speed of the horse the fighting teeth of a chimpanzee the wings of an eagle the claws of the tiger or the protective fleece of a sheep But we have discovered or invented technology we make tools where other species make physiological adaptations we have fire and all the energy-producing engines stemming from it. We travel faster than the horse fly higher than the eagle fight more devastatingly than any predator and protect our bodies with not only sheep's wool but artificial fabrics as well.

B.   If technology is stopped now most human beings will die they are already dying in gruesome famines in Africa mainly because our social institutions can't distribute food properly and partly because our technology cannot control geophysical forces such as climate we will never go "beyond" technology we may develop technologies that are nonpolluting nonobtrusive clean and quiet and completely reliable but we will no more forsake technology than we could grow the fangs of a rattlesnake

◇ PRACTICES IN PUNCTUATION: PART II

Practice 1.   Read the following paragraph from the first draft of a student's essay on astrology. In the margin are some instructor's comments given as a guide to the student for a revision. In the space provided, rewrite the paragraph, and change faulty sentence structure.

To help prove my point that astrology is really lame is my girl friend Marya. She's a Gemini. Gemini's are supposed to be bright and quick witted. [Open minded and anxious to learn new things as well as easy going.] Well, let me tell you Maryas not like that, shes, not stupid but not quick witted either. Shes not very open minded or anxious to learn either.

r.o.

Try rewriting your topic sentence not using "really lame".

Instead of repeating the words used for Geminis, use different descriptive words for Marya.

Reread the section on apostrophes and contractions.

You have the right idea, but try restructuring some of your sentences.

Practice 2.   Place semicolons, colons, and commas wherever they belong in the following sentences.

1.   The tire is ruined it is irreparable.

2.   The three new employees are John Small the young man Richard World the dark-haired one and Sam Jackson the oldest-looking of the three.

3.   Here's what I want for Christmas a new Mercedes new sails for my yacht preferably blue ones and a subscription to *Playboy*.

4.   There seems to be only one thing to do forget it.

5.   At exactly 320 P.M. he says the world will end. He predicts this on the basis of a passage from Revelations 325.

Practice 3.   Place quotation marks and commas where they should be appropriately used in the following sentences.

1.   We wanted to go but we didn't have time she explained.

2.   I thought she said that I already told you.

3.   The teacher explained the term alienation effect.

4.   A & P is a short story written by John Updike.

5.   His sister yelled Close the door.

Practice 4.   Follow the directions for each of the following tasks. If you don't understand the task, review the unit for the section that deals with the italicized word in the directions.

1.   Write an example of a *direct* quotation.

_____

2.   Write an example of an *indirect* quotation.

_____

3.   Write an example of an *exclamatory* sentence.

_____

4.   Write a sentence that uses the title of a short story, poem, or song. Use *quotation marks* correctly.

_____

_____

5. Write a sentence using a *colon* and listing at least three items in a series.

_____

_____

6. Write a sentence using your street address, city, state, and zip code. Use *commas* correctly.

_____

_____

7. Write a sentence using *parentheses.*

_____

_____

8. Write two sentences about this book, using a *semicolon* to link them as one.

_____

_____

9. Write a sentence using *dashes* correctly.

_____

_____

10. Write a sentence using an introductory clause and the correct punctuation.

_____

_____

11. Write a sentence using *therefore* correctly.

_____

_____

12. Write a sentence using the contraction for "they are." (*apostrophe* usage)

_____

_____

13. Write a sentence showing that Robert possesses some object. (*apostrophe* usage)

_____

_____

_____

14. Write a sentence using a *quote within a quote.*

_____

_____

15.   Write a sentence, not a question, using "who is . . ." as part of the sentence.

_____

_____

_____

◇ PRACTICES IN USING ABBREVIATIONS AND CAPITAL LETTERS

Practice 1.   Correct any incorrect capitalization and abbreviations in the following sentences.

1.   Our state senator, Jim Sligh, has just published an informative book, *Why Bother To Vote?*.

2.   The south lost the civil war.

3.   After his lecture on steinbeck's novel the grapes of wrath, professor Kemp called for questions.

4.   His daughter, who won a Rhodes scholarship, enrolled in harvard law school.

5.   Dr. Calm, Ph.D., is an expert on the han Dynasty, which began about 200 bc and lasted until AD 220.

6.   my class with Doctor Washout begins at 9 am est.

7.   My Dad served under Adm. Nimitz when he was in the Navy.

8.   Is my Boss a Mrs., Miss, or MS.?

Practice 2.   Correct any errors in the following paragraph.

Times of day are written a.m. and PM. Usually, these abbreviations appear in small capitals in printed material. A few other abbreviations are capitalized even though what the represent are not. for example, a bachelor of science is referred to as a B.A., northwest is nw, railroad is RR, and television is TV or T.V. Remember, though, that a common noun should not be capitalized even when it appears in a phrase that contains capitals. For instance, it's not English History, but English history; it's not the State of new York, but the state of new york.

◇ PRACTICES IN RECOGNIZING FALLACIOUS THINKING

Practice 1.   Analyze the type of fallacious reasoning being used in the following examples, and write your comments in the spaces provided.

1. All Catholics are opposed to abortion.

   _____

   _____

2. Sam Slick will make an excellent governor. His father is one of the wealthiest men in the state and has given Sam the best education possible.

   _____

   _____

3. Smoking marijuana is not detrimental to anyone. I know. I've smoked it for several years.

   _____

   _____

4. I would never vote for him. All the long-haired hippies want to see him in office.

   _____

   _____

5. If I am elected, I will end social inequality and rid this country of poverty.

   _____

   _____

6. The tax money spent on space exploration is a waste. The money would be better spent on ending poverty in this country.

   _____

   _____

7. The Russians now have a larger submarine fleet than we have; so we had better build more subs.

   _____

8. I should never have walked under that ladder this morning. That's why I had this accident.

   _____

   _____

9. Because the medicine the doctor prescribed for my father worked so well for him, he gave it to my brother when he got sick.

   _____

   _____

10. I am a Methodist because what was good for my parents is good enough for me.

_____

_____

Practice 2.   Follow the directions given for each of the following items.

  1. Name a person or group you could cite as an authority for an essay on

    a. alcoholism: _____

    b. dangers of professional boxing: _____

    c. benefits of milk: _____

    d. acupuncture: _____

    e. natural foods: _____

    f. grammar: _____

    g. babies: _____

  2. Change the following generalization to a logical statement: Because 18-year-olds can vote, they should be allowed to drink.

_____

_____

  3. Change the following statement so that it is more logical: Teenagers love rock music.

_____

_____

  4. Identify what is wrong with this statement; then change it, using a better comparison: Learning to drive is as easy as falling off a log.

_____

_____

  5. List reasonable evidence you could use for an essay on this topic: Christmas has/has not lost its true meaning.

_____

_____

  6. Rewrite the following fallacy so that it is logical: Doberman pinschers are mean dogs; they even attack their owners.

_____

_____

7. Use guilt by association to make a fallacious statement about a police officer.

_____

_____

8. What types of reasoning could you use to prove to a friend that black cats do not cause bad luck?

_____

_____

9. Discuss what is wrong with the following logic:
   Husband: Boy, you sure make lousy coffee.
   Wife: Well, you're not perfect either, you know!

_____

_____

10. Change the following statement so that it is more logical: If we don't build bigger bombs than the Russians, they will take over the world.

_____

Practice 3. Select an advertisement from a magazine, and analyze it for (1) the type of advertising claim and (2) any fallacies in reasoning suggested by the words and pictures. Do this analysis on a separate sheet of paper, attach the ad to it, and turn it in to your instructor.

◆ PRACTICES IN REVISING, EDITING, AND PROOFREADING

Practice 1. Read the following paragraph from a student essay that deals with the misleading language of advertising. Mark the paragraph for the mistakes you notice and in the space provided, write what you think needs to be done to make the paragraph better.

> Another example. All the word _help_ really means is to aid or assist, but hear are some of the ways advertisers misuse the word _help_. A certain product can help prevent cavities. This doesn't mean it will stop or prevent cavities but we don't usually play attention to that part. One more example. A product claims it can help you feel young, it doesn't say it will or can make you feel young, just that it can help you feel young. But again, we don't usually pay attention to the four-letter word _help_.

Comments:

Practice 2.   Carefully read through the following excerpt from a student draft taken from an essay dealing with the topic of losing weight. Then go back through it and mark all the items that you feel need correcting. In the space provided, write some helpful suggestions to aid the writer in another draft.

The successful method used by many weight-loss centers is called "self-administered aversion therapy. A person who wants to control the temptation for rich foods. The sight, smell, or thinking of such foods may cause an uncontrollable desire to eat. Here's how it works the person imagines himself in the kitchen. He looks up at a choclate cake on the top of the refrigerator. He wants a piece. He was really tempted. So he imagined eating a piece and getting sick. Each bite makes him sicker and sicker until he imagines he is vomiting all over his pants and shoes, this is what the overweight person continues to practice in his mind over and over again. Until the desire for the cake is gone.

Comments:

Practice 3. Read the following and mark any corrections in mechanics and punctuation. Then, in the space provided, write your comments and suggestions for revision.

LET'S DUMP INTERCOLLEGIATE SPORTS

Intercollegiate sports in American colleges and universities has gotten so big that more colleges are known by their sports teams than for the level of education they impart. Mention Ohio State, UCLA, Texas A&M, USC and dozens of other colleges and people immediately think football thanks to so much attention from the media to sports events and field jocks, our society now places more emphasis on its sports heroes and a winning team than to the true purpose of a university.

The purpose of a university is to impart knowledge and help students discover and develop their intellectual abilities in the process. But more and more, universities have become a training ground for athletes who want to be spotted by the professional teams.

In his essay, Away with big-time Athletics, Roger Williams agrees with me and says that we should do four things to change the situation. We should eliminate all athletic scholarshIps awarded on the basis of athletic ability and financial need, we should eliminate athletic dormitories and special training and tutoring to athletes, we should cut the size of the coaching staff which Williams points out is "larger than those employed by professional teams," and we should stop the recruiting of high school athletes. I agree with all this.

Williams also says:

"There would indeed by ill feeling among—and diminished contributions from—old grads who think of their alma mater primarily as a football team. Let them stew in their own pot of distorted values. A serious institution is well rid of such 'supporters'."

And values is where it's at, such emphasis on sports that is now given devalues true educational institutions.

The money that is spent on athletic scholarships should be made available to those with academic promise, not athletic promise.

Comments:

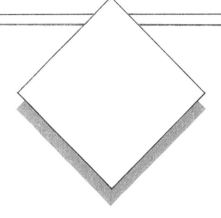

SUPPLEMENTAL READINGS

Returning to College

Andy Rooney

1   If I thought I'd live to be a hundred, I'd go back to college next fall. I was drafted into the Army at the end of my junior year and, after four years in the service, had no inclination to return to finish. By then, it seemed, I knew everything.

2   Well, as it turns out, I *don't* know everything, and I'm ready to spend some time learning. I wouldn't want to pick up where I left off. I'd like to start all over again as a freshman. You see, it isn't just the education that appeals to me. I've visited a dozen colleges in the last two years, and college life looks extraordinarily pleasant.

3   The young people on campus are all gung ho to get out and get at life. They don't seem to understand they're having one of its best parts. Here they are with no responsibility to anyone but themselves, a hundred or a thousand ready-made friends, teachers trying to help them, families at home waiting for them to return for Christmas to tell all about their triumphs, three meals a day. So it isn't gourmet food. You can't have everything.

4   Too many students don't really have much patience with the process of being educated. They think half the teachers are idiots, and I wouldn't deny this. They think the system stinks sometimes. I wouldn't deny that. They think there aren't any nice girls around/there aren't any nice boys around. I'd deny that. They just won't know what an idyllic time of life college can be until it's over. And don't tell me about the exceptions. I know about them.

5   The students are anxious to acquire the knowledge they think they need to make a buck, but they aren't really interested in education for education's sake. That's where they're wrong, and that's why I'd like to go back to college. I know now what a joy knowledge can be, independent of anything you do with it.

6   I'd take several courses in philosophy. I like the thinking process that goes with it. Philosophers are fairer than is absolutely necessary, but I like them, even the ones I think are wrong. Too much of what I know of the great philosophers comes second-hand or from condensations. I'd like to take a course in which I actually had to read Plato, Aristotle, Hume, Spinoza, Locke, John Dewey and the other great thinkers.

7   I'd like to take some calculus, too. I have absolutely no ability in that direction and not much interest, either, but there's something going on in mathematics that I don't understand, and I'd like to find out what it is. My report cards won't be mailed

to my father and mother, so I won't have to worry about marks. I bet I'll do better than when they *were* mailed.

8   I think I'd like to take a one-semester course in reading and interpreting the Bible. I haven't known many people who have actually read the Bible all the way through in an intelligent way, and it comes up so often, I'd like to be pressed to do that. There was a course in Bible at the college I attended, but I didn't take it. It was taught by the organist, and I'd want someone better than he was.

9   There are some literary classics I ought to read and I never will, unless I'm forced to by a good professor, so I'll take a few courses in English literature. I took a course that featured George Gordon Byron, usually referred to now as "Lord Byron," and I'd like to take that over again. I did very well in it the first time. I actually read all of *Don Juan* and have never gotten over how great it was. I know I could get an A in that if I took it over. I'd like to have a few easy courses.

10   My history is very weak, and I'd want several history courses. I'm not going to break my back over them, but I'd like to be refreshed about the broad outline of history. When someone says sixteenth century to me, I'd like to be able to associate it with some names and events. This is just a little conversational conceit, but that's life.

11   If I can find a good teacher, I'd certainly want to go back over English grammar and usage. He'd have to be good, because you might not think so sometimes, but I know a lot about using the language. Still, there are times when I'm stumped. I was wondering the other day what part of speech the word "please" is in the sentence, "Please don't take me seriously."

12   I've been asked to speak at several college graduation ceremonies. Maybe if I graduate, they'll ask me to speak at my own.

Man Eats Car

Natalie Goldberg

1   There was an article in the newspaper several years ago—I did not read it, it was told to me—about a yogi in India who ate a car. Not all at once, but slowly over a year's time. Now, I like a story like that. How much weight did he gain? How old was he? Did he have a full set of teeth? Even the carburetor, the steering wheel, the radio? What make was the car? Did he drink the oil?

2   I told this story to a group of third-graders in Owatonna, Minnesota. They were sitting on the blue carpet in front of me. The students looked confused and asked the most obvious question, "Why did he eat a car?," and then they commented, "Ugh!" But there was one bristling, brown-eyed student, who will be my friend forever, who just looked at me and burst into tremendous laughter, and I began laughing too. It was fantastic! A man had eaten a car! Right from the beginning there is no logic in it. It is absurd.

3   In a sense, this is how we should write. Not asking "Why?," not delicately picking among candies (or spark plugs), but voraciously, letting our minds eat up everything and spewing it out on paper with great energy. We shouldn't think, "This is a good subject for writing." "This we shouldn't talk about." Writing is everything, unconditional. There is no separation between writing, life, and the mind. If you think big enough to let people eat cars, you will be able to see that ants are elephants and men are women. You will be able to see the transparency of all forms so that all separations disappear.

4   This is what metaphor is. It is not saying that an ant is *like* an elephant. Perhaps; both are alive. No. Metaphor is saying the ant *is* an elephant. Now, logically speaking, I know there is a difference. If you put elephants and ants before me, I believe that every time I will correctly identify the elephant and the ant. So metaphor must come from a very different place than that of the logical, intelligent mind. It comes from a place that is very courageous, willing to step out of our preconceived ways of seeing things and open so large that it can see the oneness in an ant and in an elephant.

5   But don't worry about metaphors. Don't think, "I have to write metaphors to sound literary." First of all, don't be literary. Metaphors cannot be forced. If all of you does not believe that the elephant and the ant are one at the moment you write it, it will sound false. If all of you does believe it, there are some who might consider you

crazy; but it's better to be crazy than false. But how do you make your mind believe it and write metaphor?

6   Don't "make" your mind do anything. Simply step out of the way and record your thoughts as they roll through you. Writing practice softens the heart and mind, helps to keep us flexible so that rigid distinctions between apples and milk, tigers and celery, disappear. We can step through moons right into bears. You will take leaps naturally if you follow your thoughts, because the mind spontaneously takes great leaps. You know. Have you ever been able to just stay with one thought for very long? Another one arises.

7   Your mind is leaping, your writing will leap, but it won't be artificial. It will reflect the nature of first thoughts, the way we see the world when we are free from prejudice and can see the underlying principles. We are all connected. Metaphor knows this and therefore is religious. There is no separation between ants and elephants. All boundaries disappear, as though we were looking through rain or squinting our eyes at city lights.

The Floating Needle

Paul MacCready

1   A few years ago I was talking with my son, who was then 10, about how surface tension can enable a needle to float on water. I asked him how we might put down on the water's "skin" the biggest possible needle that could just barely float. As a youth I had floated needles on water, so I now suggested to my son various needle-positioning techniques based on apparatus that used hooks or electromagnets. But he said, "Why not just freeze the water, set the needle down on it and let the ice melt?"

2   Whether the technique would have worked is not significant here. The point is that even if I had worked on the challenge for days I would not have come up with his ingenious approach. Having been shaped by my experience with floating needles, my own thinking was *too patterned.* The youngster did not have my blinders on. (Incidentally, three years later that same son, making good use of balancing reflexes developed on skateboards and unicycles, became the first pilot to fly the lightweight, sun-powered Gossamer Penguin aircraft.)

3   Until the needle incident, I had never really understood why the Gossamer Albatross aircraft, which I designed, was able to win the $214,000 Henry Kremer Prize for a human-powered flight across the English Channel, when for 18 years other teams with greater resources and talents had not come close. But the needle-on-ice incident suggested a reason: every one of our serious competitors for the prize belonged to a multitalented team that included someone experienced in the structural design of airplanes. In every aircraft they built, the basic structure was conventional, albeit tailored toward human-powered flight.

4   My secret weapon was a complete lack of experience in aircraft-wing structural design while, at the same time, having a familiarity with hang gliders and fragile model airplanes. With these as conceptual guides it was straightforward for me and my team to concoct a huge 96-foot, 70-pound Gossamer aircraft with fine wires for exterior bracing. Our competitors also knew about hang gliders, but they were thwarted by knowing so much about standard techniques.

5   Thereafter, I began noticing instances in which people, myself included, had blinders on and were frustrated by barriers that really didn't exist. This led me to probe into the whole broad subject of thinking.

6   I soon found that a dominant factor in the way our minds work is the buildup of patterns that enable us to simplify the assimilation of complex inputs. But this same

"The Floating Needle" originally published in *Science Digest*, March 1983. Reprinted by permission of Paul MacCready, AeroVironment, Inc.

patterning can be a weakness as well as a strength. The patterning makes it hard for a new idea to get fair treatment. A new input is automatically distorted or filtered to adapt it to the pattern.

7   We can be trained to break away from the patterning, but our schools and our culture do not particularly foster the ability. Too often they emphasize acquiring facts, following standard procedures and being right. This is learning and reacting but not thinking. Such schooling prepares us poorly for coping with the real world.

8   Fortunately, some schools are teaching thinking skills. In Venezuela, every fourth-grade student now receives thinking-skills training. I am most familiar with the training developed by Dr. Edward de Bono, of Cambridge University in England, whose method reflects the ideas mentioned above and is the basis of the Venezuelan experiment. (The de Bono method is also being taught in the United States; I'll send details to anyone who writes me at *Science Digest.*)

9   Training in thinking skills in effect lets you see things with clearer glasses, but it doesn't tell you *what* to see. It's a bit like learning to ride a unicycle: you proceed faster if a trainer tells you some of the tricks. But you can't just read about it—you must practice to develop the skill.

10   Wouldn't it be great if someone thought up a way to measure broad thinking skills? Then a Thinking score could be included along with the Math and English scores in aptitude tests. The subject would be widely taught, and our schools would prepare people better for life's challenges.

Trust and Integrity: Easily Squandered, Hard to Regain*
Sissela Bok

1   There is strong insistence now that business ought to have a code of ethics. But codes of ethics function all too often as shields; their abstraction allows many to adhere to them while continuing their ordinary practices. In business as well as in those professions that have already developed codes, much more is needed. The codes must be but the starting point for a broad inquiry into the ethical quandaries encountered at work. Lay persons, and especially those affected by the professional practices, such as customers or patients, must be included in these efforts, and must sit on regulatory commissions. Methods of disciplining those who infringe the guidelines must be given teeth and enforced.

2   Throughout society, then, all would benefit if the incentive structure associated with deceit were changed: if the gains from deception were lowered, and honesty made more worthwhile even in the short run. Sometimes it is easy to make such a change. Universities, for instance, have found in recent years that parents of incoming students all too often misrepresent their family incomes in order to gain scholarships for their children at the expense of those in greater need of assistance. If, on the other hand, parents are told in advance that they may have to produce their income tax statements on request, such misrepresentation is much less likely to take place.

3   Very often, however, there can be no such checks—as where people communicate estimates, or vote their preference, or make sealed bids in auctions. In large organizations, for instance, specialists often communicate skewed estimates and false prognostications in order to affect the final choices made in what they regard as the "right" direction.

4   It ought not to be beyond human ingenuity to increase the incentives for honesty even in such circumstances. Many are beginning to devote thought to possible changes of this kind. Economists, in particular, are seeking procedures that reward honesty in such activities as voting, giving expert advice, bargaining, and bidding at auctions. Their efforts combine mathematical economics with policy-making in the public interest. They suggest that such changes be made in common social procedures that, when people choose strategically, it will also be in their best interest to be honest. In this way, social practices that have sprung up helter-skelter, and that at present appear to reward deception, may be altered in such a way that all benefit thereby.

*Editor's title.

Excerpt from *Lying: Moral Choice in Public and Private Life* by Sissela Bok. Copyright © 1978 by Sissela Bok. Reprinted by permission of Pantheon Books, a Division of Random House, Inc.

5   Educational institutions have a very large role to play as well. First of all, they, too, have to look to their own practices. How scrupulously honest are they in setting an example? How do they cope with cheating, with plagiarism, and with fraudulent research? What pressures encourage such behavior? To what extent, and in what disciplines, are deceptive techniques actually *taught* to students? What lines do law school courses, for instance, draw with respect to courtroom tactics, or business school courses with respect to bargaining and negotiation? Secondly, what can education bring to the training of students, in order that they may be more discerning, better able to cope with the various forms of duplicity that they will encounter in working life? Colleges and universities, as well as nursing schools, police academies, military academies, accounting schools, and many others need to consider how moral choice can best be studied and what standards can be expected, as well as upheld.

6   Some professions, such as medicine and law, have longer traditions of ethical inquiry than others; courses are springing up in these fields, and materials for teaching have been assembled. Other professions are only at the beginning of such an endeavor. But in all these fields, much too little effort is being devoted to train persons who are competent to teach such courses. As a result, existing courses are often inadequate, leaving students confirmed in their suspicion that moral choice is murky and best left to intuition.

7   In developing courses, and in training those who will teach them, there is no need to start from scratch. We are not the first to face moral problems such as those of deception. Others have experienced them, argued about them, arrived at conclusions. The structure of lies and the possible justifications have long been studied. We need to make use of the traditional approaches. We need to consider, for example, in the context of working life, why it has been thought worse to *plan* to lie than to do so on the spur of the moment; worse to induce others to lie (and thus to *teach* deception, whether in families, work places or schools) than to do so oneself; worse to lie to those with a *right* to truthful information than to others; worse to lie to those who have entrusted you with their confidence about matters important to them than to your enemies.

8   We now have resources that these earlier traditions lacked. We have access to information and to methods that can sharpen and refine the very notions of what is "helpful" and what is "harmful" among the consequences of lies. There is much room for study; but we are learning, for example, what proportion of those who are very ill *want* to be treated truthfully; what happens to adopted children who are deceived about the identity of their parents; how the public responds to government deceit. We are learning, also, much more about how the mechanisms of bias and rationalization work. Finally, we can go far beyond the anecdotes available to earlier thinkers in documenting the deceptive practices themselves.

9   These practices are not immutable. In an imperfect world, they cannot be wiped out altogether; but surely they can be reduced and counteracted. . . . Trust and integrity are precious resources, easily squandered, hard to regain. They can thrive only on a foundation of respect for veracity.

Solution to the Time Crunch: Take Your Time

Ellen Goodman

1   CASCO BAY, Me.—The tide has come in and filled up the cove. A fat, fuzzy bee has worked the last rose-hip flower in front of the cottage. I have been sitting on the porch all morning, sitting and watching. It has taken me days to come down to this speed, to this morning of utter inefficiency. Only now am I finally, truly, totally unproductive. Able to just sit and watch.

2   This has been a rushed, high-priority, overnight-express, FAX-it sort of summer. It has been as scheduled as the airline timetable that I carried in my pocketbook. By the time I left the city and office, I had reached a peak of impatience: The money machine at the bank seemed tortuously slow. The traffic was impossible. The long-distance number that I had to re-dial was annoying. Too many digits.

3   Without actually knowing it, I had upped the quota on my own production schedule. It had begun to seem important to do two things at once. To return calls while unloading the dishwasher. To ask for the check with coffee. To read a magazine in the checkout line. To use rather than waste time. The pace of work had taken over the rest of my life.

4   Now I look at newspaper photographs of Michael Dukakis speedwalking with reporters at his side, accomplishing two tasks at once—aerobic interviews—and I am amused. Somewhere, surely, there is a commuter learning Japanese on the way to work. A child is being car-pooled from one lesson to another by a parent worried about being late for gymnastics.

5   Sitting here, idle at last, I am finally conscious of the gap between being productive and simply being. At the wonderful, sensual luxury of being useless. And its rareness. Do we need vacations now to learn how to do nothing, rather than something?

6   In front of me the sides of an orchid-like wildflower open and close in the breeze like some cartoon mouth from a Disney character. I am amazed at the orange freckles that line its yellow throat. It is a wonderfully complex creation. I remember the line that accompanied that lush exhibit of Georgia O'Keeffe's paintings last winter. She wrote once: "Still—in a way—nobody sees a flower—really it is so small—we haven't time—and to see takes time, like to have a friend takes time."

7   Time. It is the priority and the missing element in our world of one-minute managers and stress clinics. But the artist knew that it wasn't possible to sandwich in an appointment for awareness (from 2 to 3 this afternoon I will pay attention to the

poppies) or to make friendship more efficient. They usually lose in the race of worka-day life.

8   Not long ago I read a report from Pittsburgh about how much time Americans waste in their lives. Five years waiting in lines. Six months at traffic lights. Eight months opening junk mail. The average married couple spends only four minutes a day in meaningful conversation. If only our tasks could be accomplished more quickly, the researchers suggested, we would have more hours for the things and people we loved.

9   Perhaps. But I am not convinced that inefficiency is our problem. Instead, it may be the passion for efficiency. The solution to the time crunch is not to move at a higher speed. It is too hard to shift out of that list-making, speed-thinking, full-throttle life into idle, the gear of human beings. The faster we try to move, the further we get from the rhythms of friendship and flowers.

10   When we rush through errands to clear a small block of free time for ourselves or our families, we may end up rushing through that "leisure" time as well. In our most productive mode we are the least open to that slow, subtle pace of caring.

11   The great myth of our work-intense era is "quality time." We believe that we can make up for the loss of days or hours, especially with each other, by concentrated minutes. But ultimately there is no way to do one-minute mothering. There is no way to pay attention in a hurry. Seeing, as Georgia O'Keeffe said, takes time. Friendship takes time. So does family. So does arriving at a sense of well-being.

12   This is what I have learned on my summer vacation—slowly. On a porch in Maine, one American is carefully lowering the national productivity. And raising the absolute value of doing nothing.

Six Decades on Wheels

Art Riddle

1   One of the first "wheeled" generations in American history is now fading away. We are referring to the people whose entire lives have been involved with the automobile, a generation whose every decision and most actions take the motor car into consideration.

2   I am one of those people, having been born in 1921. There were relatively few automobiles in America that year, and I was probably brought home from the hospital in a horse-drawn buggy.

3   But the automobile proliferated, and within six to eight years, every family on the block had one. The automobile proved a magnificent means of transportation, and although it wasn't always dependable, everyone began to view it as a necessity. As children, members of my generation became enamored of the "horseless carriage." Oh, there were problems. On long rides, we sometimes suffered car sickness and also ached from crushed fingers caught in a slamming car door. Seems like we don't hear much about either of those ailments these days.

4   As children, we had an early introduction to wheels. We rode tricycles, scooters, box scooters, and coaster wagons. Later it was roller skates and bicycles.

5   In our state, a teenager could obtain his driver's license at 14 years of age, so I bought my first auto that year (1935). It was 10 years old, a Star touring car, and cost me $25. Most of my friends bought Model T or Model A Fords. We didn't know it then, but we were being drawn into a lifelong love affair with the automobile.

6   We drove our jalopies through our high school days, and they became center-points in our lives. Most of our time and money went into those cars. We were either driving them, repairing them, or trying to improve them.

7   During our teens, we learned a lot of basics about automobiles. Driving cars built in the '20s or '30s, we changed ignition points and capacitors (then called condensers), adjusted valve tappets, and tightened connecting rod bearings. We changed pistons and piston rings when necessary, patched innumerable flat tires, cranked many an engine because the battery was dead or dying, and adjusted brakes, which at that time were activated by steel rods instead of hydraulics.

8   We became familiar with three-brush generators, vacuum tanks, and updraft carburetors. On freezing winter nights, we drained the water out of radiators and engines and replaced it the next morning from a steaming tea kettle.

"Six Decades on Wheels" reprinted from *Motor Trend Magazine*, April 1988.

9   The jalopy was fine for most activities, but if we arranged a hot date, or something equally important, we borrowed dad's car for the evening.

10   Our happy, serene high school days suddenly ended with the onslaught of World War Two. Most of us went into the military and suddenly found ourselves driving Jeeps, Dodge half-tons, or six-by-sixes. The services had an insatiable appetite for truck drivers.

11   We came marching home in 1945, and many of us entered college under the GI bill. We took our cars to campus with us and had to find part-time jobs to keep those autos running. The $65-a-month GI bill didn't cover automotive expenses.

12   Later, most of us received diplomas and moved out into the real world, where we began earning decent pay for the first time in our lives. We bought newer and bigger autos.

13   We've lived with cars ever since, and many of us now are helpless without one. We drive, rather than walk, to the liquor store a block away. We ride buses or taxis only in emergencies, and when our cars break down, we're lost.

14   When we bought our first cars in the '30s, most of America was tied together by two-lane dirt roads. Since then, we've seen the miraculous growth of highways, eight-lane freeways, and paving everywhere. Now we can easily cruise cross-country in our steel chariots.

15   Automobiles have changed since the Model Ts and the '25 Stars, but not really that much. Then, as now, an auto consisted of four wheels, an engine, some control mechanisms, a few comforts, and 5000 parts to hold it all together.

16   Today's cars run smoother, last longer, and are superbly more dependable. They have stereos, digital clocks, and air conditioning. They're quieter and shinier. But if you ever ride in a '30 Model A, you'll find the difference isn't that vast, despite more than 50 years of automotive engineering.

17   To get back to our generation on wheels, most of us are retired now. We're still driving automobiles, and we're still living our lives with the internal combustion engine. We find that our six decades with the car have seesawed in a love/hate relationship. When the auto ran "good," when it purred, we loved it. When it wouldn't start or broke down, we despised it. We felt like throwing a hard, heavy object through its smug, smart-ass windshield.

18   And yet, tin lizzie, jalopy, crate, bucket of bolts, rust bucket, steel chariot, gas guzzler, dinosaur, we're glad you've been with us on our journey through life.

Propaganda

Freda S. Sathre-Eldon, Ray W. Olson, and Clarissa I. Whitney

1   Propaganda is any systematic scheme or concerted effort to persuade others to believe in a particular practice, doctrine, or point of view. The rather common use of propaganda techniques makes them a type of persuasive communication that merits our attention. There is nothing necessarily bad or underhanded about propaganda; the same techniques are used, in varying degrees, in advertising, politics, education, religion, public relations, and even most group discussions. Nearly all information-giving and persuasive activities involve some propaganda. If we can learn to examine these techniques and logically evaluate information and issues for ourselves, we will be able to examine the issues critically, and not naively accept persuasive arguments.

2   Propaganda techniques may be used by the sincere persuader, but they may also be used by the self-serving manipulator. Manipulation is the attempt to influence others, by any means possible, to think or do what the manipulator desires them to do, as he or she seeks to achieve some selfish end or purpose. The manipulator has only his or her own interests at heart. Obviously, at times our own motives are mixed, and the line between honest persuasion and selfish manipulation becomes very thin indeed.

3   Often propagandists appeal to group standards. They also try to block or avoid any critical examination of their main points so that arguments against them will not arise and hinder or halt their persuasive effectiveness. The following are seven of the most commonly used techniques of propaganda.

4   *1. Name Calling.* Calling someone a "pinko," "fascist," "kike," or "war monger" arouses such strong emotions that the "loaded" word often blocks rational thought about the issue or person under discussion. It may also brand the person called such a name as bad, leading to his or her rejection.

5   *2. Glittering Generalities.* Superpatriots who say, "Our God-fearing, dedicated, sincere, and patriotic leader . . ." are loading the dice with vague and noble sounding generalities. If examined critically, these generalities are often blatantly inconsistent and false.

6   *3. Transfer.* Sometimes a tone of strong positive feeling is created and then transferred to the topic under discussion or to the speaker. For instance, many rallies start with the national anthem and presentation of the flag, after which the speaker attempts to pick up the good feeling and bask in the unquestioned borrowed glory.

Thus the authority, sanction, and prestige of something we respect is carried over to something or someone else.

7   *4. Testimonials.* Testimonials are endorsements of a person, idea, or product by prestigious, well-known people. Movie stars who use Brand X, or athletes who eat Brand Z cereals, are used in testimonials, but the logic behind such endorsements is questionable. Nevertheless, this technique is quite effective in selling products.

8   *5. Plain Folks.* Most politicians have their picture taken with assembly line workers and farmers, suggesting that they also are just average, ordinary, plain people. After posing for these pictures, the politician often gets into a million dollar airplane and goes back to a luxurious home, which should indicate to any thinking person that the suggested similarities have serious limitations!

9   *6. Card Stacking.* Some propagandists use the clever selection of some facts and figures, ignoring others, to present either the best or worst side of an issue. Many car manufacturers list the large number of cars they have built, but they seldom publicize the number of cars that have been recalled due to defective parts.

10   *7. The Bandwagon.* "Why not join us now? Everybody's doing it!" The aim of this approach is to make us follow the crowd. It is often successful with impulsive people who are anxious to be on the right or winning side, and who do not pause for more careful consideration of products, issues, or candidates.

11   Propagandists are often successful because many of us need to be given the "right" answers. Most of us do not like ambiguous situations and thus are susceptible to easy solutions from friends, television, newspapers, and other authorities. The passive, quiet person is many times exploited by the expert. We are vulnerable to propaganda when we tolerate one-way communication rather than talking back and critically evaluating the issues.

12   Many expert book reviewers "talk back" to books by writing their reactions to the book in the margins as they read it. This is an effective, active way of being critically involved with the book, provided that the reader owns the book!

Junkyard Journalism

Dave Barry

1   I bet you don't read the *National Enquirer,* or any of the other publications sold at supermarket check-out counters. I bet you think these publications are written for people with the intellectual depth of shrubs, people who need detailed, written instructions to put their shoes on correctly.

2   Well, you're missing a lot. I have taken to reading check-out-counter publications, and I have picked up scads of useful information. For example, a recent *Enquirer* issue contains a story headlined "Whatever Happened to the Cast of 'The Flying Nun'?" Now here is a vital story most of the so-called big-time newspapers didn't have the guts to print. I mean, while the New York *Times* and the Washington *Post* were frittering away their space on stories about Alexander Haig, millions of people all over America were tossing and turning at night, wondering what happened to the cast of "The Flying Nun." All over the country, you'd see little knots of people huddling together and asking each other: "Remember Marge Redmond, who played Sister Jacqueline in 'The Flying Nun'? Whatever happened to her?"

3   Well, the *Enquirer* has the answer. Somehow, an *Enquirer* reporter got Marge's agent to reveal that Marge has appeared in commercials for Tide, Bravo, Betty Crocker, and Ajax. "But," adds the agent, "she is perhaps best known as Sara Tucker of Sara Tucker's Inn on the Cool Whip commercials."

4   I, for one, was stunned by this revelation. Believe it or not, I had never made the connection between Sister Jacqueline and Sara Tucker. Now, of course, it seems obvious: only an actress skilled enough to perform in "The Flying Nun" would be able to convincingly portray a woman who is so deranged that she puts huge globs of Cool Whip on her desserts at what is supposed to be a good restaurant. But without the *Enquirer,* I would never have known.

5   And without the *National Examiner,* which is like the *Enquirer* except it uses even smaller words, I would never have found out that

40 Vampires Roam North America

6   This extremely scientific story reports on the research of Dr. Stephen Kaplan, a parapsychologist who founded the Vampire Research Center. I got the impression that Dr. Kaplan *is* the Vampire Research Center, but the story never makes this clear. It

also doesn't say where he got his degree in parapsychology, but we can safely assume it was someplace like Harvard.

7   Anyway, Dr. Kaplan sent questionnaires to people who requested mail from the center, and forty responded that, yes indeed, they are vampires. In a way, this cheered me up. I mean, I always thought of vampires as evil, uncooperative persons of Central European descent who never even file income tax returns, and here we have forty of them who cheerfully fill out questionnaires for the Vampire Research Center.

8   Dr. Kaplan, who (surprise!) plans to write a book about vampires, believes there are lots more vampires around. "This probably represents the tip of the vampire iceberg," he told the *Examiner*, which knows a good metaphor when it hears one. If Dr. Kaplan is correct, I imagine that before long we'll have a federal law requiring large companies to hire a certain percentage of vampires. They have been discriminated against long enough.

9   Here are some more stories you missed: "Bingo Can Restore the Will to Live On," "$50 Operation to Restore Virginity," "A Machine Chewed Up My Legs," "Cancer Ruins Sex," "Dead Man Thanks Killer" and "34 Years in a Haunted House." The last one is about a Massachusetts man and woman whose house is occupied by a ghost that does terrifying things, such as caressing the woman's brow with ghostly fingers when she's reading. By way of proof, the article is accompanied by an actual photograph of the woman reading.

10   Check-out-counter publications also perform valuable services for their readers. The *Examiner* has a psychic named Maria who uses her incredible psychic ability to answer baffling questions, such as "Dear Maria: A man I am dating keeps asking me to spank him. What should I do?" To which Maria replies: "Dump him. He's nuts." And some people have the nerve to claim that psychics are frauds.

11   But the best part of check-out-counter publications is the advertisements. They can make you rich. I, for one, never realized how much money you can make stuffing envelopes, but according to the ads in the *Enquirer* and the *Examiner*, the sky is the limit. I mean, people are willing to pay you *thousands of dollars a week* to stuff envelopes. I figure there must be a catch. For one thing, they never tell you what you have to stuff the envelopes *with*. Maybe it's poison spiders. That would explain the high pay.

12   Another ad I saw in the *Examiner* just *intrigues* me. The headline says: JESUS IS HERE. Now I am going to quote very carefully from the ad, because otherwise you won't believe me:

> Tired of money-mad ministers and physicians? Free, drugless urine cures all ills, increases energy and intelligence and is prescribed in the Bible . . . Due to its immuno-genetic qualities, urine is the only antidote for nuclear radiation . . . If you are not fully convinced that the course heralds the Second Coming of Christ, return it in perfect condition for a full refund . . .

13   The course costs seventy-five dollars; otherwise I would have sent for it already. I am very curious about it, and even more curious about the person who wrote it. I strongly suspect he's one of the people who responded to Dr. Kaplan's vampire survey.

Halfway to Dick and Jane

Jack Agueros

1   I am an only child. My parents and I always talked about my becoming a doctor. The law and politics were not highly regarded in my house. Lawyers, my mother would explain, had to defend people whether they were guilty or not, while politicians, my father would say, were all crooks. A doctor helped everybody, rich and poor, white and black. If I became a doctor, I could study hay fever and find a cure for it, my godmother would say. Also, I could take care of my parents when they were old. I liked the idea of helping, and for nineteen years my sole ambition was to study medicine.

2   My house had books, not many, but my parents encouraged me to read. As I became a good reader they bought books for me and never refused me money for their purchase. My father once built a bookcase for me. It was an important moment, for I had always believed that my father was not too happy about my being a bookworm. The atmosphere at home was always warm. We seemed to be a popular family. We entertained frequently, with two standing parties a year—at Christmas and for my birthday. Parties were always large. My father would dismantle the beds and move all the furniture so that the full two rooms could be used for dancing. My mother would cook up a storm, particularly at Christmas. *Pasteles, lechon asado, arroz con gandules*, and a lot of *coquito* to drink (meat-stuffed plantain, roast pork, rice with pigeon peas, and coconut nog). My father always brought in a band. They played without compensation and were guests at the party. They ate and drank and danced while a victrola covered the intermissions. One year my father brought home a whole pig and hung it in the foyer doorway. He and my mother prepared it by rubbing it down with oil, oregano, and garlic. After preparation, the pig was taken down and carried over to a local bakery where it was cooked and returned home. Parties always went on till daybreak, and in addition to the band, there were always volunteers to sing and declaim poetry.

3   My mother kept an immaculate household. Bedspreads (chenille seemed to be very in) and lace curtains, washed at home like everything else, were hung up on huge racks with rows of tight nails. The racks were assembled in the living room, and the moisture from the wet bedspreads would fill the apartment. In a sense, that seems

to be the lasting image of that period of my life. The house was clean. The neighbors were clean. The streets, with few cars, were clean. The buildings were clean and un-cluttered with people on the stoops. The park was clean. The visitors to my house were clean, and the relationships that my family had with other Puerto Rican families, and the Italian families that my father had met through baseball and my mother through the garment center, were clean. Second Avenue was clean and most of the apartment windows had awnings. There was always music, there seemed to be no rain, and snow did not become slush. School was fun, we wrote essays about how grand America was, we put up hunchbacked cats at Halloween, we believed Santa Claus visited everyone. I believed everyone was Catholic. I grew up with dogs, night-ingales, my godmother's guitar, rocking chair, cat, guppies, my father's occasional roosters, kept in a cage on the fire escape. Laundry delivered and collected by horse and wagon, fruits and vegetables sold the same way, windowsill refrigeration in win-ter, iceman and box in summer. The police my friends, likewise the teachers.

4   In short, the first seven or so years of my life were not too great a variation on Dick and Jane, the school book figures who, if my memory serves me correctly, were blond Anglo-Saxons, not immigrants, not migrants like the Puerto Ricans, and not the children of either immigrants or migrants.

5   My family moved in 1941 to Lexington Avenue into a larger apartment where I could have my own room. It was a light, sunny, railroad flat on the top floor of a well-kept building. I transferred to a new school, and whereas before my classmates had been mostly black, the new school had few blacks. The classes were made up of Ital-ians, Irish, Jews, and a sprinkling of Puerto Ricans. My block was populated by Jews, Italians, and Puerto Ricans.

6   And then a whole series of different events began. I went to junior high school. We played in the backyards, where we tore down fences to build fires to cook stolen potatoes. We tore up whole hedges, because the green tender limbs would not burn when they were peeled, and thus made perfect skewers for our stolen "mickies." We played tag in the abandoned buildings, tearing the plaster off the walls, tearing the wire lath off the wooden slats, tearing the wooden slats themselves, good for fires, for kites, for sword fighting. We ran up and down the fire escapes playing tag and over and across many rooftops. The war ended and the heavy Puerto Rican migration be-gan. The Irish and the Jews disappeared from the neighborhood. The Italians tried to consolidate east of Third Avenue.

7   What caused the clean and open world to end? Many things. Into an ancient neighborhood came pouring four to five times more people than it had been designed to hold. Men who came running at the promise of jobs were jobless as the war ended. They were confused. They could not see the economic forces that ruled their lives as they drank beer on the corners, reassuring themselves of good times to come while they were hell-bent toward alcoholism. The sudden surge in numbers caused new re-sentments, and prejudice was intensified. Some were forced to live in cellars, and were then characterized as cave dwellers. Kids came who were confused by the new surroundings; their Puerto Ricanness forced us against a mirror asking, "If they are Puerto Ricans, what are we?" and thus they confused us. In our confusion we were sometimes pathetically reaching out, sometimes pathologically striking out. Gangs. Drugs. Wine. Smoking. Girls. Dances and slow-drag music. Mambo. Spics, Spooks, and Wops. Territories, brother gangs, and war councils establishing rules for right of way on blocks and avenues and for seating in the local theater. Pegged pants and zip guns. Slang.

8   Dick and Jane were dead, man. Education collapsed. Every classroom had ten kids who spoke no English. Black, Italian, Puerto Rican relations in the classroom were good, but we all knew we couldn't visit one another's neighborhoods. Sometimes we could not move too freely within our own blocks. On 109th, from the lamp post west, the Latin Aces, and from the lamp post east, the Senecas, the "club" I belonged to. The kids who spoke no English became known as Marine Tigers, picked up from a popular Spanish song. (The *Marine Tiger* and the *Marine Shark* were two ships that sailed from San Juan to New York and brought over many, many migrants from the island.)

9   The neighborhood had its boundaries. Third Avenue and east, Italian. Fifth Avenue and west, black. South, there was a hill on 103rd Street known locally as Cooney's Hill. When you got to the top of the hill, something strange happened: America began, because from the hill south was where the "Americans" lived. Dick and Jane were not dead; they were alive and well in a better neighborhood.

10   When, as a group of Puerto Rican kids, we decided to go swimming to Jefferson Park Pool, we knew we risked a fight and a beating from the Italians. And when we went to La Milagrosa Church in Harlem, we knew we risked a fight and a beating from the blacks. But when we went over Cooney's Hill, we risked dirty looks, disapproving looks, and questions from the police like, "What are you doing in this neighborhood?" and "Why don't you kids go back where you belong?"

11   Where we belonged! Man, I had written compositions about America. Didn't I belong on the Central Park tennis courts, even if I didn't know how to play? Couldn't I watch Dick play? Weren't these policemen working for me too?

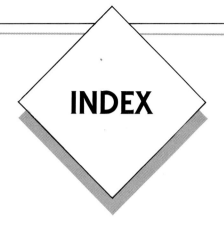

INDEX